LONDON'S
Grand Hotels

For William Morehouse
who has enjoyed staying at
some of London's grand hotels

LONDON'S
Grand Hotels

Extraordinary People, Extraordinary Service in the World's Cultural Capital

WARD MOREHOUSE III

LONDON'S GRAND HOTELS
Extraordinary People, Extraordinary Service in the
World's Cultural Capital

For information, address:
BearManor Media
P O Box 1129
Duncan, OK 73534-1129

www.BearManorMedia.com

Cover design by Bob Antler, Antler Designworks
Typesetting and layout by Greg Collins

Published in the USA by BearManor Media

ISBN: 1-59393-610-9

CONTENTS

The Itinerary

PREFACE

*L*ondon's Grand Hotels follows somewhat the format of *Life at the Top: New York's Grand Hotels*, published in 2005. With some twenty-five chapters, each dedicated to a single hotel or group of hotels which are singular for their history, guests and ambiance, *London's Grand Hotels* also includes some colorful profiles of personalities of owners and guests of The London Ritz, Claridge's, The Milestone, The Goring, Haymarket, Soho, Brown's, Mandarin Oriental Hyde Park and many others. Several chapters are devoted to a group of hotels as in the case of Firmdale Hotels, Red Carnation Hotels and Como Hotels, chronicling some of their history, famous guests and legends surrounding these their unique properties. As with *Inside New York's Grand Hotels*, the book pays special homage to theater, cinema, and literary figures who have stayed in these illustrious properties.

The choice of these two dozen hotels was largely subjective. Some are left out because I didn't have the time or the good fortune to stay there. Others, perhaps unfairly, I deemed too small for inclusion in a general hotel book by virtue of size alone. In terms of service many left out can compete with the grandest.

Again, with the hotels in this book and others that stretch in my imagination and those of my fellow travelers, it's my fervent hope they become "such stuff as dreams are made on" (Shakespeare's *The Tempest*).

Introduction

Hotels and I

The origin of *London's Grand Hotels* is a natural progression from my book *Life at the Top: Inside New York's Grand Hotels.* In the late Seventies I continued my already long and distinguished career of staying somewhere other than at home, first at an actors' club on St. James Street in London, but my introduction to the great London hotels was at The Savoy, which my father had been frequenting since the late Twenties. (We Morehouses tend to start things in the latter part of decades for some odd reason.) My brief stay at The Savoy, in a riverfront suite overlooking the Thames, inspired me to finish a book I'd already started on The Waldorf – *The Waldorf Astoria: America's Gilded Dream.* If you've read any of my earlier books on hotels, you know that I very early in life inherited my father's great love of inns (and especially of room service) but at The Savoy it was as if I'd stepped into a fairytale chateau and my very own, pre-internet, very undigital "domain" had magically appeared before me. Most of the hotels I'd patronized up to that time simply paled in comparison. I was like a double A ball rookie getting his first look at Yankee Stadium. In short, I was hooked. What video games are now to some obsessed youngsters, grand hotels became to me.

I also found many similarities between The Savoy and my most beloved New York grand hotel, The Waldorf Astoria, both in grandeur and in the single–minded devotion to service. Now that we as a species have successfully made it safely to the 21st century, service seems slap–dash, obsequious in many places. But the finest London hotels remain an eminent exception. You might say they, almost alone among earth's institutions, have held onto what was good about the 19th century.

The more I write about hotels, the more convinced I am that many people choose them primarily as a place to hobnob with bluebloods and, better still, celebrities. This, I think, is especially true of bluebloods and celebrities themselves. A hotel's décor, like a beautiful woman, is a strong attraction to anyone. Yet, subconsciously its clientele, illustrious, eccentric, or even hoi polloi – past, present and future – is an undeniable magnet. Every hotel, you see, has a history, has its regulars, and it is the people of a hotel, those who work there to be sure but also those who, for whatever reason, choose to stay there, that gives a hotel its special character. Why does a nice, clean, modern motel have little or no character? Because it has no history.

Now, if you were driving down the highway and found yourself pulling into the drive of the Bates Motel, you'd sit up and notice. Most likely you'd back up and keep driving, but you'd be intensely aware of that motel's history. You might even be intrigued (and courageous) enough to stay the night. Well, if a run–down dive like that can resonate with such history, how do you think a place like The Savoy, or The Ritz or the Connaught or Brown's feels? The very places where the business of the empire was conducted for over a century. Many of these great hotels are tourist destinations in themselves. You very well may be more impressed by The Goring than by the Tower of London. And you certainly wouldn't want to stay at the Tower! Despite its impressive, centuries–long list of guests. Actually, from what I've read, the stay at the Tower wasn't all that uncomfortable, but the checkout could be murder.

The reader may be startled at this book's departure from the usual *modus operandi* of hotel histories and travel guidebooks. This is because it's really a book about people – the personalities who build, manage and stay in London hotels, among the greatest congregation of glamour, sophistication and beauty in the world. And there's as much fascinating rhythm about London and its hotels as about New York and its hotels. Moreover, the two great cities have a distinctly different vibe. Both are great world capitals, of course, but where New York's hotels throb with power – power breakfasts, power lunches, power clients – and with money and glitz, London's great hotels just ooze class and history and romance.

Much has changed on both sides of the Atlantic, of course, since the great age of steam ships and steamer trunks. As was the case in New York up until several decades ago, London newspapers used to publish names of "Americans Staying in London Hotels." Modern day security and privacy issues have put a major damper on this practice even though names are still bandied about in various gossip columns, especially on the web. But most of what was great about London's grand hotels a century ago is still great today, and therein lies much, but certainly not all, of their great charm.

A Peculiar Proposition

Perhaps if I were a true English gentleman or even Boston Brahmin, I'd prefer posh clubs to hotels. While lolling in various luxurious lobbies in beautiful hotels the world over, but especially in London, I can never escape the sensation of being Phileas Fogg reclining in his favorite lounger in his exclusive London men's club. If ever I want to duplicate this sensation when I am home in New York, I always repair, usually with a few close friends who either understand or share my peculiar antiquated tastes, to the lobby of The Algonquin Hotel in midtown Manhattan. There my friends and I can chat while sharing a civilized cocktail or pot of tea and imagine ourselves to be denizens of an earlier, more sophisticated and less coarse age.

Well, my friends and I were thus engaged a year or so ago when the conversation, as is frequently the case when I am present, turned to great London hotels. One of my friends, knowing of my obsession, thought to corner me and make me divulge just which of the great London hotels was my absolute favorite. I replied that would be like having to choose between one's children. Well, then, my friend, undaunted, pressed, if you could only stay at one London hotel from now on, which would it be? Again I protested it was a Solomonic choice! "C'mon, Ward," another friend jocularly protested. "After all, when you travel to London you can only stay in one hotel at a time anyway. So which would it be?" I instantly replied that there certainly was no reason to remain in one hotel for the duration of any stay in London. Perhaps if one were a jet-setting CEO who flew in for a day's meeting and flew out the next day. But, the last I checked, most normal people generally travel to England for more than one night at a time. I went further to state that there was no reason, since so many of the great London hotels are so closely situated together, why one couldn't stay at a different one every single night. "Even," my first friend countered, "if you were in London for two weeks?" I replied that two weeks might be the perfect duration for just such an enterprise. "You mean, fourteen luxury hotels in fourteen nights?" my friend laughed. Then noticed that I was quite serious. "But that's like some kind of tour bus excursion nightmare, sixteen famous European cities in six nights!" the second friend argued. Not at all, I said. Not one bit the same thing. There would be no need for any rushing around from one city to the next. All that would be required after checkout each afternoon was a simple taxi ride to the next destination. I have always traveled lightly, never more than a couple of suitcases. It would be simplicity itself, little more trouble, really, than staying in the one place the whole time. "But," my first friend again protested," "you'd have to tip the staff every single day! Or would you be so cruel as to stiff the poor blighters?" Finally, my friend had a point. However, it's the rare grand design which that doesn't have at least one fly in its ointment. I still maintained that the enterprise would not only be practical, but a great deal of fun. It then dawned on me that it might also make a good subject for a book! The very book, in fact, which you are holding in your hands right now.

When I returned home that night, I immediately began to formulate my plans. After all, in this day and age it would be foolish for a gentleman to attempt to replicate Phileas Fogg's feat of circumnavigating the globe in eighty days (far too slow), but one certainly could attempt to stay in as many luxury London hotels as possible on one transatlantic trip! A most modern quest, as well as an enticing one. Moreover, there would be none of that traversing hazardous terrain which Mr. Fogg was subjected to. My sole means of transportation need only be taxicab, and, on a few occasions when the hotels in question were within eyeshot of each other, shoe leather.

As a result, for the last leg of researching this book, I had the enviable task of staying in fifteen London hotels in February and March 2009. I would get up, have an interview with the general manager or public relations person, sometimes request a late checkout time, write until my next, sometimes late, afternoon interview and then move to the next hotel. In one case, when I was staying at The Connaught and heading to the Millennium Mayfair, the London taxicab driver told me as we sped barely more than half a New York City block to the front entrance of the Millennium Mayfair Hotel around the corner from The Connaught, "I think that's the shortest cab ride I've ever had." At every hotel, I heard the same question: "how was your trip?"

"Fine," I would deadpan.

"Did you have a good flight?"

"Oh, yes," I said, not going into detail which would have required somewhat of a lengthy explanation.

The Ethos of Hotel Patronage

As I sit on a secluded Canadian island in the St. Lawrence River writing these lines, I find myself reflecting a bit on the appeal of hotels, on their essence, if you will. Just what is it that makes us love them? And in particular makes me love them. Picasso once said, *"Te mets dans mes tableaux tout ce que j'aime"* ("I represent in my paintings all that I like"). So, too, here I represent all that I like, building not only on my previous books such as *The Waldorf-Astoria: America's Gilded Dream* or *Inside The Plaza: An Intimate Portrait of the Ultimate Hotel*, but on my family's life-long passion for living in hotels. My mother, the late Broadway actress and publisher, Joan Marlowe, and my late father, drama critic and columnist Ward Morehouse, lived in Suite 1532 at The Waldorf-Astoria just before I was born. They lived at The Plaza before that and my father and stepmother subsequently lived there for another eleven years.

Ben Hecht, who co-wrote the Broadway blockbuster *The Front Page* with Charles MacArthur, once said that, "the first and most vital thing a young writer must do is to decide to be himself and find that cause that carries only his name. He must be his own cause – he must not shop around for things to join up with, ideologies to hook on to."

With *The Waldorf-Astoria: America's Gilded Dreams* I found my métier. It spoke to me loud and clear on several levels. I had become enamored with the hotel, writing several stories on it for *The Christian Science Monitor*. It was an "undiscovered country" as Hamlet says of death but one that, for me, came bursting to life, personal and professional.

I recently found a letter that had been addressed to my father at Room 1526 in The Waldorf-Astoria, a little more than a year before I was born. So my "own cause," as Hecht put it, was hotels and because my parents were also in it, the theater. Hotels and theaters – as well as hotels as theater – became my material. And not only the rich and famous. They included rich, and poor, high and the mighty and the low, and self–doubters and even self–loathers. The personalities of "backstage" crews, from managers to maids, often proved as fine a literary fodder as captains of industry and the arts. Do you know who Nathan Cummings was? – maybe not. In his day, he was a business giant like Conrad Hilton. The Sara Lee cakes king lived at The Waldorf–Astoria with his vast and valuable collection of art. He could have afforded to live anywhere he liked, but he chose The Waldorf? Why? Just ask General Douglas Macarthur. After more than a decade in the Far East, running the Pacific theater of war during WWII and then for several years all but ruling the nation of Japan singlehandedly, he returned to a hero's welcome in America and a ticker tape parade up Broadway. But where did he choose to settle down the last years of his remarkable life? At the Waldorf Towers.

The more I've thought about hotels in New York, London, and around the world, the more I've come to the conclusion that while many of the finest are beautiful to look at and stay in, they would be practically nothing without the vision of the people who own them, manage them, and work in them. You cannot separate a great hotel from a great manager – in fact, a great hotel represents the will, wishes and, sometimes, whims of a great manager to a remarkable degree. The late general manager of The Waldorf–Astoria, Gene Scanlan (as well as the current one, Eric Long) was really the essence of the hotel. A complete gentleman; admired by his staff as much as he advised them. Just so, Michael Shepard is as much the London Hilton Park Lane or The Savoy as Geoffrey Gelardi is The Lanesborough or Anthony Lee, the Connaught. Take away these managers, bring in competent substitutes, and you're left with competence. But the essence of a hotel is like the essence of great theater – and just as intangible. It's like a father or a mother watching over their children, with the difference being the children are both guests and staff. As I said, my own love of hotels I inherited. My father lived in some twenty-nine hotels in New York alone. That was during a different time than today, when many hotels welcomed long–term "permanents" which time has faded dramatically following the Sixties.

It occurred to me the other day that there is much about New York City that my father would not only not recognize but would not understand. Not to mention not approve of. New York City with only three daily newspapers? Soon to be two or one or possibly even none if things continue the way they're going.

Inconceivable!   Why, not that long ago Manhattan's newsies hawked no fewer than two dozen papers. There were morning papers and afternoon papers, not including the late editions. Broadway still puts on shows, but nothing like the ones my father was accustomed to.   What would my dad make of *Shrek, the Musical?* I shudder to think. The producers should thank god my father is no longer reviewing! But there is one place my father would still recognize, and still feel at home in, and that's Manhattan's great luxury hotels. And the same would be true if he flew or sailed to England. The great hotels as well as the great service and great tradition are still going strong.

There is something about hotels that defies either their history or rational categorization, just as, in an ambient sense, a hotel stands apart from its neighbors and the world. They are islands; not in the stream of sameness of apartment or townhouse. Their welcome mat is open to all with the means to pay or the desire to serve. Moreover, hoteliers of great hotels make you feel like you have "arrived." Like a parent dotes on a child and has infinite expectations for that child, so, too, to an excellent front desk manager you are kings and queens of your realm and castle.

London hotels are also about repeating the past. People come back the same way they visit their grandmother every summer – and for the same reason, to be doted over for a time before returning to the rat race. Spending time at a great London hotel can also be like spending some time with that great girlfriend you never had. Years ago you spotted her walking along Green Park or Piccadilly and thought to yourself, "She's too good for me. But someday. Someday!" And you dutifully saved up and worked hard and one day you really could spend a night or a weekend at that dream hotel.

"I wouldn't ask too much of her," Nick Carraway says to Jay Gatsby about the aristocratic Daisy in Fitzgerald's *Great Gatsby*. Gatsby replies incredulously, "Can you repeat the past? Why of course you can!" If, like Gatsby, you've got the money!

Welcome to the present, the future – and the past. May I take your bags?

Fancy Rock Island
Rockport, Ontario
Canada
June 2009

20218395

Chapter 1

Some Preliminaries While Crossing the Atlantic

There is a common misconception that all grand hotels are ultra expensive, similar to preferential orchestra seats on Broadway or the West End. Expensive, they often are. There is, at the same time, extraordinary value to be found at some of these palaces.

Moreover, I don't think there's a simple luxury in this world that quite compares to room service, a love that goes back generations in my family. After all, my father wanted "Room Service, please!" on his tombstone. He didn't get his inscription in the end but he certainly enjoyed his passion while he adored hotels around the world.

In this book you'll also visit leading theatrical luminaries of the last century who set up shop, so to speak, in The Savoy Grill, The Ritz Bar and similar venues.

The book is also about people and theater. Hotels, people, theater. In my mind, at any rate, it's hard to separate them! The serious nature of London hotels, their dedication to service, is akin to the serious nature of theater and theatergoers.

Glenn Young (publisher of Glenn Young Books, formerly publisher of Applause Theatre and Cinema Books, owned and operated by Hal Leonard), who published my book on The Plaza Hotel, had recently seen a serious piece of theater in London. "By chance," he recounted to me, "Prince Charles had been to the same performance three times. This says so much about the theater – and about him. There are plays that everybody is interested in. And he arrives at the theater by himself with his wife, Camilla, and two security men who are just to the side. But, you know, they don't rope everything off, and he sits down at the last minute. And they get up the same time everyone else does. They are part of the culture, whereas our culture is fragmented. I've been going to the theater all my life, and I've never seen a politician."

Here is another telling story, perhaps peculiar to English culture, as recounted in *Life of the Party. The Biography of Pamela Digby*

Churchill Hayward Harriman, by Christopher Ogden (Little, Brown & Co., 1994):

"An urban Lady Baillie who specialized in café society, Emerald staged enchanting meals at her London home at a circular table of lapis lazuli which reflected the candlelight and the gilt epergne of the naked nymphs and naiads centerpiece. Her guests were an eclectic mixture of handsome men, social wits, clever women, writers, musicians, diplomats and politicians . . .

"With the onset of the Blitz, she shut up her house and table, but the gatherings continued when she moved into The Dorchester. Her hotel salon was packed with so much valuable French furniture – a welter of velvet and gilt, busts by Houdon and Mestrovic – that it looked as though Sotheby's were using Emerald's quarters as a storeroom.

"Pamela, young, pretty and well connected, was always welcome. She had learned a great deal from observing Emerald entertain . . . In March, 1941, within days of her twenty-first birthday, she was in high spirits walking down The Dorchester corridor to Lady Cunard's suite. . . . Emerald hugged her and introduced her to two Americans who had just arrived in London: John Gilbert Winant, the incoming U.S. Ambassador . . . and Averell Harriman, Franklin Roosevelt's Lend–Lease expediter. Harriman smiled at the young beauty. She stared back. He was the most beautiful man she had ever seen."

Needless to add the American and the young lady were at long last wed, in 1971 – and I'd bet the reception was held at some fabulous London hotel.

If there's any one thing that sets London hotels apart from great and grand hotels in other cities, it is their afternoon teas. Jasmine Birtles, a financial expert and TV presenter, who runs the website www.moneymagpie.com, full of tips on money-making and saving, says she loves London hotels most for their teas. "Some people gauge the quality of an establishment by its restrooms. Others by its wine list. Me, I will immediately fall in love with a hotel that does a really excellent traditional afternoon English tea," she told me in an interview for this book.

"I always used to swear by the cream teas at the dear old Basil Street Hotel in Knightsbridge. A wonderful hotel, quintessentially English, crumbly, slightly tatty and good quality, I had a genuine sense of loss when it closed a couple of years ago. Since its closure (it was bought by developers to turn into luxury apartments; such is the way with property in London right now), I have been on the hunt for a hotel to replace it. It's been fun.

"Personally, for all-round excellence, quality of food, crockery and choice of loose-leaf teas (very important for the tea aficionado like myself) I really don't think you can go higher than tea at Claridge's. Again, with Claridge's there is still that 'best of British' feel about the place. Not tatty and crumbly like the old Basil was, but here 'improvements' and 'modernisations' have been done in a manner that retains the old-world style that makes it so elegant and comfortable. Even its new art, such as the amazing chandelier in the lounge, works with the more traditional fittings.

"Unlike so many of the big chain hotels, Claridge's has kept its character – a soothing fact in these times of corporate homogeneity. It also offers food that is clearly made on the premises – scones that are out of the oven rather than a packet (even some of the very expensive chains produce scones that are clearly fresh from the microwave). Gordon Ramsay's restaurant is also the height of great quality. I'm looking forward to visiting again some time soon for dinner. . . .

"If I want to up the cool factor, particularly if I am meeting friends or business contacts, I find myself drawn back again and again to the Charlotte Street Hotel and it's even cooler sister, the Soho Hotel. I have dined, partied and even watched films in both of these hotels. Both are so convenient for media-types like myself. They're both right in the heart of media-land in London and are constantly busy. These are not places to repair to for a quiet drink every now and then. They're buzzing, happening and great for star spotting.

"The fact that both of them have screening rooms makes them very popular with film people and P.R. execs, keen to show off their latest product on celluloid to interested journalists. I have regularly met P.R. contacts for lunch, tea or drinks at the Charlotte Street Hotel, and the buzz of the place certainly helps to concentrate the mind. The Soho Hotel has some quieter spots too, though, including lounges with huge sofas that you can curl up in and have a long, intimate conversation with a close friend. (Another of my favorite methods of relaxing in London!)

"For daytime sunshine (yes, we do get some occasionally in this rainy city) you really can't beat the Landmark hotel on the Euston Road, just in front of Marylebone Station. This is another hotel that locals often walk by without realizing what glories lie behind the modest entrance.

"I remember my first visit to this place in the early Nineties just after it had opened for the first time. I had been warned but I didn't realize how magnificent its atrium was. Quite often in London we have fabulously bright, sunny days with a biting cold wind. This was one of those and I can recommend the Landmark as the best place in town to be on a day like that. As you walk into the atrium, you are astounded by the bright sunshine pouring through the massive glass roof and the warmth of the place, set off by indoor palm trees. This is a place to while away the hours of a cold but sunny afternoon. You get the best of both worlds: sunshine and indoor warmth at the same time.

"My first visit was as a reporter for a national paper, interviewing the British women's Olympic rowing team. They had been given one of the wonderful inside-facing suites in which to be photographed and they couldn't stop talking about how wonderful it was. This is certainly the place for a romantic weekend. You might never go out the front door, particularly if the wind is chilly.

"My latest surprise find among London hotels has to be the Park Plaza on the Albert Embankment, which is the south side of the Thames. We Londoners don't expect to find anything particularly cool around this area so it was quite a shock to me to realize just how high quality this hotel is and how staggering the view! Get one of the rooms overlooking the Thames and you have a full, floor–to–ceiling, million–dollar view of the Houses of Parliament. It has a modern, Japanese–style fit to the public areas, and the food is a very high quality. If you want one of the best hotel views in London, this has to be it."

Ah, wouldn't it be "loverly," as Eliza always says, to just trail around Londontown in the wonderfully tasteful care of a guide like that? Unfortunately, she's a very busy lady, but I hope to provide you a similar service as we stroll around Piccadilly and environs over the next few weeks of high–falutin' hotel-hopping.

Many American writers have had love affairs with London, too. One of these was playwright Robert Sherwood, who wrote *Abe Lincoln in Illinois* and *The Petrified Forest*, the latter of which propelled Humphrey Bogart rapidly to film stardom after several earlier failed cracks at it. "He never lost his love for the giant city of London, for the serenity of the surrounding countryside, for the charm of the roadside inns and the geniality and humanity of the pubs," my father once wrote of Sherwood.

As with strictly theatrical productions, London's hotels are as deferential to dukes as they are to the captains and princes of movies and theater. And are patronized by them. Of course, actual dukes are a pretty rare commodity these days. They tend to be the aging brothers of kings (and about whom it seems a little silly to still be referring to them as princes), or, as in the case of the Duke of Edinburgh, a former monarch himself. But there are still plenty of other impressive, genuine upper royalty to come pay a visit. The Ritz has the distinction of having the "royal seal," and Queen Elizabeth hosts parties, large and small, there.

The Queen's presence, however, is seen in the unlikeliest hotels in what was once the British Empire. Take Canada, for instance. In The Gladstone, Toronto's oldest, continuously–operated hotel built in 1889, there is a photo of Queen Elizabeth II visiting one of the artist–decorated bedrooms. She also has a "royal suite" in the Royal York Hotel for whenever she comes to Toronto. Not too long ago a rather large fuss was made when Her Highness made the trip across the Atlantic to take part in the 400th anniversary of the founding of Jamestown, in Virginia. She stayed in a hotel there that she stayed in when she came over half a century earlier for the 350th bash. Of course, a few centuries before that, the British crown happened to actually own Virginia and a few other colonies along the Atlantic seaboard.

But besides The Ritz, royalty has been regulars at Claridge's, The Goring and The Savoy, among others.

Moreover, it is impossible to separate London hotels, in the travel sense, from the West End theaters. "I think London (theater) is more exciting because the palate is wider and it is deeper," said Glenn Young. "In other words, you have an appetite for theater. If there's a great restoration comedy and you have the right people in it, it will run in the West End. If there is a Wycherly or Congreve play, it will find its way to the West End. They have artists who have been trained in it and appreciate it, and they have an audience whose palate has been seeded with subtle tastes. The palate here in New York is much more narrow." Although that may be changing, as the 2008–2009 season illustrated so favorably.

But like New York, London is a frame of mind – albeit a glamorous, cacophonous, gaudy, resilient, delectable frame of mind. Novelist Ford Madox Ford started *The English Review* in 1900 and published the writings of D. H. Lawrence, Ezra Pound, T. S. Eliot and others. His novels include *The Good Soldier* (1915), *A Man Could Stand Up* (1926) and *Last Post* (1928). Ford left England for good in 1922 and lived in France and the United States. But in his autobiography, *It Was the Nightingales*, his love for London lives on. "To be a Londoner is a singular, amorphous state," he wrote in the book, published in 1933. "It is a frame of mind rather than a fact separated by domicile. The passion for London is a passion for vast easinesses and freedoms in which you may swim as in a tepid and tranquil sea."

Personally, I like to think London not only makes American entertainers more civilized but more talented, more vulnerable. There's a palpable, symbiotic, artistic majesty in the air within the vicinity of Piccadilly and Covent Garden as much as the stately sapience surrounding Buckingham Palace. Singers and actors seem to reflect it. I saw superb American chanteuse Maude Maggert in London in February 2008. She didn't sing better than at New York's Algonquin Hotel. She seemed more enchanting. But the most telling thing about London hotels is that they are in one way like great theater – they are permanent, especially in the masterful hands of their employees. Employees don't retire; they die out of their jobs,, just as old, sometimes forgotten plays have a place in the commercial West End because of the love that the actors and audiences have for them. Permanence.

I took a young rock singer, with whom I had a purely platonic relationship (too bad at the time, I thought) to Simpson's on the Strand. When I left the table to go to the men's room, a very proper lady, albeit somewhat of a witch, lectured the singer about "selling herself" to an older man. What shocked me most was being called an older man, even though I was twice her age. I guess some things have changed in London since the 19th century – back when a gent had to work like the devil until he was fifty just to be able to support a young wife!

Just as the roots of America's Declaration of Independence can be found in some of the more enlightened parts of English law, and certainly in a little ancient document they have over here called the Magna Carta, and which "inalienable rights" would come back to bite merry Old England when the original thirteen colonies declared their Independence, grand American hotels gained much by example and custom as well as majesty from

London's grand hotels. One has to look no further than Geoffrey Gelardi's grandfather who had a secure footing quite literally in London and in New York, as manager of The Savoy and The Waldorf Towers of The Waldorf–Astoria simultaneously!

Additionally, I've thought a lot about the difference in hotels in London and, for example, New York. There are the obvious differences: the castle–like antiquity of many London hotels overshadows all but a few of New York's palaces like The Plaza and Waldorf–Astoria. There are the parks, which though even Hyde Park is hard put to rival Central Park, are more numerous than New York's green stretches.

Well, it's hard for the hotels of any city to beat the picturesqueness of The Lanesborough, overlooking the ancestral home of the Dukes of Wellington and Green and Hyde Parks; The Savoy with the Thames at its windowsills figuratively and almost literally; The Metropolitan, with its gigantic picture window vistas of Hyde Park, or the spectacle of Big Ben and the London Eye from a round turret suite of the Mandarin Oriental Hyde Park – one of three such suites. But I think the Four Season's Canary Wharf, with its bird's–eye view of the snaking Thames, Big Ben and the Tower Bridge, may have them all beat for sheer tranquility and glamour. From its 142 ultra–chic, contemporary guest rooms and suites with American black walnut furnishings to Quadrato, with its Northern Italian cuisine that the greatest of Italian tenors would practically die for, London's finest health club and Olympic–sized swimming pool, itself appearing like some sort of liquid luxury liner moored on a curl of The Thames, the Four Seasons Canary Wharf has set new standards for romantic rest and relaxation.

Aside from teas, cuisine at London hotels has gone in the last several decades from the oftentimes barely passable to the at-times extraordinary. Actor Kevin Kline, in awe of the late English acting giant, John Gielgud, supposedly once asked him what was the key to great actors, whereupon Gielgud replied somewhat cryptically, "London hotels have the best food."

"London boasts some of the most famous hotels in the world – temples of luxury like Claridge's and The Dorchester and more recent arrivals like the Four Seasons," trumpeted the 2006 edition of *Frommer's London*. Who ought to know.

These and many other thoughts traversed my mind as I reclined in my coach plane seat. (I'm a journalist, after all, not a duke.) I cast my mind ahead to the hotels I expected to visit in the coming weeks. In some cases I already knew the hotel general managers. In others, I had stayed at hotel, told the managers so, and said I wanted an interview with them. This was the case with Stuart Procter, General Manager of The Stafford. I'm including my letter to him. In no case did I ever ask for a complimentary room; in most cases, I was most generously offered one, sometimes a two- or three-night stay. Sometimes, to paraphrase that great philosopher Mel Brooks, even if you can't be king, it's still good to be a journalist!

I wrote to Mr. Procter: "I will be in London from February 6 to March 7 finishing my book *London's Grand Hotels: Extraordinary People, Extraordinary Service in the World's Cultural Capital.* I would like to interview you for my chapter on The Stafford as well as for stories for my syndicated TV show called "The New Yorkers," which is seen by an estimated half million people in New York and Florida. I will also be doing stories on London luxury hotels offering special savings in these difficult economic times for *TravelSmart Newsletter* and Travelsmartnewsletter.com, for which I do the monthly "Checking In . . ." hotels column. I also have a travel section on the increasingly popular website Broadwayafterdark.com."

As I gazed out my plane window at the great ocean sweeping beneath me, I was also struck by the difference between New York and London hotels. In New York, they go straight up – from The Waldorf to The Ritz Tower to the "new" I. M. Pei–designed Four Seasons, which Pei freely admitted he took some inspiration from The Waldorf and its soaring towers. Up, up, up, the hotels go. Of course, this is true of Manhattan real estate in general – only so much space on that expensive little piece of property named Manhattan Island. In London, where space, though still dear, is nonetheless more plentiful, hotels seem to take their cue from Buckingham and other palaces. Sure, you have the London Hilton Mayfair soaring above Buckingham Palace and its well-guarded, manicured grounds. But mostly they, the hotels, hug the streets and parks and riverbanks like scintillating caterpillars, alive with music and dance and history.

Forbes magazine, which is forever, publishing top ten, or top fifty or one-hundred lists of all the things most of us can't afford anyway, recently came out with a "most expensive cities" list, and in which London proved to be more costly to live in than Manhattan. That surprised me. Of course, this is a list that was topped by Moscow, of all places. Well, of course Moscow is expensive. Once you find yourself there you'd spend anything to get out. But London? Expense is relative, though. And, as I stated at the beginning of the book, "bargains" are to be found even in London's otherwise priciest hotels. It's one of the things I'm going to be on the lookout for over the next few weeks.

For Anne Hampton Calloway, the extraordinarily gifted cabaret and Broadway star, London's hotels are only part of the excitement she feels every time she's in London. "Every bit of London is worth experiencing and walking in. And whenever I'm there I feel I'm with my people!"

As we burn jet fuel on our trip over, I am not unmindful of the hot topic of the decade, global warming. I won't go so far as argue that staying at luxury London hotels will save the planet, but I will mention an interesting quote I found in a terrific book by *New Yorker* writer David Hale, published in 1988, called *How To Get Lost and Found On London.*

"Any city in Europe, any city that came before the automobile, is greener than most US cities. The trouble with most American cities is they really didn't start building until they had cars. London had a head start by centuries because so much happened before the car. Because they are not as automobile dependent as we are. . . . At almost every corner in London there is a village green or public garden or a tree filled square where you can recede from the rush and smell the flowers. "

So, you see, just by being in London for the next few weeks, I'll be lowering my carbon footprint.

The book also notes: "Belgravia, south of Hyde Park Corner, is where newborn Rolls-Royce limousines go to nurse." The Goring and the Halkin, two of the hotels on our itinerary, are located in Belgravia. Belgravia dates back to 1826 when Earn Grosvernor got a Parliamentary permit to build a square surrounded by terraced houses.

Hold on. The stewardess is telling me to put my tray up and fasten my seat belt. We're approaching Heathrow. The great adventure is about to begin. Where will we go? What wonders will we find? How much will it cost? These and many other important issues will be answered, or at least addressed. So welcome to London's grand hotels. I hope you enjoy reading about them as much as I enjoyed staying in them.

Chapter 2

Heathrow Baggage Check and Partial Itinerary

I remember in one of my father's columns, in which he was writing about circumnavigating the globe, he talked about visiting twelve or fourteen countries in twice as many days. Well – I can't claim that yet! But in the last five trips to research and write *London's Grand Hotels: Extraordinary People, Extraordinary Service in the World's Cultural Capital*, I stayed at fourteen hotels in twenty–three days.

My extraordinary London excursion took me, for instance, to what I like to think of as one of London's grandest "country houses" in the middle of London, almost like the Vanderbilt mansion on Fifth Avenue and 58th Street, which was razed in the late 1920's for Bergdorf Goodman's. This is The Lanesborough on Hyde Park Corner overlooking both Hyde and Green Parks as well as the rust–like tinged mansion that has been the home of the Dukes of Wellington.

At The Lanesborough I felt like aristocracy, but I have also dipped my toes into the razzamatazz 21st century at The Metropolitan, which was hosting a kick–off party for London's Fashion Week. Breathless views of Hyde Park out of the floor–to–ceiling picture window.

I ventured back into time and reestablished polished beauty in a suite at the world–famous Connaught Hotel on San Carlos Place. The Connaught is arguably one of the greatest hotels in the world, along with The Lanesborough, Claridge's and The London Ritz. I enjoyed two nights of utter luxuriousness at The Connaught, in fact.

I went to East London and the fabulous Four Seasons Canary Wharf, with the best view of the Thames of any London hotel with the exception of The Savoy, which at the time of my visit was closed for renovations (scheduled for reopening some time in 2010).

I came down a little closer to earth another night by staying at the Mela "White House" Hotel near Regent Park, a complimentary night's stay along with my round–trip British Airlines ticket. I was pleasantly surprised by the Mela – comfortable, clean and ultra high–tech. No buttons in the elevator. You press your floor at a kiosk on the ground floor; an electronic arrow points out which elevator to use and you're off!

I had left my bags at The Milestone on Hyde Park and the following night stayed there after having dinner with The Milestone's incredibly hard–working public relations person, Annell Kendall, and Julia Record, formerly head of public relations for the Savoy Group of Hotels. I occupied the most outlandishly theatrical suite I ever stayed in, in the "Mistinguett Suite" named after the famous French music hall entertainer and film star.

If you'd like an expert assessment of the current "state" of grand London hotels, you couldn't do better than to heed the words of Trisha Wilson, President/Founder Wilson Associates/Interior Architectural Design. Ms. Wilson has, among many others, designed Chairman Kwek's fabulous St. Regis Hotel in Singapore. (Visit the chapters on Bailey's and The Millennium Mayfair for much more on the intriguing Chairman.) I made so bold as to ask Ms. Wilson for her opinion on London hotels' over-all interior design and she was gracious enough to respond:

"Hospitality interior design in London pays strong attention to British traditions. Hotels continue to modernize their guest experiences and services. I have found service is carefully inte-grated into the design, as seen at the Lanesborough, the Ritz-Carlton and the Berkeley. Often old facades reveal inspirational interiors magically blending a mix of hand crafted English furni-ture with unique modern twists through brilliant use of color and detailing."

I couldn't agree more. That's the great thing about London's best hotels – all the latest conveniences and styling inside, and all that great historical architecture outside. It's a very tough act for other world capitals to follow.

At another juncture in my excursions, I ventured into the more modern, upscale hostelries, gleamingly new inside and out. I arrived at "41" – that's it, the whole name of the hotel, just the number 41. Like The Milestone a Red Carnation hotel, it was where I thought the service equaled or even surpassed The Milestone. For one thing, it's all on one floor, a sort of ranch–style hotel in the sky, if you will, the top floor of what used to be the ballroom of Reubens Hotel. Because of the renovations, I didn't stay at The Savoy this time around, or the even–more–historic Bailey's or One Aldwych or Dukes, but they are all described here along with The Chesterfield, London Hilton Mayfair, Grosvenor House and many others. Enjoy!!

But I'm getting ahead of myself. I'm like a kid in a candy shop when I land in London. I really do wish I could stay in all of these great hotels at the same time! I want to gorge myself on all of them.

The following chapters more or less follow the chronology of London luxury hotels, from the most venerable, Brown's, to the spanking newest, Tim and Kit Kemp's hip, modernist boutique establishments. It's difficult to determine which is, in fact, older than which in some instances, because some hotels have sprouted up in much older buildings, while others have gone through various name changes and renovations. But in my journeys I tried to follow the general time line of London's grand hotels – in part to help me remember where I was and where I was going next, but also to provide the reader of this book a sort of "time-traveler's" idea of how, why and when these marvelous hotels came into existence. London is the locale, after all, of H.G. Wells' famous time-traveler. His adventures may have been more dramatic than mine, but I guarantee you that mine have been far more luxurious than his.

Chapter 3

Brown's Hotel

"A very warm welcome to Brown's and I do hope you have been made to feel at home," wrote Nina Colls, publicity director for Brown's, apologizing in a hand-written missive that she could not greet me personally. Think nothing of it, Nina. I'd already by that time been made to feel quite at home by any number of other Brown's employees.

I was far from the first Yankee to settle in at the hotel.

Broadway lyricist Ira Gasman ("The Life") was working on a song that the late Zero Mostel was to sing in the film *The Front*, which also starred Woody Allen, moonlighting from his own directorial efforts to play the titular role of a blacklist-era literary frontman. One evening, the cast and creative team were having dinner at Brown's in London, and Gasman leaned over to grumble to Allen that Mostel "is constantly changing the words in the song I wrote. What should I do?!"

"You know what?" Allen replied. "Take the money and run!"

For years after Senator Joe McCarthy and friends decided to make a little political hay for themselves by going after supposed Commies in the film business, a number of top screenwriters were not allowed to work openly for any of the major studios or television networks. The way everyone involved got around this was to have someone act as a go-between, pretending to have written a script by one of the blacklisted writers. Woody Allen may have been earnest in his advice, but he had also not long before that directed a comedy titled *Take the Money and Run*, starring himself as a hapless, two-bit crook. Whatever the case, Mr. Gasman could at least comfort himself that he was working for a producer who treated his employees to such a swell hotel.

Because Brown's itself is front, back, actual and the genuine article, ever since James Brown (no relation to the soul singer, at least that I'm aware of) and his wife, who was a lady's maid to Lord Byron's widow, opened their hotel with just one townhouse on Dover Street. Brown's was 172 years new, with 117 guest rooms and suites, in 2009. I like to think of Brown's as a sort of semi-secluded retreat from bustling Piccadilly Circus or even Bond Street and Kensington. Like a small island of trees in the French or English countryside of vast brown and green fields. The surrounding streets are almost that quiet, especially on weekends. You might even hear the hushed anticipation of Alexander Graham Bell making London's first phone call from Brown's.

Nearly 200 years after Brown assembled his five townhouses, Sir Rocco Forte, the indefatigable chairman of The Rocco Forte Collection, who formerly owned Brown's when it was a Trust House Forte hotel between 1968–1996, restored and renovated the now eleven town–houses in all its simplicity with a 21st century flair in redecorating its rooms.

"Did Brown's start out as an extension of the English country house in some way for people coming down to the city from their houses?" I asked Brown's fantastic public relations director.

"It started out that way, yes. It literally started out as somewhere people who lived in the country and didn't have a townhouse could come and stay," said Colls. Regardless of how the hotel started out, what perhaps is most remarkable about it is the state of preservation it is in a couple of hundred years down the pike. My P.R. friend offered a comment on that, too: "We're lucky here. When Sir Rocco bought the hotel, he and his sister, Olga Polizzi who is The Rocco Forte Collection Director of Design, were very keen to retain the wonderful British Heritage but bring it up to the 21st century, whilst giving the hotel a contemporary twist. And I feel they have done this perfectly, harmoniously blending them together."

Legends lived, got married, wrote and held convivial court within the hotel's celebrated walls. Rudyard Kipling finished his most famous tale, *The Jungle Book*, on an antique desk which is still within the hotel. Franklin D. Roosevelt spent several nights of his honeymoon here, and Theodore Roosevelt (a distant cousin to FDR, by the by) got married while staying at the hotel.

About that first phone call, the hotel's then owner, Henry Ford (again, no relation to the motor company), later recalled that Alexander Graham Bell came to the hotel with "a large handbag" which contained not clothing, but an almost spectral collection of wires and instruments, "declaring it was an invention which would enable the human voice to be carried along a pair of wires." Bell had come to London to try to interest the British government in his invention and was anxious to try it out first. By a stroke of good fortune the Fords had installed a private telegraph line between the hotel and their home in Ravenscourt Park, so Bell fixed up the instrument and, after the first complete failure, the inventor tried again between two and three a.m., when no one was using the line, and they spoke to each other with astonishing clarity. It is understood that many distinguished individuals subsequently visited Brown's to use the telephone, and these included Sir Arthur Conan Doyle, J. M. Barrie, Robert Louis Stevenson and Oscar Wilde.

In 1980, Stephen King stayed at Brown's and started the story that would later become the novel *Misery* – from Rudyard Kipling's alcove desk. Which itself sounds like a pretty good basis for a ghost story.

Today, following a £24 million renovation completed in December 2005, Brown's 117 guest rooms (including 29 suites) combines 18th century charm with Olga Polizzi's stylish, contemporary, chic designs and color schemes.

The man behind Brown's nowadays is Sir Rocco Forte, Chairman of The Rocco Forte Collection – and formerly Chairman of Forte plc, the company Sir Charles, his father, founded. Knighted in 1994 for his contribution to the U.K. Tourism Industry, Sir Rocco is the proud possessor of one of the finest collections of hotels in Europe. His hotel empire is growing to include Eastern Europe and the Middle East.

A passionate sportsman and family man, as well as hotelier, Sir Rocco finished an "Ironman" event in 2005 in [Klagenfurt], Austria, in 11 hours and 40 minutes, or second in his age range.

I stayed at Rocco Forte's Hotel Amigo in Brussels, located in a building that has parts going back to 1522 when the Brussels City Council bought it for a prison. The [Blaton] family turned it into a hotel in 1957 in time for the city's Universal Exhibition the following year. Olga Polizzi, Sir Rocco's sister and Director of Design for his entire collection, helped transform it into the best luxury hotel in the city, located a short stone's throw from "Manneken Pis," Brussell's most famous tourist attraction. Its fresh, modern interior design compliments its exterior historic character and charm. It has 154 rooms and 19 suites, also refurbished by Ms. Polizzi, who is clearly a very busy, as well as very talented, lady.

At Brown's everything is a work of art. Take the "Staying In

. . ." menu, for example. With its orange and black cover it seems as appetizing as the advertised dishes of "Steamed Wild Sea Bass with Wilted Alexanders" and "Treacle-cured Salmon with Pickled Cucumber Salad." Dom Perignon 1999 is £185 a bottle while Louis Roederer Cristal is £240. The Donovan Bar is one of the most attractive and coziest in London, with its so-called "naughty corner," complete with artful, nude photographs by the famed British photographer, Terence Donovan. Here Mrs. Polizzi blended the original stained glass window from the 1800's hotel, alongside not only these fifty photographs, but also a leather bar designed by Bill Amberg.

Brown's own archives provide a cornucopia of historic dates and events, including when "ranch man" Teddy Roosevelt stayed at the hotel before his marriage to his second wife, Edith Kermit Carow.

First, I take you back to the year 1859, when founding father James John Ford first bought the hotel. James hailed from Wiltshire and, when he arrived in London, he socked away a few pounds working in the Oxford Street livery and stable trade. More importantly, in this same year he produced a son, Henry, who was destined to thrive in the family hotel business.

In 1871, the hotel got a couple of special guests when the Emperor Napoleon III and the Empress Eugenie stopped in for a bit. The couple, it seems, were fleeing one of those periodic political upheavals they were always having in France about this time. On the present occasion, the Franco-Prussian War had just ended and established the third republic. After that, there was not much room at any French inn for the Emperor and Empress. Skip ahead a few years to 1876, when that momentous moment I already related to you about Alexander Graham Bell took place at Brown's Hotel.

In 1882, Henry Ford (honest, no relation to the Model T fellow) took the reins at Brown's – for the next 46 years! Among other important innovations, he put in the colorful window boxes which are still in evidence today and serve as a legacy to his memory. Henry, like his father, wanted Brown's to be a "private" hotel. A place where the rich and famous could spend time in a home-like atmosphere and escape their worldly cares and fame (but not, of course, forgo the good service they'd grown accustomed to). Hardworking, prescient Henry then installed a lift (elevator) sometime in the 1880s. It was one of the first in all of

London. He also established a smoking room – or gentlemen only, of course (and which no longer exists anyway courtesy of the recent UK no-smoking laws) – as well as the very first hotel restaurant, which is to say a fine dining establishment actually within the walls of the hotel. Before this brilliant innovation, guests either dined in their rooms or hired one of the available sixteen dining suites.

Many years before it became commonplace, electricity was installed in the hotel in 1884. Brown's relied on an oil-driven generator in the basement to provide the juice, probably a very shrewd idea in those early days of not terribly reliable DC current. (One of the problems with DC is that, unlike AC, it cannot travel very far. Having your very own generator on the premises, then, made stunningly good sense.)

In 1885, the bathrooms arrived, referred to in one local paper as a "fixed bath," and described, no doubt condescendingly, as a novelty. Perhaps it was bathing itself which was the real novelty for that Fleet Street correspondent? Sir Rocco refurbished all of these with not only luxurious Bush hammered limestone, or mosaic and marble, but equipped the signature suites with double bathtubs – complete with a television at the foot!

Theodore Roosevelt stayed at Brown's in 1886 before wedding Edith Kermit Carow. (They got hitched at St. George's Church in Hanover Square.) The hotel still proudly displays a mounted copy of the marriage certificate. One of the more interesting entries on the form is "occupation." The future President of the United States listed himself simply as "ranchman."

From 1886 to 1894, the Count de Paris, the Pretender to the French throne (although perhaps that's not quite the way he would have put it himself), dwelt in royal comfort at Brown's. He even held Court, of a sort, there in his suite. The great Cecil Rhodes, namesake of Rhodesia as well as founder of the Rhodes scholarships and source of a great many tall tales, stayed at Brown's regularly. Okay, one quick tale from Mark Twain. Since you asked. According to Mr. Twain, Cecil Rhodes once got a fabulous jump on a stock market tip, and the start of his great fortune – out of the belly of a great white shark. After swallowing the London newspaper, the shark had swum the Atlantic faster than the swiftest ship of the line in that day. Apocryphal, no doubt, but a good one.

Not content to sit on his laurels, Henry Ford acquired St.

George's Hotel in Albemarle Street. (The hotel, incidentally, had been named after that same church where the Roosevelts got married.) Fortuitously, the hotel backed up to Brown's. Today, the merged buildings still serve as the heart of the hotel. This was also the time that a fifth floor was added. The newly enlarged hotel still was called Brown's but St. George was not entirely driven from the field. The hotel's logo and stationery still proudly exhibit evidence of St. George's. There is also a stained glass image of good old George in The Donovan Bar, formerly known as St. George's Bar and the plaques on the outside of the hotel still say "Brown's and St George's Hotels." Not that St. George doesn't otherwise get his due in London – being the patron saint of England for the past couple thousand years or so – but it's always nice to be remembered.

Lord Kelvin (he of the thermometer of the same name) led the international Niagara Commission meeting at Brown's in 1890. The commission decided it'd be a good idea that water should be used to conduct electricity "using the Niagara Falls." Well, Lord K. would know, but conducting electricity through water sounds a little hazardous to me. Maybe he meant water should be used to generate power hydroelectrically? The point is that Lord K., a very smart individual, liked Brown's.

Rudyard Kipling, he of The *Jungle Book* fame, first stayed at Brown's on his honeymoon but returned frequently – not with other brides, by himself or with his wife. He found the hotel conducive to his writing. Today one of the hotel's two Royal Suites is named after him. Queen Victoria also visited the hotel on a regular basis as she adored the Traditional Afternoon Tea in what is now the English Tea Room, although she never stayed overnight. Of course, Buckingham Palace was practically around the corner.

Reaching at last the 20th century, we find three more townhouses appended to the whole of the hotel. This permitted for overall structural alterations as well as expansion.

As I mentioned earlier, in 1905, that other Roosevelt, Franklin, and his bride Eleanor stayed at Brown's on their honeymoon. Eleanor was, of course, T.R.'s niece, so maybe she got the recommendation from uncle Teddy. We do know that Mrs. R. wrote about her stay at the hotel in her autobiography, *The Lady of the White House*, wherein, she recollected, "We were given the royal suite at Brown's Hotel, with a sitting room so large that I could not find anything that I put down." Seems like a rather petty complaint to me, but so be it.

During the First World War, Queen Elizabeth of the Belgians (England's own QEII was as yet a few years in the future) stayed at Brown's with her entire family. Belgium really didn't make out too well in either of the World Wars. Such a pleasant, unassuming country, too.

London and Brown's was surely the place for exiled royals of all stripes. From 1924 to 1935 it was King George II of Hellenes' turn to turn up. He'd been exiled from Greece. He became, in fact, the hotel's longest royal resident and, once again, the hotel served as *de facto* royal court. Before heading back to Greece, the good king even decorated the hotel's manager with the Knight's Cross of the Royal Order of the Phoenix and to honor this, The Hellenic Suite is the name of Brown's other Royal Suite. King George was, by the way, a cousin or some relation to the future Prince Phillip, consort of England's future Queen Elizabeth. Of course, that romance was a number of years later. But who knows? Maybe Brown's played an indirect role as royal cupid? Pure speculation on my part, but all these royal folks were pretty cheek-by-jowl at times.

Case in point: in 1936, Haile Selassi, Emperor of Ethiopia, stayed at the hotel too. And *he* was a refugee from Mussolini's pre-WWII adventures in Africa. King Zog of Albania then showed up in 1939. They should have just started the United Nations right there at Brown's. Certainly the accommodations, and the room service, would have been better than at the General Secretariat.

In 1941, the Dutch government in (what else) exile declared war on Japan from the hotel. That has got to be some kind of first. Not that it got the Dutch very far. Next thing they knew, the Dutch East Indies were captured by the Japanese. On the other hand, the Dutch government was still enjoying Brown's hospitality so perhaps it wasn't so bad.

Dame Agatha Christie, queen of crime writers and inventor of Hercule Poirot (among others), was another famous frequenter of the hotel. She based her book *At Bertram's Hotel* on Brown's.

Brown's was purchased in 1968 by Trust House Limited, an entity that later transformed into Forte plc. The ownership then changed hands in the takeover of Forte plc in 1996. In July 2003, Sir Rocco acquired it again to be an integral property within his new luxurious collection of hotels – The Rocco Forte Collection. And, at least for the time being, the onrush of exiled royals abated! Whew!

But to me one of the most intriguing historical events, or series of events, to occur at Brown's was the strange case of "The Lindbergh Reports" in a book called *The Lindbergh Report: The Untold Story of Lindbergh's Report of September 22, 1938* by Matthew B. Wills.

The first part of the book's title refers to the report Charles A. Lindbergh wrote in connection with his tour of German air power at the time of the Nazi war machine's buildup in the Thirties.

Some critics have even blamed Lindbergh for British Prime Minister Neville Chamberlain's appeasement of Adolph Hitler in the Munich Agreement. According to Wills, Lindbergh's estimation of "comparative European air strengths were contained in a letter from Lindbergh to Ambassador Joseph P. Kennedy, which Lindbergh began drafting in long hand at Brown's Hotel in London after dinner on Wednesday, September 21, 1938." Wills goes on to say, "He finished it the next morning, had it typed by an embassy secretary, signed it and gave it to Herschel Johnson for delivery to Ambassador Kennedy. [Ambassador Kennedy, of course, was the father of Jack, Bobby and Teddy, as well as a bit of a character in his own right.] It was not an analysis of comparative air strengths. It was much more a statement of opinion, but it was couched in terms that were calculated to alarm all who were concerned about the survival of England. Lindbergh wrote, 'I do not believe civilization ever faced a greater crisis. Germany now has the means of destroying London, Paris, and Prague if she wishes to do so . . . It seems to be essential to avoid a general European war in the near future at almost any cost.'"

Wills quoted Lindbergh's wife, Anne Morrow Lindbergh, in her book *War Within and Without, Diaries and Letters 1939-1944* as saying her husband's reputed influence was exaggerated:

"His estimates of comparative European air strengths were rumored to have influenced Prime Minister Neville Chamberlain in his decision to go to Munich and to persuade the Czechs to yield to Hitler's demands. The truth is that Lindbergh never spoke about German Air Power to Chamberlain or to the Secretary of State for Air, Sir Kingsley Wood. His reports to other air officials were no doubt repeated, but there is no evidence that these were influential in the decisions at Munich."

But, according to Wills, even if U.S. Ambassador Joseph P. Kennedy succeeded in getting the "report" to Chamberlain before he tried to appease Hitler, Chamberlain of his own accord, dreaded that the Germans had the capacity to destroy London. Nevertheless, according to the author, there is evidence the report strongly influenced him. Wills stated that, "Chamberlain may well have received a summary of Lindbergh's report at Heston aerodrome on the morning of September 22, but it seems probable that he did not get the entire report until shortly before his flight to Munich on September 29. The late James Reston [the fabled future correspondent of *The New York Times*] covered the Munich Crisis from London. He was then a 28-year-old, new reporter for the Associated Press. In his memoir published over fifty years later, Reston wrote, '[Ambassador Kennedy] not only agreed with Charles Lindbergh's judgment that the Luftwaffe could lick the air forces of Britain, France, and Russia combined but also handed a memorandum of the Lindbergh opinions to Chamberlain when the prime minister set off to see Hitler at Munich.' Reston had not gained the reputation as the most influential journalist of his generation by using facts carelessly. He most likely learned of Kennedy's action days after the event at an informal, off-the-record meeting where Kennedy had pontificated on his role in the crisis."

Though it's uncertain how much influence Lindbergh's air expertise had on Neville Chamberlain, it is no mystery how much of an effect the great aviator had on public opinion on the war in the United States. He was one of the major figures advocating that America stay neutral during the coming world conflict, and at first his views prevailed. The irony is, had he succeeded in keeping America entirely out of World War II, Brown's Hotel, along with the rest of England, would have been lost to Germany. Nevertheless, I find it truly remarkable how often a great old hotel plays a role, large or small, in great world events. Great men and women of history, it seems, like great hotels like Brown's. And every time you or I stay at such fabled places, we can breathe in and share a little of that reflected grandeur and glory.

Now, however, it's time for me to leave history and Brown's behind as I pack up and head off to my next great destination: Claridge's.

Chapter 4

Claridge's

"When I die, I don't want to go to heaven; I want to go to Claridge's." So said the great love of Katharine Hepburn's life, Spencer Tracy, who lived at Claridge's in London. I use the word "live" advisedly. Walk into the foyer, with its graceful window – staircase to the "heaven" of rooms above – and you at once feel at home whether you are landed gentry from a castle back home or a tiny apartment in New York City or Paris. Its rich yellow walls, mirrored white pillars and gentle, coffered ceiling lighting make one wonder if this isn't indeed heaven.

Martin Riskin, who has had executive positions in three of New York City's greatest hotels – The Waldorf-Astoria, The Plaza and the Pierre – traveled to London and the Continent frequently for both business and pleasure. The nephew of virtuoso violinist Jascha Heifetz, Riskin saw his acclaimed uncle occasionally in London. He happens to be an expert on the subject of Claridge's Hotel, which is only one of the reasons I was chatting with him.

"London's great Claridge's Hotel has served as the host for numerous celebrities over the years," Mr. Riskin told me, after I had luxuriously ensconced myself in one of his hotel's world-renowned, superbly appointed rooms, then trailed downstairs to confer with him. "With its superb service and utmost discretion, stars as well as wealthy guests have felt the utmost in comfort staying here. Claridge's is an oasis, no matter what takes place in the bustling city."

Of course, he feels somewhat obligated now to prove his point with one of the many wonderful Claridge's anecdotes:

"Many years ago the superb violinist Jascha Heifetz returned to Claridge's following his sold-out concert. As usual, the evening manager greeted Mr. Heifetz cordially and the great musician just nodded and was heard to mutter: 'Happy Birthday, ha!' as he headed to the elevator. The manager was naturally puzzled by this, until a couple who had attended the performance returned to the hotel and mentioned an amusing incident.

"It appears a lady who was at the concert sent a note to Jascha Heifetz during the intermission. That day was her husband's birthday and she requested Heifetz to play 'Happy Birthday' for him. Before the second part began, the great musician announced receiving the note. He said he would be happy to oblige, however, he had left the music home. A few evenings later Heifetz gave a command performance for the King and Queen. Afterward, the royal couple chatted with him. The King said 'Mr. Heifetz, I noticed that at the conclusion of your wonderful recital you smiled at the Queen.' Heifetz was quite flustered and quickly replied 'but your Majesty, she smiled at me first!'"

I stayed at Claridge's for the first time just before Christmas 2005, and it was unlike any hotel experience I ever had. It was as if I were an actor in a Noël Coward play: in an art–deco suite that was a stage set at The Haymarket or Duchess or another West End historic playhouse.   The closets, with thick, perfectly curved wooden doors, were the same ones titled and theatrical royalty used, and I almost reverently hung my lonely, single suit and shirt in one of them.

Though Claridge's as we know it opened in 1898, there had been a hotel on the site ever since James Mivart opened one at 51 Brook Street in 1812. Sixteen years later he connected five townhouses to make one hotel, and royalty of the day, like Grand Duke Alexander, flocked to Mivart's new inn. Probably not too many American tourists during that first year of operation, seeing as we were at the time at war with England. More's the pity.

William Claridge ran a separate hotel at 49 Brook Street, and he and his wife, Marianne, ran the townhouses from 49 to the corner.   Richard D'Oyly Carte, who built The Savoy (and Savoy Theatre) purchased Claridge's such as it was, demolished it and opened it anew, retaining its name, in 1898. Landed gentry stayed at The Savoy much the same as their counterparts, more industrialists than gentry, did in New York at The Waldorf–Astoria which opened in 1893, and, later, The Plaza, which opened in 1907, first as temporary expedients for in–town mansions which became too costly and burdensome to keep up.

New York's Waldorf–Astoria may be the world's greatest Art Deco palace. Claridge's, on the other hand, is Art Deco on a more human scale, with its horseshoe lights strung along subdued white light glass panels.

Katharine Hepburn once upon a time raised eyebrows by coming down to the lobby in slacks, but few very things ruffle the perpetually unruffled feathers of the staff of Claridge's. One former executive of Time-Warner I know once informed a Claridge's butler that she was waiting for dinner for her husband. "Yes, Madame. You're waiting for dinner for your husband," the butler replayed without the slightest tinge of disbelief.

"The truck drivers in London whistle at me when I walk around in slacks and I get strange looks from the desk clerks at Claridge's, but I do love those British," Katharine Hepburn once told my father in an interview. "They're the toughest race in the world. They can go through anything and they have a passionate belief in themselves." (Here my dad inquires after her next stage role.) "My next play? I never know. I don't like to talk about any plans that I might have; it's a phobia with me. But I do know that there's an enormous field of absolutely fascinating stuff to do in the theater – so many fine things just lying around." Ah, yes, those were the days. On Broadway, at least.

"Hell, I like seeing plays," Ms. Hepburn continued. *"Death of a Salesman* has been my favorite for some time. I think Elia Kazan is the best damn director there is. George Cukor is wonderful – I've been with him a thousand times. I loved working with John Huston on *The African Queen* and it's always been fun doing pictures with Spencer Tracy. Spence is a great, great actor. He has such simplicity. I respect him and I love him." (Next inquiry, about Ms. Hepburn's daily routine.) " I love walking, as I've said. I walk around the reservoir in Central Park very often and you're always meeting the same people."

Incidentally, I believe I had the last newspaper interview with Hepburn before she died. It was in 2000 at her seaside home in Connecticut.

I talked – very briefly! – to design doyenne Diane von Furstenberg not long ago at the National Arts Club in New York. I told her of my impending trip and asked after her favorite London hotel. Without any noticeable hesitation she said Claridge's. I later talked to one of her associates who stayed for drinks at the Club and she told me Diane was also designing some rooms at Claridge's.

This website I happened across seems thrilled about the prospect:

"We may remind you that this isn't the first we've heard

about Ms. von Furstenberg's fondness for Claridge's: her Resort 2009 Collection was hotel-inspired, and she actually deemed a portion of her Florence runway show 'the Hotel Life,' showcasing ensembles of Wedgwood blue and a hotel key pattern directly influenced by the style of Claridge's. . . . Plus, she has had her hand in a couple of other hotel-related projects already: remember she worked with W Hotels to produce the DVF Emergency Fashion Kit ($320) that includes her black wrap dress, a thong and a garment bag. Also, waitresses at the Hollywood Roosevelt's lounge are outfitted in the designer's signature wrap dress (best uniform ever, maybe?)"

Like most of London's historic grand hotels, Claridge's, has attracted dozens of fine shops around it. W. Somerset Maugham's wife, Syrie, opened one on Duke Street. But in his biography of Maugham, called *Maugham, A Biography*, Ted Morgan says the playwright and novelist went out of his way to avoid his wife's shop. "Forgive me, dear Beverly (Beverly Nichols, a journalist), but I could not bear to look through the window and see what my wife might be doing," Morgan quotes Maugham as saying as he avoided walking past her little establishment.

My father interviewed him (Maugham, that is) during World War II after he'd fled both London and his home on the French Riviera. "We were in the library of Nelson Doubleday's home at Oyster Bay, where I'd finally succeeded in tracking him down after barely missing him, over the course of a decade, at Shepheards's in Cairo, at the Pera Palace in Istanbul, The Savoy Grill in London and the Twenty-One Club in New York," my father – place-name-dropping somewhat shamelessly – wrote in an interview for *Stage Magazine*. "He now wore a brown sports coat and gray trousers, part of his scant wardrobe. Only recently inhabiting a London bomb shelter, he left England with a blanket, three days' provisions, a suitcase, a sack for soiled linen and boots, and three dollars.

"'I managed to get to America with six suits,' he said. 'I have that suitcase, and nothing else in the world. I don't know what's happened to my home on the Riviera. I suppose the Italians are using it. My books, my pictures – everything is there. I don't know how long I shall stay in America, or where to go when I leave. I have jobs of work to do. I expect to earn a bit of money. The British Government has taken all my money, but I'm asking them to allow me enough to live on.'"

"I was astounded," he told my father of the success of the play *Rain*, based on his story of the same name, and which ran on Broadway starting in 1922. "I absolutely couldn't believe it . . . Poor Jeanne Eagels. What a magnificent actress! I thought her performance was amazing. I saw the part played in many cities and many languages but no one touched her. Death took a great actress from us . . . Isn't it strange how short lives are in the theatre? Careers. People struggle to get to the top, they stay there precariously for a while, and then they're no longer on the top and they're forgotten."

Poor Jeanne. She died tragically young at 39. A great loss to Broadway. Here's an excerpt from my father's writing about the play and Ms. Eagels:

"*Rain* came into the Maxine Elliott Theater on a November evening in 1922, and the opening brought forth an emotional demonstration never exceeded in the theater of this country and century. First-nighters stood and screamed when the curtain fell upon Sadie's denunciation of [Reverend] Davidson at the close of the second act; they were as wild as spectators at a football game . . . I occupied a seat in the rear of the balcony on that opening night and experienced one of the most genuinely stirring moments in all my theater going years in the final scene of the third act when Sadie's long-silent phonograph broke into the haunting strains of 'Wabash Blues,' her gesture of complete disgust with all mankind."

Rain, one of the most popular short stories ever printed, was also turned into the movie musical *Miss Sadie Thompson*, starring Rita Hayworth and Jose Ferrer, in 1953. Why am I going on so much about this story? Well, when one spends time in London, one expects a fair amount of rain, doesn't one?

Back to Claridge's, "You'll expect Fred Astaire and Ginger Rogers to emerge dancing at any minute," Frommer's guidebook says:

"If you want to live in the total lap of luxury, at an even tonier address than The Connaught and The Dorchester, make it Claridge's . . . . Diva Joan Collins may have staged her latest marriage here, but now Kate Moss is spotted in the hip bar. Elizabeth Hurley strolls through the lobby, and *chef extraordinaire* Gordon Ramsay is loud-mouthing it in the kitchen . . . what would Queen Victoria have said about his fiery temper?!"

Hundreds of years of collective experience of the staff and

tradition of Claridge's mean pinpoint perfection for the guest. Peter Timmons, Executive Chef at the Greenbrier, one of the greatest resort hotels in the world, defends Ramsay's unique temperament as well as his extraordinary talent. For one thing, Timmons says, Ramsay is a perfectionist and has a right to demand perfection of his staff.

"You can't get away from the heritage – it is so important. And the building itself is so beautiful and it had the gorgeous art deco richness," Gil Christophers told me. "And when it was done in the early 1930's, it was pushing the boundaries of Art Deco then; they really were brave . . . But now we enjoy that. . . . Claridge's has come into its own again in the past eight years. It was refurbished about five years ago, and it was done so sympathetically."

Gordon Ramsay has "become a celebrity chef at Claridge's," Christophers continued. "He was a big name but not as big a name as he is today. Claridge's is as important to Gordon as Gordon is important to Claridge's. It's a very happy relationship . . . ."

"You're extremely proud of what you do – because that's what gets you up in the morning," the Executive Chef of Claridge's main dining room told me. "Today that's totally different than it was yesterday . . . the flavor of everything has changed from the day before."

Pride in job longevity is a hallmark of many employees at London's grand hotels. "I've actually always been here. I've always worked here," a chef at Claridge's told me.

Gil chimed in, "We have a ballroom and we have six other rooms, all of which are full pretty much every day – with two or three things a day. So Martin, our chef, could be booking dining for 200 and then deliver 80. We could be doing a cocktail party for 700 which, I think, we're doing tonight. Its operation is huge and it's a hotel operation as opposed to a simple 80-seat restaurant.

"Different people do different things – I mean a hotel is hospitality," Martin said. "It's someone's house. So it is 24/7, whereas with a restaurant, they close every day.

"Actually, what happened before it made business sense, because it was one kitchen creating food for all these rooms and the restaurants and all the other operations of the hotel.

"I think part of the condition was that they brought a staff to Claridge's and it is a wonderful hotel and should deserve a star because I think people . . . again, it gave us an opportunity to reform on what we were doing. We've upgraded our functions and used our private events menus for lovely, elaborate canapés. So it gave us the opportunity really to focus on what we are doing.

"This area really didn't do any business at all. It was sort of a meeting area in the hotel and people would come and have a drink and a coffee, and now we've got quite a substantial breakfast and lunch."

On a tour of the kitchen, Martin continued, "This is a trophy that one of the pastry chefs has won for dessert of the year. It's just been delivered today. It's a funny little thing. Achievement is great as well. And here are some of those lovely things that are left over from the old days of the restaurant – things that we still use. This is a duck press. (Tour d'Argent in Paris is known for duck dishes.) I actually do an interactive dining in the kitchen. Main kitchen, filled with room service . . . private events. So the preparation of everything is [done] here."

"We don't make any pretense to be the least expensive in town or anything like that. We try not to be greedy. But it's beautifully served . . . good value for money," Gil said. "In here we have breakfast . . . and this sauce section on the side here . . . and so many things to do with meat, game, poultry. And then you're in the fish and the vegetable section."

"There are [four] rooms on the Sixth Floor which we supply from the kitchen . . . and a bit of maintenance going in here. . . . Afternoon tea is here; we'll do well over a hundred for afternoon tea."

"A team of fourteen works pastry at Claridge's. The first person who comes in does bakery at 4:30," Martin said. "Our snacks are biscuits, our sorbets, ice creams – you name it, it's made here,." I'm told by one of the chefs at Claridge's.

Afternoon tea is one thing – tea, sandwiches, scones, pastry – High Tea quite another, especially at Claridge's. One executive chef discovered inspiration from Claridge's archives and today's High Tea differs little from those in the 1930's. The menu for High Tea at Claridge's consists of your choice of Eggs on Toast, scrambled, poached or boiled with soldiers, Welsh Rarebit from the original Thirties recipe, Fresh Sardines on Toast or Mushrooms on Toast, all served with Crumpets or Teacakes and a selection of cakes and tea from a choice of over thirty different blends. High Tea has been served in the Reading Room at Claridge's from 5:00 p.m. until 6:30 p.m. while Afternoon Tea is served from 3:00 p.m. until 5:30 p.m. in the Foyer and Reading Room.

A press note on High Tea at Claridge's goes, in part, like this:

"Picture the scene. It is early evening in November and the nights have drawn right in. It is dark, it is cold and a misty rain is falling, shining silver in London's lights. You are wrapped in layers of cashmere and wool but still your nose and toes are freezing. Nevertheless it is with heels tapping and a singing heart that you enter the warmth and elegance of Claridge's, to sit next to a roaring fire and feast on welsh rarebit or boiled eggs with soldiers, followed by hot crumpets, lemon cake and of course, lashings of hot tea. What could possibly be better than that!

"Claridge's is delighted to be re–introducing the glorious tradition of High Tea to winter evenings. Taken a little later than the Afternoon Tea which Claridge's is so famous for, High Tea is served between 5 p.m. and 6.30 p.m., making it both a marvelously warming end to a cold afternoon and a pleasantly early supper – especially before the theatre.

"Whilst planning his menu for High Tea, Executive Chef, Martyn Nail, sought inspiration from Claridge's archives and today's High Tea differs little from that served in the 1930s, when, of course, the newly refurbished, art deco Claridge's had firmly established itself as *the* destination for London's smart set."

◊◊◊

High Tea at Claridge's

Eggs on Toast
Scrambled, poached or boiled with soldiers
or
Welsh Rarebit
(from the original 30's recipe)
or
Fresh Sardines on toast
or
Mushrooms on toast

Crumpets or Teacakes

A selection of cakes

Tea, from a choice of over 30 different blends

High Tea will be served in the Reading Room at Claridge's from 5.00pm until 6.30pm and is £35.

Afternoon Tea will continue to be served from 3.00 until 5.30pm in the Foyer and Reading Room, until November 25th when Christmas Tea will usurp both. High Tea and Afternoon Tea will be available again from January 7th.

◊◊◊

Sipping a spot of tea herself, Gil turned to Martyn: "I was telling him [that is, me, Ward] about you doing your sandwiches every day and about being consistent with a nice amount of filling. It's discipline and skill to get them all the same size."

Maybourne Style, a magazine devoted to The Berkeley, Claridge's and The Connaught when the three were the Maybourne Group, captured the essence of the perfect blend of caviar and champagne in a piece by Bill Prince. Here's a tasty snippet of his report:

"Top dog beluga didn't disappoint: peppercorn–sized eggs play an entirely different symphony on the taste buds. Words like 'earthy,' 'oaken' and 'powerful' often spring unbidden when beluga is consumed for the first time. Caviar royalty needs champagne royalty, so we matched beluga with a glass of Cristal (£46.50). First made for the Russian imperial family, Cristal is easily the equal of beluga in terms of power and its kaleidoscope of flavors.

"Neither champagne nor caviar, once opened, keeps for very long – a great excuse for indulging in the three C's today."

While things may appear to run like clockwork, a "school of hard knocks" may be an apt description of part of the Claridge's learning curve.

"I can remember, I'd been here a couple weeks, not even a couple weeks, a couple of days," Martyn, the Executive Chef, told me. "And the sous chef, the man that was in charge, asked for this creamed spinach." He (Martyn) made it, placed it on the pass, walked straight back and, before he knew it, it was running down his back! "It wasn't seasoned enough! . . . It was actually quite a big china dish. It was quite heavy! . . . That's the nature of the environment as it was then. But it was tough. It was a big kitchen of over eighty people. . . . I have an amazing team in the kitchen. There is the sort of core and then the people that aren't so passionate about what they do. But you need them to garnish 2,000 pieces of canapé. It's different people and the different styles of people make the teams."

My additional notes on Claridge's: *Average age was quite high amongst guests; hard to raise prices for them so revenue suffered . . . Claridge's doesn't have pool, carpark, many things but do have service and staff . . . hard work — everything has to be perfect, all the time, every day — it's a massive undertaking . . . kitchen staff is a very young team . . . you could go into kitchen with a stack of notes and say 'today we need to be great' — it wouldn't make any difference because the dedication is there every day . . . not unusual to have challenging kitchen requests at challenging hours . . . customer, 94, comes for lunch every day; association with hotel goes back to Fifties . . . extraordinary Savoy reputation as British and American officers from WWII who lived/used Savoy have nostalgic memories of the service they received in severely difficult times . . . Claridge's always had a substantial Jewish clientele . . . these elderly people tell stories to their family who carry on "love" of Savoy or Claridge's (goodwill can't be bought) . . .*

Bing Crosby and Bob Hope used the wide, carpeted corridors as putting "greens." Winston Churchill moved in after his ouster in the 1945 General Election as Prime Minister; he had declared Suite 212 the Yugoslavia Suite when Crown Prince Alexander II was born there on July 17th of that year. Yugoslavian soil, or so the legend goes, was sprinkled on his bed so the Crown Prince could be born on his own country's soil!

Well, that in a nutshell is the story of London's grand hotels – they make everyone from Crown Princes to crowned clowns feel at home.

Home to more foreign kings and dignitaries than Windsor Castle, there was such a sea of crowned heads at Claridge's when Princess Elizabeth of Yugoslavia was married in 1961 that, when a harried telephone operator was asked to be connected to the Queen, he asked, "which one?"

Scott and Zelda Fitzgerald stayed at Claridge's just after *This Side of Paradise* had been published in the early Twenties in

England. They were impressed with the amenities, but their lack of friends there cast a pall on their stay. "Claridge's in London served strawberries in a gold dish, but the room was an inside room and gray all day, and the waiter didn't care whether we left or not, and he was our only contact," Zelda wrote. Of course, we know now, Zelda could be a bit depressed from time to time.

Perhaps the Fitzgeralds were at Claridge's recuperating from all the gay times in New York after the publication of Scott's first novel, *This Side of Paradise*, which helped seal his reputation as the inventor of the Jazz Age. "Like a fairy-story hero and heroine they lived in a world in which the important things were romance and thrills – both of which could be bought on a roof garden in New York if you just had enough money," wrote Arthur Mizener in *The Far Side of Paradise*, a biography of F. Scott Fitzgerald.

In a letter to his daughter, Scotty (Francis Fitzgerald Lanahan), in 1938, Scott has this to say about Zelda, who by this time has been in mental institutions: "When I was your age . . . I lived with a great dream. The dream grew and I learned how to speak of it and to make people listen. Then the dream divided one day when I decided to marry your mother after all, even though I knew she was spoiled and meant no good to me. I was sorry immediately I had married her, but being patient in those days, made the best of it and got to love her in another way . . . But I was a man divided – she wanted me to work too much for her and not enough for my dream."

It is a long way from the days of Churchill, Audrey Hepburn and the dining frenzy created by Gordon Ramsay at his restaurant, Gordon Ramsay at Claridge's, to when Claridge's was, originally, Mivant's, a conglomeration of five adjacent Brook Street homes. In 1854, the establishment was renamed Claridge's.

The "new" hotel, which opened in 1898, and like The Connaught, Ritz, Dorchester and now Lanesborough has "seen them all," from Cary Grant to Katharine Hepburn, who successfully did manage to break the house rules by wearing those slacks.

"It was like her uniform. She always wore a scarf and when I was in a play with her (in the 1970's), she even required me and another understudy to wear what she did – off stage," actress/writer Caitlin O'Heany, once told me. Of course, by the time Ms. H. strolled down the staircase at Claridge's in those sporty trousers, she was a sort of world royalty herself. It is very difficult for anyone to say 'no' to royalty in Britain, especially if you work at a hotel with the history of Claridge's. So Kate got to keep her slacks, and Bing Crosby and Bob Hope were permitted to putt, putt, their way to theater, radio, record and movie fame in the storied corridors of Claridge's Hotel.

Broadway producer Marty Richards, who produced the original production of *Chicago* on Broadway, *The Life*, and has been working on producing a Broadway musical of Woody Allen's hit movie *Bullets Over Broadway*, says, "Claridge's has always been my favorite hotel. I stay there all the time."

For some Broadway stars, the task of choosing a London hotel may be even as daunting as getting a starring role on Broadway. James Barbour, who starred in the megamusical *Tale of Two Cities*, shot the PBS special on the musical in London. "There are so many great hotels in London, how do you pick a favorite?!" he asked me. Sorry, I am the last one to ask. I can't make up my mind either.

World-renowned interior designer David Linley, also an English Lord, as in Lord Linley, designed suites at Claridge's as well as (what I think is) his *piece de la resistance* in The Goring restaurant. Lord Linley, by the way, is also Queen Elizabeth's cousin. He told *Tatler's* Camilla Long for a piece published in *Maybourne Style*, that "Claridge's is a delicate creature. I felt strongly we should create somewhere that felt familiar, rather than make a design statement. So not just plonking pieces of furniture down, but having global understanding of what you're dealing with . . . I've had an association with Claridge's over many years – it's a special place for me. I've seen many happy occasions here; parties as a child, and my wife spent her last night here before our wedding."

No time for sentimentalizing, however. I have to push off to my next destination. Well, what do you know! My suitcase has already been packed up for me by the staff. How considerate. Of course, if I were a more suspicious person I might think someone was giving me a little hint. No matter. Have to be running anyway. Goodbye, Claridge's, hello Bailey's.

Chapter 5

Stopping at Bailey's

My grand tour continued its spectacular grandness next at the Millennium Bailey's Hotel – located at 140 Gloucester Road in the heart of fashionable Kensington, less than a minute's walk from Gloucester Road tube station (that's London lingo for subway station for those of you new to "Britishisms").

Bailey's is an undiscovered London treasure. I spent nearly a week at the hotel and loved every minute, from the almost suite-sized single room to the ambiance, location and ultra-friendly staff.

Feeling more like a Victorian townhouse than a hotel, Bailey's suggests New York's historic Algonquin Hotel. Its authentic Victorian decor with sweeping staircases and real fireplaces exude nostalgia. *Vive la difference* between Bailey's and the adjoining Millennium Gloucester Hotel. A full-service, felicitous "convention hotel" with ball and function rooms, it would be at home in the New York Hilton or Sheraton Center. Yet, as sleek and modern as it is, it boasts the Bombay Brasserie, London's finest Indian restaurant.

The hotel's conference center (known as the Millennium Conference Center), which interconnects the Bailey's and the Millennium Gloucester, seems big enough for an auto show, which it has been used for! Its promotion profile states: "Our venue offers a choice of twenty-five versatile conferencing and banqueting suites, suitable for both business and social functions and capable of accommodating two to 500 delegates. About 17,000 sq. ft. of meeting and event space have been carefully re-designed and refurbished to provide total flexibility along with state-of-the-art technical equipment including 10 mb uncontested SDSL broadband, Wi-Fi, screening facilities and intelligent lighting. The hotel also has a full civil wedding ceremony license for all of its rooms. AV equipment is also available for hire and a dedicated staff will be on-hand for your event." I love that full civil wedding license point, the way it's slipped in there among all the other amenities, like having your shoes shined. To top this off, combining both the Bailey's and Gloucester hotels, their facilities can offer some 820 rooms, making them one of the most expansive facilities which can hold world-class conferences, conventions and meetings – small and large scale.

But Millennium is not easy to position in the hotel world. Its chairman, Singapore born and based Kwek Leng Beng (or, as he is most commonly called, Chairman Kwek, one of the wealthiest men in the world) has a passion for history and the arts. He restored Broadway's Hudson Theatre (a subject which I wrote about in full in my book *Discovering the Hudson*) and owns The Millennium Biltmore Hotel in Los Angeles, which was "the" Oscars hotel for several years. He and his company defy traditional corporate profiles. Some of his hotels are extraordinarily modern, sleek; others notably historic, embodying the rich tapestry of old-world architecture and heritage. He seems to have not only a love and appreciation for great hotels around the world but almost a hobbyist's affection for them, like a classic car buff or stamp collector. He wants passionately to share his love of hotels not only with his guests, of course, but with all around the world. Of course, collecting beautiful hotels is not a hobby for everyone!

At the invitation of Chairman Kwek, I had the pleasure of dining at the Bugis Street Brasserie, located at the Millennium Gloucester, which adjoins the Bailey's. It offers authentic Singaporean, Malaysian and Chinese cuisine with house specialties that include *Mee Goreng* (Malay-style fried noodles) and *Nasi Goreng* (Malay-style fried rice), fish fillets stir-fried with black pepper sauce and aromatic crispy duck.

In what sounds more like a documentary film than one of the best hotelier's effort to go the extra mile, Millennium & Copthorne Hotels plc donated a grand piano to the Wai Wai, an Indian tribe in Guyana, according to an article in *Caribbean Best* in March 2001. I think this story will give you far better insights to Chairman Kwek's unique relationship to his hotels, to people and to the world than I can.

In a tale seemingly right out of *King Solomon's Mines*, an explorer by the name of Colonel John Blashford-Snell (honest, that's his real name) had been conducting an expedition into the remote regions of equatorial Guyana. During which he came upon the minute Amerindian Wai Wai tribe and befriended them. So much so that he found himself promising to bring them back a grand piano. What did the tribe want with a piano and just how did the Colonel imagine he could physically transport such a delicate, enormous object into the jungle, are both intriguing questions. The natives dwell in the forest at the edge of the Essequibo River in the extreme south of Guyana. The Colonel had already brought the 190-member tribe much needed medical supplies, the sort of things adventurers imagine that primitive tribes would like. But, no, the Wai Wai tribe wanted a grand piano.

Apparently as the Colonel was departing the village, a priest by the name of Elessa asked him to bring back a grand piano for the tiny church there. The Colonel knew of course that the cleric was requesting the near impossible. Although it may be an occupational hazard for priests to expect the impossible, Elessa had certainly confidence in God, and also, it seems, in the Colonel.

Finding a sponsor for the grand piano back in England was the relatively easy part. As noted, Chairman Kwek's company Millennium Hotels & Resorts offered to foot the bill on the musical instrument. Meanwhile, the explorer got in touch with BWIA, who offered to transport the piano to Trinidad. After that, the explorer would have to rely on his own devices. So he and his team (and the grand piano) planned to take small planes into the Guyanese interior. Then, when that was no longer practical, they would hoof it the rest of the way back to the Wai Wai village.

But, wait. You didn't think it was going to be that easy, Colonel, did you? Just as they were leaving London (with the grand piano), they were informed by the Guyanese government that the Wai Wai had had to relocate – the entire village – because they'd been rather rudely flooded out of their old neighborhood. They'd moved upriver from Akou to Masekenari. Moreover, they now urgently needed, what else, medical supplies! As well as school books and tools with which to build a whole new village.

Still undaunted, the Colonel pushed off from London with seven other members of his new expedition. In addition to the rather large grand piano, they carried a supply of medicine and the other necessities. The team arrived by small plane in Guyana's interior, 350 miles from the capital of Georgetown. Then, for three days, they lugged their cargo through the steaming jungle, crossing rope bridges, then rode by canoe the last leg of the trip up to the Wai Wai's new settlement.

Some in the group feared that the piano strings might not have survived all this damp hot weather, not to mention all the jostling. To everyone's amazement (except, no doubt, for the priest) everything was in perfect working order. The piano was uncrated in the middle of town and the villagers erupted with a cry of delight – which must have seemed to make it all worthwhile for the Colonel. Next, one of the expedition members taught several of the tribesmen how to play and care for their new instrument. Not much later, an open–air concert (the town concert hall must have been booked) was held. The Wai Wai tribe performed native songs and their own compositions.

Just think of it. Delivering a grand piano from London to the South American jungle. Now, that's what I call room service! Those top London hoteliers, they don't seem to be able to say no to anything.

Millennium Hotels' own history of Bailey's, which it commissioned, pretty much tells it like it was, and is, and I am tacking fairly close to their official account in the following description.

First and foremost, Bailey's is one of the oldest hotels in London still standing, and operating. Moreover, like many a refined and beautiful London lady, it has a fascinating history. Unlike most London ladies, the hotel's history stretches back to 1876. Perhaps not too surprisingly the story of the hotel begins with a gentleman by the name of the Right Honourable Sir James Bailey, MP, who was born in 1840 and died in 1910. Among his many other remarkable achievements in life during the better part of the Victorian age, Mr. Bailey was the original owner of the hotel which came to bear his name. Mr. Bailey and his hotel are also inseparable from the history of the particular section of Kensington which houses the hotel. Mr. Bailey's hotel, through ingenuity, luck and much hard work managed to survive not only the turn of the century, and the unfortunate death of Mr. Bailey, but two world wars, subsequent changes in ownership and at least one serious threat of demolition. Frankly, given all this turmoil of over one and a quarter centuries, it is practically amazing that the hotel has managed to hang on to its original structure. Someone who stayed there in the 1870's probably wouldn't even have any trouble recognizing the place today, assuming that person was extremely long–lived, that is. The hotel in fact is in itself a fairly important London architectural landmark, and not simply as a result of its longevity and tenacity. The hotel is one of the defining characteristics of its unique neighborhood, Kensington.

One of the important things to remember about London is that it really is not one city but a number of neighboring towns that sort of grew together over the centuries. In fact, London only recently got her first mayor. Even as late as the 19th century, Westminster was really a different place than Kensington. This is one of the reasons why many of the areas of Greater London have such different, and distinct, characters. Take for example the advertisement that James Bailey himself employed to promote his hotel in its earlier days, in which he referred to Kensington as "the healthiest and most fashionable part of London." Anyone who has read Dickens or any of the other great English novelists of the 18th and 19th centuries knows full well that there were, alas, certain sections of town which were distinctly unhealthy. Plumbing, remember, was itself once a luxury. Kensington, being somewhat removed from the more congested central parts of the city was practically out in the country in James Bailey's day. However, more important to the hotel's purposes, it was situated in a section that was more likely to attract London's aristocrats and the more successful members of that new, upwardly mobile class the bourgeoisie. In short, rich people. Kensington had one other attractive quality for the Right Honourable owner, and that was the relative scarcity of nearby hotels at the time of its founding. James Bailey had the local upper class market to himself. Better still, the area, while removed from the trouble spots, was nonetheless close enough to the city's main attractions and social and business centers. Why, it even had a brand new "underground railway" that could zip hotel guests to central London in as little as five minutes, as well as to "all parts of London." No doubt, even the swells liked to use the underground when it was new. Mr. Bailey's hotel was also conveniently situated near the Royal Albert Hall, Hyde Park, the National History Museum, the Royal Horticultural and Kensington Gardens. And for those guests who wished not to descend underground to get around, the original hotel boasted no fewer than nine stables, which housed "well-appointed" carriages to convey guests to wherever lay their heart's desire. No ratty dog carts for these folks!

It's very interesting to read in the hotel's history that there were actually very few hotels, as such, in all of London at this time. And the aim of James Bailey in constructing his hotel was to provide accommodations on par with the local royal establishments or, at least, to be "not inferior to Buckingham Palace,

Buckingham Gate." Thanks to changes in the social order and to the Industrial Revolution, there was now apparently a need to suitably house the town's nouveau riche, as well as its old rich. The colorful travelers' inns and boarding houses just would no longer suffice, apparently.

As for James Bailey's own personal history, he was the son of William Bailey, who was a farmer in Mattishall, Norfolk. James did not, it seems, take to farming life as he absconded early in life for London. Not that he entirely turned his back on Mattishall, but clearly he was an ambitious young fellow. When he made his fortune in the capital, he did donate a beautiful organ to his local parish church in Mattishall.

It is unknown, however, what exactly prompted James Bailey to head for London at the age of twenty, which was in the year 1860. Rumor has it that he began his professional life as a butler shortly after arrival. This, remember, was a time when a large household, not to mention a palace or a hotel, required an enormous amount of daily labor. Not only was there no electricity, there were really none of the labor-saving devices we so take for granted today. Everything depended on two types of power – horse power and human sweat. It is known that, at some later date, James Bailey managed to acquire the Harrington Hotel, which like Bailey's is also located in Gloucester Road. As bright as he was hardworking, Bailey enlarged his new purchase, a practice he would continue when he constructed the future Bailey's itself. What everyone at Bailey's today would love to know about their progenitor is just how he managed to finance these considerable purchases – on a butler's salary! Which, in those days, could not have been very considerable. Presumably, he was also something of a financial wizard. Or extremely frugal! Most likely, he used his good name and managed to borrow the money, then made good on it.

One of the few things the remarkable Mr. Bailey did not do all by himself was actually build the structure of Bailey's Hotel. A well-known property owner by the name of H. B. Alexander, it seems, arranged the construction of the hotel with the assistance of the developers Charles Aldin, Jr. and William Aldin. The Aldins were quite well known in the Kensington area at this time, and had developed many other projects, including James Bailey's first hotel, the Harrington Hotel at 25 Gloucester Road. (Of course, this does raise the question of who was Mr. Harrington?) The Aldins, busy as bees, also built the houses and shops which surrounded Mr. Bailey's new hotel. Indeed, it must have been a most prosperous time, in Kensington at any rate. The name of the actual architect of the hotel is unknown, even though in that day this must have been a construction project that created what we in this day would call serious buzz. On the other hand, architects were not the celebrities then that they are now, so this anonymity is perhaps not so peculiar.

Whoever the fellow was, his design began a new architectural fashion in Kensington. Before Bailey's went up, the neighborhood was populated with buildings that had fronts, according to the London Survey, of "white Ipswich, Suffolk, Gault or Beart's patent bricks." I have no idea what any of that is, but it certainly doesn't sound too attractive. James Bailey's new hotel, on the other hand, was constructed with red bricks with "white dressings of bath stone." The upshot was that red brick became a viable building material for swanky addresses. Overall, the hotel conforms to most other fashions of the Victorian age, but this red-and-white bricks effect became a distinguishing characteristic of Kensington, and has lasted to the current day. Not too surprisingly, since it is most appealing.

If you, as an American, were confused enough at the British calling elevators "lifts," what would you have made of the Bailey's Hotel's brand new "ascending rooms?" True, they were just simple elevators, but the term "ascending room" still conjures up for me the image of an entire hotel room that goes up and down. The new building also boasted a "safe room," which also sounds quite intriguing, but which, again, simply referred to a metal safe. More important still, there were bathrooms on every floor. This was quite the luxury back then, when private baths were practically unheard of, even in the great houses and palaces. The luxurious "bath room" is a fairly modern concept. Back then, they were just privies and closets with tubs in them. Very utilitarian.

Apparently, Bailey's was a big international hit from the moment it opened its doors. At least we know that the great American author of, among other things, "The Luck of Roaring Camp," Bret Harte checked in during the first year of operation. Also, Eduard Strauss, the younger brother of the more renowned Austrian composer Johann Strauss, stopped by about the same time. More importantly to Mr. Bailey's bottom line, British royals flocked to its spectacular Victorian grand ballroom. Bailey's had arrived!

James Bailey himself did not reside in his beautiful new hotel. He'd bought 4 Harrington Gardens nearby for his private home. At this time he also owned the South Kensington Hotel in Queensgate Terrace, so he was becoming quite the Victorian Age real estate mogul. Then, in 1877, Mr. B built up Bailey's down Courtfield Road with extensions and, in 1881, those nine stables were leveled to make room for a garden and other extensions. Today, this area is home to the Bombay Brasserie. Not yet ready to rest on his laurels, Mr. B had new bedrooms installed in 1883 and, in 1890, a new elevator system and electric lights in all the rooms. This was quite forward thinking. Many people at that time still thought electric lights were dangerous. (Actually, Edison's rather clumsy DC current was prone to killing the odd horse in the street that had the misfortune to step on the buried cable.)

By this time Bailey's Hotel had grown to over 300 rooms and even Mr. B could no longer resist not living there – he'd moved himself and his entire family into the place. To make life easier for Mr. B, the hotel also served as domicile to about thirty–five of the staff members, helping to serve the customers better. Bailey's was becoming quite the tight–knit little hospitality community. You know you like your boss when you live in the same house with him. Especially if it's possible he might ring you up for room service at two in the morning.

Despite the expense and trouble to cross the Atlantic in this era (don't forget, the *Titanic* disaster wasn't until 1912), America and Britain may have been closer then than they are now – at least culturally. In any case, many of Bailey's early customers were Americans, both on business and pleasure trips. The Survey of London tellingly quotes a tourist guide of the era (1891, to be precise), commending Bailey's Hotel for its "cozy, homelike atmosphere, which is enhanced by rich and substantial surroundings." Sounds like at least a four–star recommendation to me. The guide went on to commend the wine, too, as well as the sanitary arrangements and, a little more peculiar to us in this age, the fire. Remember, back then before central heating, the fireplace in your room was much more than decorative. In fact, this is probably why the luxurious private bath took so long to come along – first, when you had to haul the hot water up by pail (before indoor plumbing) and then, when the only really warm room was one with a roaring fireplace. Ah, but we take so much for granted these days.

After all this whirlwind of activity, James Bailey in the 1890s would grow somewhat tired of the hotel business. First he sold off both of his hotels to Spiers and Pond Limited in 1894. Probably this change of heart was due to his newly booming career as a London official. He served at this time on the boards of Harrods and D. H. Evans – both world famous department stores, only the former not quite as much as the latter. Then in 1895 Mr. B was elected a Member of Parliament for the Walworth division of Newington, a post he would hold onto until 1906. He also busied himself as a Kensington vestryman from 1878 to 1894, as Deputy Lieutenant for Norfolk and as a Justice of the Peace in Essex. As you can see, his energy had not dwindled in the slightest. Oh, yes, a vestryman is a member of a local church's operational body, or vestry. Mr. B with all that extra time still on his hands was also a founding member of the Constitutional Club. This doesn't surprise me. Obviously, the Club was open only to gentlemen with iron constitutions like Mr. B's. For all this selfless, endless service, Mr. B was at last knighted in 1905 and five years later he died at his home in Rutland Gate. He left an estate of 245,000 pounds sterling. Which even now is a heck of a lot of dough. But no wonder, really. He was so darn busy his whole life he probably never had a free moment in which to spend a farthing.

We sadly leave Mr. Bailey but his hotel goes gloriously on without him.

When first erected, the hotel had virtually no competition in the area, but this changed by 1914, when there were no fewer than fourteen hotels in eighteen buildings, all situated in Cromwell Road and Harrington Gardens. Which, if you're keeping score at home, is the area roughly south of the southwest corner of Hyde Park. Not surprisingly, this phenomenal growth in the London hospitality industry tailed off at the start of the First World War. But it also changed very little in the years between the two World Wars. (There was a little event going on at the time called a worldwide Depression.) But, by 1939, the start of the Second World War, a major part of the Kensington area had been purchased with plans to build numerous new hotels. Many of these, however, were merely houses converted to use as hotels, unlike Bailey's, which had been designed and built from scratch as a luxury guest establishment. In short, the new competition was not, pleasant as they no doubt were, that intimidating custom–wise.

You may have heard or read about the inconveniences much of the city of London suffered at the hands of the Luftwaffe during WWII. Well, Bailey's did not, alas, pass through the conflict without its share of nicks and scrapes. In fact, in October of 1940, an incendiary bomb hit it square on, starting a major fire and causing, of course, much damage to the hotel's building. Some of this war damage would not be repaired until the early Fifties. The last to be reinstated were the badly damaged fourth and fifth floors. The hotel was not open during the whole of the war. The hotel's records here are a little incomplete, but it is believed the hotel served as a provisional hospital or even a shelter. Now that's what I call waiting out the war in style! None of these dingy tube stations for me! I want the ambassador suite, please! You don't suppose there was room service available during the blitz, do you? Probably not. Even the fabled English hospitality has its limits, after all.

In 1945, the hotel suffered again, with a fire in the staff quarters. Ceilings and floorboards were damaged and the entire hotel was evacuated. The structure, however, was not threatened, thank goodness. During the early Fifties, rather extensive alterations were carried out on the hotel, in fact. New bathrooms were installed in 1954, for instance. (It must be very hard for hotels to keep pace with bathroom technology; must cost a fortune to keep installing those newfangled fixtures. After all, a bed is a bed. A chair a chair. But every few years, showers and tubs keep getting ritzier and ritzier.) The new owners were not satisfied, however, and at the end of the Fifties, they made further major alterations, the highlight of which was a brand new bar. By now they must have had all their customers covered – those who check in and want nothing but a nice hot bath, and those who check in and want nothing but a nice chilled cocktail.

Despite all this new activity, however, the hotel actually came under the threat of demolition at about this same time. The Royal Borough of Kensington and Chelsea rode to the rescue, declaring that it would deeply regret such a loss to the neighborhood, arguing that the hotel forms an integral part of the area because of its historical value. Hear, hear! Disaster was indeed averted. There have, though, been many changeovers in management and ownership since Mr. B was laid to rest. In 1988, for instance, Bailey's was completely restored before it was taken over from the Taj Group by Securum Hotel Holdings (the actual transaction took place in 1992). Only a couple of years later, in 1994, the hotel was then acquired by City Developments Limited (CDL).

Never fear, however, despite all this financial finagling as well as two world wars, Bailey's has maintained most of its original structure. The original main hall is almost untouched, with its large marble pillars, grand staircase, stained glass windows and Victorian plasterwork. Today, Bailey's is a four-star hotel, with 211 rooms and has not relinquished one iota of its prestige. Of course, beautiful old pillars are lovely to look at, but a modern hotel has to change with the times and all of the rooms offer all the modern conveniences in addition to the great cultural and architectural history. The cost of a room has also changed somewhat since Mr. B built his beautiful hotel. In the 1890's, rooms supposedly went for a dollar a night for a single. Perhaps more surprisingly, by the 1970's that had gone up to only twelve pounds a night. By 1986 the cost had hit forty pounds and by the present millennium, about 145 pounds. It makes one wonder if Mr. H. G. Wells' time machine is still available in London. The use of it for even one night could save you a bundle on a hotel stay. On the other hand, they didn't have Wi-Fi in 1890. What they did have back then was once described as "homelike atmosphere which is enhanced by the rich and substantial surroundings." Moreover, the site that the prescient Mr. B chose is still a propitious one for a hotel, still not too close and not too far from most of what one wishes to visit in town. Needless to say the service at the hotel has never suffered a setback and the atmosphere of both the hotel and Kensington are as sanguine as ever. In short, the hotel still has all that made it so attractive to guests for over a hundred years, in addition to the Wi-Fi and all the other modern conveniences. At Bailey's, as at so many of the great luxury London hotels, a traveler truly is getting the best of both worlds, the past and the present.

Chapter 6

The Connaught

Taking a tour of The Connaught with General Manager Anthony Lee must have been like listening to Cary Grant talk about his film career in "Evenings with Cary Grant," which he toured colleges with shortly before his death at age 84. There is an ease mixed with reverence and splashes of fun.

"Geoffrey [Gelardi, General Manager of The Lanesborough] and I know each other very well – we have good fun together," Lee told me as we started on our tour. "The Penthouse. It's 280 square meters. It's all about the design; it's about the feeling of intimacy; it's like a Mayfair apartment. This whole place, in one way, is about coming home. We've got regular guests that love it; it's more personalized. We give more time. The world is out there when you want to grab it. But here we are, condensing thirty hours into every 24–hour day for every CEO . . . in a very genuine way."

Talking about the recession in early 2009, he continues, visibly bracing himself a bit, "We got ourselves ready several months ago and, as painful as that was, I think we are in a very strong position now to meet the economic climate. We're doing well."

Ralph Lauren thought so much of the staircase here at The Connaught, he had it replicated in his flagship New York store at 72nd Street and Madison Avenue. Not to mention The Connaught is the only hotel he stays at in London. For many it's London's only hotel. Gloriously renovated, complete with an entirely new ultra–modern section, The Connaught drips service. Like near-neighbor Claridge's, you can do no wrong. Murder, of course, is a no–no; short of this, however, it is as Cole Porter describes it in his song, "Anything Goes."

Imagine a hotel that never lays off anyone from its staff. Imagine one in which there are three staff members to every guest. One where more than eighty percent of the guests are repeat visitors. And listen to General Manager Anthony Lee: Guests guests "come because they feel at home here and because we do not pretend to be a glamorous hotel and we do not ascribe to artificiality or current fashions. We are what we are, a down-to-earth home where guests are comfortable and at ease."

You have imagined The Connaught.

Originally called the Coburg Hotel, named after Prince Albert of Saxe-Coburg, Consort of Queen Victoria, the Duke of Westminster's building originally occupied the area where Carlos Place was carved in Mayfair like an inviting   left arm off Grosvenor Square. In 1917 it was renamed The Connaught after Queen Victoria's third son, Prince Arthur, the Duke of Connaught.

Over the years. Andrew Anspach, manager of the Algonquin Hotel in New York, never stayed anywhere else. Today, most of its guests think of The Connaught as their London residence. They even want to stay in the same room year after year, decade after decade.

From the window of my suite, I can see a curved English street that even Dickens couldn't have painted in words. There's a cute English house, maybe it was a carriage house originally but it's pink ... across the street there's One Carlos Place ... I've got a little balcony outside this room on the second floor and a curved street that is idyllic, maybe out of Peter Pan! The bathrooms are magnificent; the ceilings are magnificent; the walls are magnificent; every-thing is magnificent! I am staying in room Room 103 and already, though this is the first time I've ever been here, am getting an overwhelming desire to come back, to treat this place as though it were my home.

I feel like I have arrived! . . .

This is where Charles de Gaulle stayed after WWII. It was in the Marie Antoinette Suite that Charles de Gaulle, who had moved to The Connaught, met Churchill and Eisenhower for meetings during World War II. Churchill and Eisenhower I can understand. Both had their down-to-earth side. But de Gaulle? The only place I can picture the super-erect de Gaulle at home is on a parade reviewing stand. But even he must have let down his hair (figuratively) at The Connaught. If they can make him feel at home, you know they're good.

"There has been a great deal of interest in The Connaught in recent months following the £70 million restoration of what many regard as their 'London home' when in town," the new Connaught brochure reads. "The Coburg Bar has been voted number one bar by London's *Time Out*; award-winning Hélène Darroze unveiled what is proving to be the finest dining experience in town and we also celebrated the successful opening of the new David Collins-

designed Connaught bar. With summer and London's social season now in full swing, it is our sincere hope that we shall have the
pleasure of welcoming you back to The Connaught to witness the
evolution of a London legend."

The £70 million restoration of the Connaught, completed in
2008, catapulted this Olympian destination of taste and luxury
once again to the international acclaim The Connaught has
enjoyed since it opened. French chef Hélène Darroze has made
her "Hélène Darroze at the Connaught" one of the most thrilling
dining experiences in London. Food expert Jasper Gerard
describes her "La Caviar D'Aquitaine" as "so fresh and sumptuous
that if you could eat only one dish for the rest of your life, this
might be it." Darroze, a [two]-Michelin star chef oversees all the
cuisine at The Connaught, including the renowned semi-circular
Connaught Grill. And if you're unfamiliar with the Michelin grad-
ing system, don't be misled. A two-star Michelin restaurant is
positively stratospheric. Three stars is the absolute top and that's
given only to a handful of restaurants around the world, and
those are the kinds of haute-cuisine places where even the French
have trouble pronouncing the menu items.

The Connaught has also reinvented its butler service to
ensure every whim is satisfied, from sumptuous, in-room afternoon snacks to unpacking and pressing the finest suits and other
garments. My own Connaught butler, Oriental and as friendly
and attentive as if he had walked out of an Astaire–Rogers movie,
appeared minutes after the press of a button, just as his counter-
part at The Lanesborough had done. A fellow could get spoiled
by that kind of service.

Noël Coward presented an entirely different kind of butler
in his play, *Ways and Means*, a light comedy in three scenes.
Stevens, the ever-so-proper butler, sounds utterly amazed when
the destitute, highbrow couple, Toby and Stella, ask him to burgle
their neighbor, a house guest like them, in the next room.

"Oh, Madame – I don't think I dare!" Stevens exclaims.

Stevens is so proper, in fact, that after relieving their fellow
house guest of her francs, he refuses to share in the loot, with this
caveat: "I'd rather not, sir, if you don't mind – I'd rather you had
the money," he replies gallantly. "I happened to find these on the
dressing table – they'll do me nicely." Coward goes on to relate in
the stage directions that Stevens "produces several diamond
bracelets, some rings, and a jeweled cigarette case."

I'm not advocating for a moment the idea that any butler at The Connaught, Lanesborough, Ritz or any other grand and glorious hotel in London could ever stoop to being a thief. What I am saying is that summoning a butler, even at £355 per night, can be a liberating experience. Liberating for many who vainly labor to meet their daily and weekly expenses – and more, much more. So even for a few fleeting moments, one has indeed arrived – not at a place, station, or stardom. But at the almost indescribable feeling of "somebodyness" that comes over one. It cannot be measured by money or time. So is it worth £355 pounds? For one thing, there will never be a day when you can't say, "well, my butler was always there in a minute," or some such thought! It's like a friend of mine who produced an off-Broadway play. He lost every penny but it was a great memory. Not that anyone loses anything staying in ultra–luxury. Yes, money can go for other more utilitarian things. But there will always be utilitarian things. How often in life do you get a taste of what it's like to be royalty? The upper crust does crackle with a certain indescribable electricity.

Guest hotels, as Peter King notes in his book on The Connaught, do difficult if not impossible things as if they were simple, unsurprising tasks. "Clearly, a readiness for everything can only result from a very special kind of management," King writes in *"The Connaught Story."* "To achieve greatness, a hotel must be managed by a man whose commercial skills are enhanced by an artist's feel for style, and a pioneer's pleasure in change."

King is referring to Paolo Zago, who was born near Venice and worked at small and great hotels on the road to becoming General Manager of The Connaught. When he was first made head of The Connaught, he said that, "for six months I did nothing, absolutely nothing, but watch, listen, learn – and take notes. And it did not take long to realize that if The Connaught did not exist, it would have to be invented."

Zago's further comments to King about not wanting to make any precipitous moves are telling and worth including. They are typical of the approach of most of the hoteliers in this book. Zago said, "What I recognized, and what I struggled there many years to maintain, is the continuity of good taste, dignity and old–fashioned values, while allowing the hotel to evolve naturally. In a business now plagued by the disease of mediocrity and standardism, I've tried to make [concessions] and am proud to consider myself with my staff the guardian, the custodian of a great tradition."

In fact, the hotel has only had six general managers since it opened in 1897, thus allowing it to "hold on to its unmatched, idiosyncratic and intimate brand of five-star luxury," according to The Connaught website. Six general managers in over a century. There have been more popes than that.

Reflecting pensively from my suite at The Connaught in 2009 – the Grosvenor Suite, to be more specific – I quietly note that my living room has gold leaf on a plaster ceiling, a beautiful chandelier, a great wooden fireplace with marble interior; and beautiful original art – pastoral scenes and floral prints. There's a flat screen TV in every room, including bathrooms; orchids and flowers everywhere . . . fixtures are very solid silver coin, marble bathroom, marble floor . . . sailing yachts in bathroom; beautiful Mount Street, Mayfair view. I get exhausted thinking about what it must take to polish everything just in my room.

Anthony Lee, General Manager of The Connaught, makes sure even his guests' dogs are happy. I've interviewed him several times over the past few years, and I always come away feeling like I stayed in the best hotel in London, which The Connaught may very well be.

Mr. Lee told me, "Lauren Bacall was over here this summer filming for three months and she rang me from New York to apologize. I have a very close relationship with her. I met her at the Bel Air – we went swimming together last year, and I'm best friends with her dog, Sophie! The dog can now send emails, leave voice mail, you know, I teach the dog all sorts of tricks! She said it's the first time 'I've ever stayed any place else' 'cause she's used to staying in an apartment when taking filming commitments that she had and she wanted me to know that she's in town and that we'll catch up for a drink while she's here. But she rang me personally to apologize the fact that she's not at The Connaught, which is the first time she's ever stayed any place else.

" . . . I think a hotel, apart from the character of the place, I think the key to success of the hotel that can retain its guests and bring them back time and time again is the staff. When people ask me what I do, apart from the kidding around and saying I do the washing up, basically I feel that I am the keeper of the soul of The Connaught. . . . A little bit like cooking, it takes three things to make what I call a great hotel, and that is the building, the guests and the staff. And like cooking you blend it together, you nurture them together and you create what I call the soul.

" . . . I've got a 1927 wine list – two of them, actually – perfectly preserved, which I found in an archive here. Look brand new. But some of the vintages from eighteen hundred and something on it and the prices; bills where you paid extra for the fireplace to be lit in your room at the Connaught, in shillings and pence and farthings, and it's history.

" . . . I think people from the past used to fear it. It was a very impenetrable fortress, The Connaught. It didn't matter who you were or how much money you had – unless you were introduced by somebody who was a guest of The Connaught, you couldn't get in. It was literally like that. It was a personal introduction system. I remember that time; it was at the tail end of when I first arrived. Of course we're not so strict nowadays. Much more open, in fact. So much so that the whole warmth of the place hopefully wraps around you when you come in. I think it's a little like an insurance policy – you don't always appreciate it, although we try to spoil everybody that's here. We love doing it. If you're under pressure of business and something goes wrong, that is when you really appreciate what our professional team can do. That's why I say it's a bit like an insurance policy. You hope you never need it, but when you do need it, you want to make sure it's a good one. So, you know, all of a sudden, whatever, your flight can go belly up or something happens, our concierge team here are second to none in the world. They've got a finger dipped in everything and anything, and the wonderful thing about everybody that works here is they are like a well-oiled machine. They make the impossible happen.

"One of the compliments I've had time and time again from many guests is if they had to fall ill anywhere in the world, they would want to fall ill at The Connaught! I take that as a compliment because of the way that the staff care for you, and we've got great chemists and a great house doctor who will come and see you at the hotel.

"Jack [Nicholson] was staying with us. He used to come back still with the makeup on from filming. He used to come in the door – I remember him coming in the front door – it was about 98 degrees outside, summer heat wave. And he came in with mask and coat! Crazy! He came in the door like this, in his Joker makeup from *Batman.* And he went up the staircase and he kind of slow motion took two or three steps at a time, clear up the staircase. He went up to the top of the balcony – 98 degrees outside – he had his glasses on and this crazy, nasty coat. . . . And looking up at this guy with mask and coat on who ought to be passing out from the heat! He's fun. Danny DeVito's funny, too. When those two get together, well you know, he's this short man rolling around in this big limousine, going out and coming back at 4 a.m. absolutely – well, . . . Oliver Reed, too, was a dangerous one. There was a time when The Connaught was very formal, and we had a little tea over there. . . . And he came in with a Scotsman's kilt on – in true Scotsman's style with nothing on underneath. And he came in on a Sunday afternoon. There I was, dressed in – in those days they used to have black tails, stiff white collar, you know, very traditional. Oliver's the sort of man that if you look at him wrong, he'll break your jaw . . . like 'what are you looking at me like that for?' And he sat there on the couch giving a full view to all our guests! He was well and truly inebriated. Dealing with people is very interesting. Anyway, long story short, I did persuade him to finally come out the door with me. He then wanted to play doorman for ten minutes before finally leaving.

"Even I let my hair down, you see, when I'm out of here. Everybody thinks that I hang up the suit, put it in the cupboard, take it out in the morning. But I'm a normal person."

The conversation lighted upon Van Johnson. "He asked me to come up urgently. So I came up and asked, 'what's wrong?' 'The scales.' 'You always like to have scales in your room.' 'Not in metric!' he said. 'By the time I figure them out, I nearly pass out. Put them back into stones for me!'"

That's The Connaught for you. Leaving absolutely no stones unturned.

Nor was Van the only Hollywood nobility to patronize The Connaught. "Betty" Bacall used to stay at both The Connaught and The Savoy some years after she and Bogie were married. Bogart used to call Lauren Bacall "Baby," and the late New York *Post* and syndicated columnist Earl Wilson was on hand at the 21 Club, one of Bogie's favorite New York haunts, when he recalled in his book *The Show Business Nobody Knows* that the normally crusty thrice-married film star was, as Wilson put it, "wearing his heart on his sleeve" after a few drinks. "Let's drink one for Baby!" Bogart proclaimed loud and clear to some of the ruffled patrons . . . "I'll let you in on a secret. I'm in love again – at my age! . . . As soon as I get my divorce, I'm going to marry Baby!" When someone at another table remonstrated the erstwhile screen gangster for being "very boring," Bogart laughed, adding, "Do you mind – I'm in love!"

Now, let's see. What's next on the agenda? Well, what do you know. Time to visit the Millennium Mayfair.

Chapter 7

The Millennium Hotel Mayfair

In its own refined and understated way, the Millennium Hotel London Mayfair is on par with the very best hotels in London, including Claridge's and The London Ritz. Of course, it lacks the gilded physicality of The Ritz, the incredible tradition and *savoir faire* of Claridge's. But it has that most important commodity: "location, location, location." The Times real estate benchmark, and indeed its location in Mayfair on Grosvenor Square near Hyde Park and the elegant Park Lane, give it a cozy lived-in feeling, especially for longer-stay guests that's hard to imagine at The Ritz or The Savoy.

The Millennium Mayfair is part of the worldwide empire of one of the greatest hoteliers in the world. That man is Chairman Kwek, Kwek Leng Beng of the Hong Leong Group and the Millennium & Copthorne Hotels plc worldwide. He's the boss. But he's not only the boss. His personal tastes are reflected in his hotels. He has a great knack for real estate. That's part of the equation, certainly. But he also had a knack for presentation – and money.

His hotels in London include The Millennium Hotel Mayfair, Bailey's (built in the 1890's), Gloucester and Knightsbridge as well as the well known 833–room Copthorne Tara Hotel located in a quiet corner of the Royal Borough of Kensington and Chelsea. Chairman Kwek loves London, its antiquity, charm, history. But he's also there to make a profit.

Wikipedia, the online encyclopedia, is as good a place as any to find the basic facts of the Chairman's background. The following is what the Wik has to say about him, somewhat revised by more recent information I've obtained:

"Kwek's father, the late Kwek Hong Png left Fujian province as a penniless teenager for Singapore and subsequently founded the Hong Leong Group there. Kwek Leng Beng was trained as a lawyer in London, but chose to join the family business in the early 1960's. He became Executive Chairman in 1990 and went on to establish an international reputation for his leadership of the Hong Leong Group Singapore, a conglomerate with more than 250 companies, including eleven listed ones.

"Kwek is the Executive Chairman of City Developments Limited (CDL), an international property and hotel conglomerate and a leading real estate developer listed on the Singapore Exchange Limited. The CDL Group operates in twenty countries in Asia, Europe, North America and New Zealand/Australia and has over 300 subsidiaries and associated companies including five companies listed on the stock exchanges of London, Hong Kong, New Zealand and Philippines. CDL has a market capitalization of over US$6 billion (at its peak, it reached over US$10 billion) and is in the top 5 percent of listed companies in Singapore. It is also the second-biggest property developer in Southeast Asia.

"Kwek Leng Beng also chairs Millennium & Copthorne (M&C) Hotels plc, which is a London-listed international hotel group of which 54 percent share belongs to CDL. M&C is ranked 34th among the world's top international hotel groups (Index of 325 World's largest hotel groups, July 2009, *Hotels* magazine) and has a portfolio of over 120 hotels with over 36,000 rooms in eighteen countries.

"Kwek's Hong Leong Group of companies also owns Hong Leong Finance, Singapore's largest finance company, with a network of twenty-eight branch offices. Kwek Leng Beng was a member of the Board of Trustees of the Singapore Management University. He also holds an honorary doctorate (DUniv) from Oxford Brookes University. Kwek oversees the Singaporean operations of the Hong Leong Group while his cousin and fellow billionaire Quek Leng Chan oversees the Malaysian operations."

One can also turn to a more established source of information, Reuters, to get additional info on the prodigiously hardworking Chairman:

"Kwek Leng Beng has been the Chairman of M&C since its incorporation. He is the Executive Chairman of the Hong Leong Group Singapore, and CDL. He is also Chairman and Managing Director of Hong Leong Finance Limited and City e-Solutions Limited and the Chairman of Hong Leong Asia Ltd. Mr Kwek's achievements have also captured the attention of the academic institutions. He was conferred: Honorary Doctorate of Business Administration in Hospitality from Johnson & Wales University (Rhode Island, US), where students have an opportunity to pur-

sue career education in business, hospitality, culinary arts or technology; Honorary Doctorate from Oxford Brookes University (UK)
whose citation traced how Mr. Kwek, who joined the family business in the early 1960s, had gone on to establish an international
reputation for his leadership of the Hong Leong Group, as well as
being an active supporter of higher education in Singapore.

"Mr. Kwek also serves as a Member of the INSEAD East Asia
Council. France-based INSEAD is one of the world' leading and
largest graduate business schools which bring together people,
cultures and ideas from around the world. Mr. Kwek is a Member
of the Action Community of Entrepreneurship (ACE), which
involves both the private and public sectors to create a more
entrepreneurial environment in Singapore for small and medium
enterprises.

"Mr. Kwek has distinguished himself in property investment
and development, hotel ownership and management, financial
services and industrial enterprises. Today, he sits on the flagship
of a multi-billion empire worth over US$21 billion in diversified
premium assets worldwide and stocks traded on seven of the
world's stock markets. He currently heads a worldwide staff
strength of some 40,000 across a range of businesses in Asia-
Pacific, the Middle East, Europe and North America. Mr Kwek also
played a pivotal advisory role in Las Vegas Sands Corporation's
successful bid for Singapore's high profile Integrated Resort project at the Marina Bay."

Even a partial account of the Chairman's career provides
insight as to why he is a billionaire and you and I are not.

By the by, another of Chairman Kwek's great London properties is the Millennium Hotel London Knightsbridge, which
counts many designer stars of today such as Gucci, Chanel and
other designer boutiques as its close neighbors. Conveniently
located at 17 Sloane Street, the hotel is just two minutes from the
world famous Harrods Department Store and Hyde Park. Sloane
Street has always been on par with Bond Street (which is five minutes away from the Millennium Mayfair). These two streets, which
house many of the world's famous, top fashion brands, have long
earned their reputation as London's most exclusive, chic shopping
belts. Transportation is a breeze as the Knightsbridge underground tube station a just a good nine iron golf shot of 150 yards
away. Its MU Restaurant and Cocktail Bar is a destination for local
fashionistas with its innovative Asia-accented French cuisine.

According to ZillionTech's Knowledge Repository, Chairman Kwek used to "sit in the lobby of King's Hotel at Havelock Road in the Seventies in Singapore and pray that guests would check in. 'When they arrived, I cheered and my spirits lifted,' he recalls."

Real estate was the family business when Chairman Kwek was young. During that time, it was common for developers to enter the hospitality market as an auxiliary business. There was never any intention to start a chain of hotels, which has now become quite fashionable. That formula would change dramatically when young Kwek eventually took control of the company.

But back in 1967, Chairman Kwek's father asked him to tender for a land site, to build the King's Hotel. This milestone heralded the company's venture into the hotel arena. In 1970, when his father's company opened King's Hotel in Singapore, Kwek Leng Beng was assigned the task of managing it. This sounded like it might be a dream job, hanging around a beautiful hotel all day, but it was really a sort of business baptism by fire. With little knowledge or experience in managing hotels, the young Kwek was thrown into the deep end of the pool.. He was either going to swim or sink.

Meanwhile, Kwek's father was managing the smaller Orchid Inn Hotel at Dunearn Road, which had fewer rooms than King's but the father made more money with it than the son did with King's. Learning why that was so would be the young Kwek's first lesson in the hotel business.

Chairman Kwek persevered. In 1998, King's Hotel was rebranded Copthorne King's. He was rebranding several of his hotels in Singapore after having acquired the Copthorne hotel chain and integrated it into the Millennium Hotels. Name recognition is very big in hotels, and Copthorne was well known. The newly dubbed Copthorne King's also underwent extensive renovations at this same time, to the tune of $15 million (in Singapore dollars) or approximately US$10.7 million.

Over the years, King's proved to be quite the excellent training ground for the young Kwek. He learned how to navigate through economic downturns, what to do with an over-supply of hotel rooms and how to balance the waxing and waning flow of tourists to Singapore. In the process, King's blossomed from its original 175 rooms to 310 Zen-inspired rooms today. The hotel mostly caters to businessmen these days. The great thing about businessmen is that they show up at your hotel even if the weather's lousy! Not like those finicky tourists.

Chairman Kwek must have studied his new trade very hard, because today, his company owns over 120 hotels across five continents. There is still a soft spot in the Chairman's heart, however, for his first hotel, King's. Having practically raised it from a pup, and having bought the land it occupies for just under a million in Singapore bucks in 1967. Of course, today, that same property, which encompasses the land and the hotel building itself, is worth northwards of S$120 million (US$86.4 million). As the Chairman himself has explained it, "If you work backwards, this means that the investment at King's has enjoyed a 10.5 percent annual compounded rate of return, without even taking into account the good dividends received yearly on this property." Pretty good return on your Singapore dollar, yes?

In fact, Chairman Kwek firmly believes that "real estate is the key to becoming rich in this part of the world (East Asia)." Not that it won't earn you a nice living in other parts of the world. The Chairman's company also owns Los Angeles' Millennium Biltmore Hotel, where they used to throw that Oscar shindig every year before they moved it to that big ugly auditorium place. And the company also owns Chicago's Millennium Knickerbocker, where a fellow by the name of Al Capone once hung out in the Twenties.

But Copthorne King's will always be home for the Chairman. He affectionately calls King's "the mother of all hotels." Rightfully so. After all, this is where he started as a rookie. This is where he learned the ropes of the business. Much sweat (literally) and perseverance went into building the hotel and, sentimentally, it was also the family's first hotel investment. He returns to it every chance his busy international schedule permits, and when he's in town, he's sure to visit it weekly. He likes to dine there with family members, business associates and tennis buddies. You can most often find him at the hotel's famous long Penang Peranakan buffet table. The Chairman is partial to the Penang Hokkien mee. He also likes the King's Tient Court restaurant. Well, if you worked as hard as the Chairman, you'd have a pretty good appetite too.

I have stayed at the Mayfair Millennium several times, actually three in all, and these stays were progressively better. My most recent suite at the Millennium Hotel Mayfair had a large bedroom, a mid-sized living room, and two bathrooms. I had an especially long stay, about a week, in 2007 when I interviewed Chairman Kwek. The consummate host, I met Chairman Kwek for dinner at the L'Atelier de Joël Robuchon Restaurant, steps from the bright lights of Piccadilly Circus. I understand from the Chairman that he has plans to revamp the Mayfair and make it a flagship establishment for M&C Hotels plc.

"I will tell you why we have more hotels here than in New York," he said. "The gross operating profit – margin – in London is better than in New York."

"Does the high cost of operating in New York – the unions and . . . ?" I asked.

"Yes, the hotel industry has no unions in the UK."

"I refused a sale on the UN Plaza," he went on. It's a little difficult to keep the Chairman focused on one nation's hotels at a time. He tends to think globally. Here he's referring to an offer for his UN Plaza hotel in Manhattan that, apparently, he could refuse. "I didn't need the money and New York has always been a great city for hotels . . . There is only one UN. How many hotels around the world can call themselves the UN Plaza?"

In fact, it's a little hard for anyone to keep track of all the hotels the Chairman manages, or owns, or both. A colleague of his told me, "In the absolute number of hotels that they (Copthorne) actually own, rather than help people to manage, I think Chairman Kwek is the leader. They own over 90 hotels around the world, and I don't think there is any individual or company that owns that many hotels. Others may manage many, many, more." That's the real estate mogul in the Chairman. He just has this thing for acquiring property that he inherited from his pop. When you or I find a hotel we like in a beautiful location, we book a room. The Chairman buys the place.

"We created the first hospitality REIT [real estate investment trust] in Singapore and it has been performing very well," the Chairman continued. "In the first eighteen months after its listing, the share price had already gone up by 300 percent." Today, after the financial crisis and the rebound in the stock market, the share price has increased about 100 percent against its initial listing price.

"Is it still a good investment – Singapore?" I asked.

"Singapore just released a projection on Friday, and growth will be four to six percent against last year of eight to nine percent." (This was said in the context before the 2007/08 global meltdown.)

Chairman Kwek is also developing hotels in India – business

class price without the grand ballroom and conference centers. "When this budget hotel is developed and its earnings are stabilized, we hope to achieve about US$150 per room," he said.

His hotel in Paris is The Millennium Hotel Paris Opéra. I stayed there just before my book on his Broadway Hudson Theater was published. I was astonished to find myself sitting in the rounded living room in the hotel, looking out at the busy Boulevard Haussman and the pinnacle of the Paris Opera House. Part of me can sense the Germans approaching Paris in the famous movie *Casablanca*; another part of me: Hemingway's *A Moveable Feast*, his views of Paris as the epitome of literature, music, art and just plain life.

Here after writing *Life at the Top: Inside New York's Grand Hotels* I'm planning another book about hotels, but can't help but marvel at Chairman Kwek's far-flung hotel empire, at once modern and sleek, and alternately historic, grand, brimming with the best of the past and blending this with the best of the present and future.

As I indicated, the Millennium Mayfair is one of many hotels Millennium he owns in London. Bailey's is a traditional hotel, and historic, another of the Chairman's London properties. Built in the 1890s, it's right next to the Gloucester Hotel in Kensington, which is, surprise surprise, also a Millennium Hotel.

I got another rare opportunity to sit and chat with Chairman Kwek one late fall afternoon in 2008, in the posh restaurant of his Millennium Knightsbridge Hotel in the heart of London's fashionable shopping – Sloane Street. Our talk ranged from Gucci, Fendi and other designer shops that line the fabled street, to the hotel across the water in New York City, to the Hudson Theatre.

"This hotel, it was a Holiday Inn long time ago," he said, referring to the hotel we were in at the moment, as we tasted a special noodle dish. "They had a swimming pool on this level, and then somebody from South Africa took it over. Then during the recession, American Express offered me this deal. And I fully refurbished the hotel."

In 1995, his Hong Kong listed CDL Hotels International acquired the Copthorne group with hotels in the UK, France and Germany. The Copthorne hotels, his London hotels and other hotels were pooled together into the Millennium and Copthorne (M&C) Hotels plc and floated on the London Stock Exchange in 1996. M&C took over the business undertakings and hotel assets under CDL Hotels International. Both Copthorne and Millennium brands have been growing since.

Along with the Knightsbridge Hotel in which my conversation took place, Chairman Kwek owns the Millennium Gloucester and the Millennium Bailey's Hotel in London. The Chairman once took Steve Wynn to the Bombay Brasserie, an Indian restaurant which has made a name for itself as a favorite of celebrities, at Millennium Bailey's. "Was he considering becoming a partner?" I asked. "No, no. He was here, at that time, when London was supposed to be – England was supposed to be – opening up to international casino operators and owners, so he was looking at London, and I happened to be here. I've known him a year. So we talked and I took him to see the Bailey's Hotel. He liked the Bombay Brasserie which he said he could envision a similar concept to be placed in one of his establishments in Las Vegas."

Chairman Kwek spends two-thirds of each year in Singapore where his Hong Leong Group is headquartered and where he was born and raised. The other third of the time he spends playing an active role in the asset management of his vast hotel and other holdings around the globe. He views himself as a real estate developer first, a hotelier second, learning much about real estate from his late father.

"My father came from China originally," he said. "He started as a building materials supplier and he went into real estate, not as a developer at first. His first love was real estate. I took over the chairmanship of Hong Leong Group in 1990, although I had been actively leading several companies within the group before that."

The Chairman, ever practical, talked about his group of hotels, including the historical Biltmore Los Angeles where the Academy Awards ceremonies were once held, after they were first at The Roosevelt. "I'm not trying to build a huge hotel chain like Starwood or Intercontinental. I just can't do that as I don't have critical mass. But I, unlike the purely hotel-trained people, have real estate experience. M&C has consistently adopted a twin strategy of being both an owner and operator of hotels. For instance, with the Biltmore Hotel, I see the potential of maximizing the plot ratio and I plan to convert, at the right time, some of the offices within the Biltmore, and hope to re-configure some two hundred rooms into condominiums."

Chairman Kwek explained he was a real maverick in the

hotel business. "I'm a contrarian in the sense that many hotel companies want to get all the management contracts they can, around the world. My approach to hotels is not only management but also owning the real estate. I have an extra strategy. With many of my hotels like the Biltmore, we can eventually convert a significant part, if not, the entire site (where it makes business sense) into condominiums or other uses. I've also introduced branded residences into Singapore by developing the St. Regis Hotel in Singapore, which has adjoining St. Regis Residences where residents are able to tap the hotel services. Today, The St. Regis Hotel, Singapore, is one of the world's best luxury hotels."

Since its grand opening in April 2008, The St. Regis Singapore has earned prestigious accolades and been named one of the best new hotels by renowned publications, including Condé Nast Traveller Hot List 2008, Travel + Leisure IT list 2008, Robb Report Best of the Best List 2008, and Elite Traveller's 101 Top Suites in the World.

I was still ruminating on how the Chairman's hotels are, for him, also real estate. "The hotels have another life," I said.

"They have another life," he said. "So what we want to do now is to seriously look at some of our hotels, to reposition them, bringing some of the hotels to a much higher standard. In fact I have a designer doing a prototype design of the rooms for me in Singapore. The design is "East Meets West." It's a fusion between East and West because I strongly believe that, you know, Chinese travel will become the dominant traveling force in years to come. In four or five years, they will be the greatest travelers.   And I want them to feel that they are at home when they travel. It's not exactly Asian design. It's the luxury of the West, and a touch of the East."

In fact, a number of rooms at the Millennium Biltmore have been designed this way. "The Biltmore, which currently has about 683 rooms, could have been converted into an 850 room hotel, I think" he said. "The previous owner of the Biltmore left two floors empty with structures that could be partitioned and made into additional hotels rooms. We have plans to covert one of the office blocks into residences at the appropriate time. Because, downtown Los Angeles is getting very popular. People living in L.A. have found that they have to drive for two to three hours every morning, be stuck in traffic jams before they can come downtown. So the condominium prices there are very good now. And it is fashionable to have condominiums inside the hotel providing the hotel services to the condominiums."

These were plans that were shared when the market outlook was brighter in 2006. Although the plans were already drawn up, in light of the global financial meltdown in 2007/08, this redevelopment initiative was put on hold as it was deemed unsustainable given the challenging economic conditions. Perhaps, one day, at the right time, when the economy stabilizes and there is growth, they may revisit this idea.

I admitted to the Chairman that I was curious about his own lodging preferences.

"When in London, sometimes I stay in my hotel, sometimes I stay in my apartment," the Chairman explained. "In fact," he said, "when you have a chance, there is another historic hotel called Millennium Hotel Paris Opéra, located in the heart of business area, close to the major stores of the Faubourg Saint Honoré and the Place Vendome and to the main monuments. It's a small hotel, only 167 rooms, it's not far from the Grand Opera House. But uniquely, (and not many know this), when you stand in front of the hotel, facing it, from the side view of the hotel, you get a beautiful vista of Sacré-Coeur Basilica up high on Montmartre."

Later, the Chairman drove me to his Bailey's Hotel and the Gloucester Hotel, both in Kensington, in his Rolls-Royce. I assumed he would have a chauffeur. When I got into the back seat, he motioned me to sit in the front seat because he was driving. Bailey's, a truly historic hotel, was built in 1876 and is near Kensington Gardens, Hyde Park and the National History Museum.

Getting back to the Millennium Mayfair, a number of the houses around Grosvenor Square date back before the American Revolutionary War. Much more commercial than residential these days, Grosvenor Square, like nearby Berkeley Square, was one of London's most fashionable residential addresses until WWII. But before and after the war, the private houses were razed, replaced by hotels, embassies, and neo-Georgian apartment flats.

I have a special affection for Grosvenor Square as I stayed in a suite with my son and his mother when I first interviewed Kwek Leng Beng, or The Chairman as he is called. Our suite overlooked the park and I took special comfort from the statue of American president Franklin Delano Roosevelt in the park.

Former U.S. presidential candidate Adlai E. Stevenson died

outside after leaving the American Embassy. His companion Marietta Tree says his last words were, "Do not walk so fast . . . and do hold your head up, Marietta."

She recounted later that, "We walked around the neighborhood a little bit and where his house had been where he had lived with his family at the end of the war, there was now an apartment house and he said that makes me feel so old. Indeed, the whole walk made him feel very not so much nostalgic but so much older. As we were walking along the street he said do not walk quite so fast and do hold your head up Marietta. I was burrowing ahead trying to get to the park as quickly as possible and then the next thing I knew, I turned around and I saw he'd gone white, gray really, and he fell and his hand brushed me as he fell and he hit the pavement with the most terrible crack and I thought he'd fractured his skull."

The homes around Grosvenor Square were where "the Bentley Boys," English versions of F. Scott Fitzgerald's idle, rich and playful American counterparts and ex-patriots, held all-day parties. I had thought they were the owners of the Bentley Motor Car showrooms on Berkeley Square. But their name came from their predilection for green Bentley sports cars. Some of their names seemed to fit their reputation – especially "Woolf" Barvato; the others were Tim Birkin, Glen Kidston and Bernard Rubin.

London hotels are now known for their food as well as their décor, history and celebrity. One of the best meals I ever had, in fact, was at AVISTA at the Millennium Mayfair. The famed Italian restaurant with its refined regional Italian cuisine was a sumptuous gastronomic feast. It was here, too, that Chef Brian Turner had his restaurant, Brian Turner's, for several years, and I greatly enjoyed that. Great hotels are complimented by great chefs and vice versa. But AVISTA continues to charm palates of locals and world travelers alike.

Brian Turner writes in his autobiography Yorkshire Lad: "I think there are several reasons for our present-day passion for cooking. One, I believe, is our lack, after the war, of a 'gastro culture' in Britain. Other European countries had long-established food traditions, but we had little in a culinary sense to fall back on. After the post-war years of rationing and food shortages, we had much more 'room' than other cultures in which to grow and develop, and this we started to do very rapidly. When traveling abroad on holiday began to be popular in the 1950s and 1960s, we encountered many food influences, brought them back, and absorbed them into our new burgeoning style. Because we had so far to go, we had to catch up quickly, and in some cases I think we've overtaken some of our neighbors. London is now considered by some to be the gastronomic center of Europe, although personally I don't believe this is the case. It's more to do with that rapid catching up in so short a time.

"In tandem with this, chefs began to be more visible. Although I've emphasized elsewhere how much myself and Richard Shepherd were in the vanguard in this respect, I think it was really Silvano Trompetto at The Savoy who began the 'socialisation' of chefs, Escoffier and Carême, and later chefs like Käufeler and Virot, were all names to conjure with, but they remained firmly in their kitchens. Trompetto, however, used to walk round the Grill and River Rooms, in his whites and tall chef's hat, occasionally stopping to talk. He would only stay for a brief time, and it was all very formal, but it was a start, a move towards transforming the perceived role of a chef from tradesman, or 'skivvy' even, to professional. The enthusiastic 'amateurs' mentioned before – the George Perry–Smiths and John Toveys – took the idea further, talking to and moving among the tables, making food and eating out more customer–friendly. The open kitchens of places like the Capital contributed another facet, and in a huge majority of new restaurants opening today you can see and watch the brigade at work. And I think the advent of plate service – where the chef dictates how the food will look on the plate (one of the more valuable legacies of nouvelle cuisine) – was influential as well. The chef was now an artist, having come full circle from a lowly role in a subterranean kitchen. I suppose I could be characterized as the end result of that evolution, a chef–patron who cooks, walks round and sits down to chat and drink. In fact, quite often nowadays I leave the cooking in the very capable hands of Jon Jon, and work the room with the restaurant manager, currently the invaluable Louise–Anne Hewitt. I pride myself on going to the door, hanging coats up, answering the telephone, taking orders, then serving. It's very satisfying to be involved in the whole business of a restaurant, particularly when it's small and it's mine!"

In March, 2009, I had dinner at the Millennium Mayfair Hotel's Shogun restaurant in the charming company of that indefatigable London hotel PR legend, Julia Record. The Shogun is a highly reputed Japanese restaurant offering a full range of deliciously exotic fare to suit just about any palate. The earth-toned room is the coziest "dungeon" you've ever seen, with racks of feathered arrows, Japanese watercolors and other intriguing period touches decorating it. Chairman Kwek touts it as the most authentic and best sushi and sashimi restaurant. It's certainly the one he enjoys most.

Just over 400 years earlier Guy (also known as Guido) Fawkes, was imprisoned in the former underground Mayfair prison housing the restaurant. Guy Fawkes Day is celebrated on November 5, on the anniversary of his attempt to blow up the Houses of Parliament in protest to systematic discrimination against English Roman Catholics. Julia and I had a more enjoyable experience than Mr. Fawkes, I suspect, as we were treated to an unforgettable quadruple course Sushi and other appetizing entries there for dinner.

Next to Bailey's is the Millennium Gloucester with over 600 guest rooms. A convention hotel in every way, with every size meeting space, one of them is roomy enough to oblige automobiles. The guest rooms have direct dial telephone, trouser press, Guestlink TV, in-room movies and satellite, coffee and tea making facilities, en suite bathroom and hairdryer. Guests staying in the Millennium Club Rooms have access to a private Millennium Club Lounge where they can enjoy complimentary breakfasts, evening cocktails and coffee throughout the day. South West 7 has Italian cuisine in a rich, warm ambiance. Bugis Street Brasserie serves authentic Singaporean Chinese food and a selection of Asian dishes. Back Page Sports Bar has a true London Pub atmosphere while Humphrey's Bar is a cosmopolitan lobby bar with live music.

The last time I spoke with him just before the financial crisis hit, Chairman Kwek said he had no specific plans to buy additional properties in the U.S. market. "I have a policy that you cannot pinpoint acquisitions and say, in effect, 'Next year I'm going to acquire ten hotels' because the conditions may not be conducive. Also, opportunities may not come knocking at your door. Conversely, when the golden opportunity does knock at your door, you have to seize it."

Spoken like a true hotelier. After all, what is the hotel business, other than lots of people always knocking at your door? Originally, it was simply about sheltering people for a night.

Travelers, particularly in England, traversed the various king's roads and since it often took days to get anywhere, the coach had to put up someplace at night. Eventually, however, a different tradition began to take hold in the best of London's hotels. And that was the tradition of gentlemanly "service." It's not really surprising in a country famous for not only its nobility but for its butlers, that the British would have a particularly good knack for making people feel right at home.

Chapter 8

The Savoy

If The Lanesborough Hotel, in the words of internationally renowned interior designer Trisha Williams, makes her feel as close to royalty as she may ever get, The Savoy is "home" to me. Part of it is like The Plaza Hotel; it's where my father stayed so long. In reality in terms of time spent at one place it, along with The Plaza, were really the places he spent the longest time. At a party he threw just before the making of *The African Queen*, one guest told Humphrey Bogart Africa was no place to take a lady, Lauren Bacall. "She's going, pal." "But," the guest interjected. "She's going." "Bogart and Ward liked each other," said Rebecca Morehouse, who is my stepmother and was married to my father, Ward Morehouse, for seventeen years. Bogart and my father had known each other since the Twenties, when Bogart was on Broadway in those fairly vacuous "Tennis anyone?" roles. Bogart was then in my father's movie, *Big City Blues*, before landing the role of gangster Duke Mantee in *The Petrified Forest*. (He repeated the role in the movies at the urging of star Leslie Howard, who would not do the movie version otherwise.) Bogart, of course, had been best known in his early career, playing tough gangsters. He once admitted, Ezra Goodman reports in his book, *The Fifty-Year Decline and Fall of Hollywood*, that "physically, I'm not tough. I may think tough. I would say I'm kinda tough and calloused inside. I could use a foot more in height and fifty more pounds and fifteen years off my age and then God help all you." Goodman quotes Bogey's wife, Lauren Bacall, as saying Bogart's face looked "as if somebody'd stepped on it." Goodman in the same book calls Bacall "a sort of Humphrey Bogart in skirts." Bogart was dramatic and so was my father.

Just as you cannot separate celebrities, authors, playwrights and actors from London's hotels, it's hard to separate the shop-lined broad avenues and quaint byways of Mayfair, The Strand, Piccadilly and Covent Garden from the finest of hotels. It's as if they are part of the stage setting. So the Omega store in its own way is as much a part of nearby Brown's as are Kipling and Lindbergh who stayed at the hotel.

Tallulah Bankhead lived in a townhouse on Farm Street in the West End. When my father interviewed her there her love bird "Gaylord" was perched nearby. The interview was a bit disconcerting for him as Bankhead, like Marilyn Monroe after her, seldom wore underwear. She once proclaimed she "was as pure as the driven slush." Mae West famously said she was once Snow White – but just drifted!

No one quite ever described shopping in London quite like the late singer Rudy Vallee. In his book, *My Time Is Your Time*, the name of his theme song, he says London is a shopper's delight. Vallee started as a musician and singer in bands, then graduated to radio, then became Number 1 – for a while. In the 1960s he had a huge comeback starring in the Broadway musical, *How To Succeed In Business Without Really Trying.* Vallee, who was at the time playing saxophone at The Savoy Hotel, wrote,. "Any time I could seize a moment off from the saxophonic chores, I would frequent the shops along Bond Street which catered to the sartorial needs of the man. As far as clothes are concerned, (and in many other ways . . .) England is a man's country. . . . I amassed a collection of around two hundred pairs of socks, about two hundred and fifty ties, suits and coats tailored with Chesterfield style, then in vogue." Sounds like Rudy could have given even Céesar Ritz a run for his money in the clothes horse stakes.

Vallee writes of his Savoy experience, "I played every evening: upstairs in the beautiful, pillared, red-carpeted main dining room, where dined such personalities as Tetrazzini, Marconi (who lived for a time at the Seville Hotel in New York; The Seville is now The Carlton), Fokker, the German aircraft inventor, diplomats, artists, actors, etc.; and early in the morning downstairs in the large ballroom with its floor set on springs, playing opposite the large Savoy Orpheanum, a band of some twenty-two pieces which rivaled Paul Whiteman's aggregation in its brilliance and beauty of tone."

Vallee had been persuaded to remain in London longer than he originally anticipated to get a "royal appointment" to teach the Prince of Wales to play the sax. "I could not wait for the Prince's return from Africa so I might become the regal saxophone tutor," Vallee added.

The Savoy opened in 1889, after the success of The Savoy

Theatre where Richard D'Oyly Carte stepped out onto the 27-foot deep stage, dwarfed by the 30-foot high proscenium arch and smashed a glowing electric light bulb as black-tie audience members gasped. They had just witnessed a performance of Gilbert and Sullivan's comic opera *Patience* and the impresario wanted to demonstrate the safety of the newfangled electric light bulb. The theater, unlike the venerable Haymarket or smaller Comic Opera Theatres and their neighbors was the first London theater to be lit entirely by electricity. The gold, satin curtain behind him shimmered in the reflection of 1200 incandescent bulbs and gaslights were – except on those rare occasions when the 120-horse power generator conked out – history. *Iolanthe, The Mikado, The Gondoliers*, and other shows premiered at the Theatre. When The Savoy Hotel itself premiered eight years later, the Theatre's entrance was moved to the hotel's courtyard off The Strand where it remains today.

The Savoy compiled some history and, for accuracy's sake, I give it to you more–or–less verbatim:

The Savoy opened its doors to an eager public in 1889, the brainchild of the Gilbert and Sullivan impresario Richard D'Oyly Carte. Built on the site of a former palace, the hotel took five years and vast expenses to complete and incorporated unheard of features, including full electric lighting and what for the time was a startling number of baths: 67 in total. Richard D'Oyly Carte had laid the foundations for The Savoy's heritage – British style and tradition coupled with innovation.

Masterful timing resulted in a glittering first season and D'Oyly Carte ensured The Savoy's continued success by employing celebrated Swiss hotelier César Ritz to be its Manager, accompanied by Maître Chef Auguste Escoffier, and Louis Echenard, a master of wine, as Maître d'hotel. Other notables over the years who had "Savoy" on their resume included Guccio Gucci, who began his professional life at the hotel – as a dishwasher, and Harry Craddock, Head Barman of the American Bar, who helped create cocktail culture in London.

Escoffier created dishes for Sarah Bernhardt, Lily Langtry, Dame Nellie Melba and the Prince of Wales, later

Edward VII; Ritz instituted the impeccable service, attention to detail and creativity which that came to be the hallmark of the hotel.

In the ensuing years the hotel saw numerous expansions, always incorporating the latest amenities and facilities and a degree of self-sufficiency. The Savoy would not rely on the vagaries of the outside world for power or water, or indeed for roasted coffee.

The Savoy has always sparkled with glittering parties. One of the most famous was the Gondola dinner, hosted by Champagne millionaire and Wall Street financier George Kessler, in July 1905. Venice was recreated in the old forecourt, lit by 400 Venetian lamps. The centerpiece was a silk-lined gondola decorated with 12,000 fresh carnations. There was a baby elephant, a five-foot birthday cake and arias sung by the tenor Caruso, who was paid £450.

From these very lavish early beginnings to the present day, The Savoy has played host to London's most talked about gatherings. The Savoy has hosted the South Bank Show Awards and Evening Standard Film Awards. The hotel is also proud to be hotel sponsor and host of the pre-party event for the BAFTA Television Awards. Other events of note at the hotel include the Wimbledon Ball and the announcement of the Samuel Johnson Book Awards.

In 1923 the two Savoy dance bands, The Savoy Orpheans and The Savoy Havana Band, became the first to broadcast regularly from a hotel. The BBC's "Dance Music from The Savoy Hotel in London" was broadcast to millions worldwide. In the Ballroom Gershwin gave London its first performance of "Rhapsody in Blue" and Carroll Gibbons played nightly. Today, the Thames Foyer, where Strauss conducted, Caruso sang and Pavlova danced in cabaret, continues to feature live music, with a resident piano player tickling the ivories during Afternoon Tea service and evening cocktail hour.

Always a magnet for the well known and well heeled, by 1914 the hotel and the Savoy Grill had established itself as a rendezvous for leading stars, impresarios and critics. Royalty patronized The Savoy in such numbers that the special bell heralding their arrival had to be abandoned.

From the end of the First World War into the Thirties, Maharajas took up residence with glittering retinues, Pavlova danced, the Archbishop of Canterbury attended the cabaret.   Eccentricities were catered for without hesitation, including opera singer's Luisa Tetrazzini's crocodile!

Winston Churchill was a famously devoted Savoyard. He visited The Savoy every week when he was in London and was present at the great occasion when Mrs. Eleanor Roosevelt was the guest of honor of the Pilgrim Society. The restaurant was closed to the public and a thousand guests attended, including the newly-married Princess Elizabeth and Prince Philip.   Other famous newlyweds to visit The Savoy included Elizabeth Taylor and first husband Nicky Hilton, who celebrated their honeymoon here.

Past stars of the silver screen such as Cary Grant, James Stewart, Frank Sinatra, Gene Kelly, Fred Astaire, Katharine Hepburn and Laurence Olivier and recent celebrity guests including Catherine Zeta-Jones and Michael Douglas, Robert De Niro and Pamela Anderson have long been attracted to The Savoy's Art Deco glamour and understated elegance.   The connection with Hollywood continues as the hotel has played "leading lady" in a number of recent movies, including *Notting Hill, Entrapment* and *Dirty Pretty Things*.

Now proudly a Fairmont Hotel, the 263-room Savoy offers 19,000 square feet of distinctive function space, stunning Thames views and an incomparable location steps from Covent Garden, the West End theaters, Trafalgar Square and the City financial district.   Its famous features include the Michelin-starred Savoy Grill, the American Bar, and one of two rooftop pools in the city. In January 2005, The Savoy was noted on both the "Condé Nast *Traveler* Gold List" and the "*Travel + Leisure* 500" alongside other celebrated Fairmont Hotels and Resorts.

Quite a history. Though I can't help wondering if Pavlova

actually danced with the Archbishop of Canterbury at that cabaret. And what was a Hilton doing staying at The Savoy? Miss Taylor may have had something to do with that.

Nor were Taylor–Hilton the first power Hollywood couple to grace the hotel. Vivien Leigh and Laurence Olivier first met there in their lustrous youth, before their international fame in Hollywood, before Nazi bombs hit The Savoy and destroyed some of the fanciful London churches and other landmarks they loved and killed nearly 30,000 Londoners.

The Thames sparkled in the moonlight as Big Ben solemnly stood guard upriver. It was 11:45 p.m., fashionable time in London town to have dinner at The Savoy. Seated only a few tables apart were two actors destined to change the history of romance as well as theater and film. Vivien Leigh and Laurence Olivier. Olivier looked at her and not only beheld one of the most beautiful women he had ever seen but felt a connection he didn't fully understand. Here were two people, beautiful and talented to an extreme, thrown momentarily together. He had recently seen her in her first London success, *The Mask of Virtue* which even the sternest newspaper critics had praised her performance in. But despite his proximity to the stage, it was not at all the same as viewing her in The Savoy's candlelit River Terrace.

The two did not actually meet until she went backstage to see him in a production of *Romeo and Juliet* in which Olivier and John Gielgud alternately played the roles of the romantic Romeo and dashing Mercutio at the Theatre Royal. "She decided to go backstage to congratulate him on his performance in *Romeo and Juliet,*" writes Anne Edwards in her biography of Vivien Leigh, *Vivien Leigh.* "There were a few people in his dressing room when she arrived, but he was aware of her presence as soon as she entered. . . . Olivier thought her the most beautiful woman he had ever seen. He asked her courteously if she had any theater plans after telling her he had seen her in *The Mask of Virtue* and had been impressed with her ability."

"'I'm Vivien Leigh, and I just had to tell you how marvelous you were,'" she told Olivier. He thought, Edwards says, she was the most beautiful woman he had ever seen and he asked her to lunch with him to discuss her own theatrical plans.

She told him she had been offered the part in a play called *The Happy Hypocrite* opposite Ivor Novello, who had been compared to Noël Coward and was, at the time, a kind of English theater's answer to a young John Barrymore. Olivier suggested she take the role and at that very moment became her mentor.

During World War II, Alec Guinness in his book *Blessings in Disguise* says just how magnetic Vivien Leigh could be even to total strangers. While stationed in North Africa, Leigh, who was touring in a pre–Northern African invasion play tried to get Guinness and a fellow officer a ride back to their ship.

"She button–holed, with all her wheedling charm, a starry-eyed Admiral," he wrote. "Caressing the lapels of his uniform, admiring his campaign ribbons, she suddenly asked him what he was doing for the next few hours. His eyes danced with excitement as he blushingly replied, 'Nothing!'

"'Then,' Vivien went on, 'you won't be needing your car. . . . I have two darling friends here, and they've simply got to be driven back to a little place.'"

My father once took Rebecca Morehouse, who worked for *The Atlanta Journal*, *Time* and *Playbill*, to dinner with Vivien Leigh and Laurence Olivier one night at their place in Christ Church Street.

"Ward knew them, I did not," Rebecca said. "So I'm at table with Scarlett O'Hara and her celebrated, handsome actor-husband, the most famous couple in the world.

"They knew the pain of separation. He was on Broadway in a play when she was playing Scarlett in California. Her impatience to finish the picture was all about him, being with him. When they could arrange it, it wasn't easy, they got on planes and met in the middle of the country, some place with an airport, where didn't matter. 'We did terrible things all over your beautiful country,' Vivien said cheerfully, with no apparent regret."

Long after the famous thespian twosome divorced, my father visited Leigh in her dressing room when she was appearing in *Duel of Angels*, her last play on Broadway. On her dressing table, in a silver frame, was a photo of "Larry."

The Savoy is also the story of a thousand and one tales of wayfarers who have fallen in love like Vivien Leigh, although often without similar notoriety.

Even Big Ben, however, may have swing–and–swayed ever so slightly to the strains of The Savoy Ballroom of the London premier of George Gershwin's "Rhapsody in Blue." No stranger to the most popular of music, the BBC's Prince of Music was broadcast from The Savoy Hotel to millions around the globe.

Greer Garson is best known to American movie audiences as the courageous British wife and mom during the early days of World War II in the film *Mrs. Miniver*. That heartfelt epic of Greer and her family coping with the Nazi bombing and Dunkirk, released in 1942, just as America was entering the war, may have done as much to boost support for the war cause in the States as Edward R. Murrow's dramatic radio reports from a battered London. But *Miniver* was not Ms. Garson's introduction to Hollywood. That historic occasion took place years earlier in the British capital.

One evening, Hollywood mogul Louis B. Mayer was so enchanted with Greer Garson's innocent beauty in a mediocre melodrama playing at the St. James Theater by the name of *Old Music* that he invited her for supper at the Savoy Grill after her performance. Already aware of Mayer's predilection for "discovering" Hollywood's next major star only after accepting his romantic overtures, Garson raced home, changed into more demure clothes, and persuaded her mother to come along to the Savoy Grill. Greer must have put on a good performance because she landed a $500-a-week contract – Mayer's opening gambit with a lot of his lady stars – and soon after reported to the West Coast, though to little if any work at first. When she later retreated to London to make *Goodbye Mr. Chips*, playing the dying wife, she was nominated for an Oscar and returned to America an international star.

My own show business experience in London is so far limited to presenting that American rock singer, named EJ, in several venues including the famous military "In and Out Club" on St. James Square (and which once served duty as Nancy Astor's townhouse). She was quite a hit with those who assembled in the great hall, which had once been Lady Astor's dining room. Later in the evening, she serenaded some of the admirals who were the backbone of the club's membership. Another high point was getting her to sing several Cole Porter shows in The Savoy's American Bar even though piano music, and not singers, was the room's music staple. These were small personal triumphs set against the larger hope of seeing the musical I helped co-write the book for produced on the West End.

The New York Times liked *The Actors*, then a production of my play, *My Four Mothers*, was packed at Jan Hus Theatre. Coming to The Savoy the winter of the same year opened up the idea that I would actually make it as a successful playwright. A few years later I penned a book on The Waldorf-Astoria that would propel me into the world of great hotels and their history of which the book on London hotels is the culmination. From 2005 to 2008 I stayed in The Savoy three times, each time in a riverfront suite.

That jaunt promoting an American rock singer in 2005 may have been the most unusual as I was accompanied by three friends of hers as well. They stayed in one room of the suite; I in the other. I went to bed early; they reemerged from the clubs they had visited late and I was relieved that they were safe if not entirely sound and probably more than a little high. But, perhaps, my best productive effort in London was introducing EJ to the handsome young journalist who became her boyfriend.

But really all my experiences at The Savoy have been both wonderful and unusual. I first stayed there after my play, *The Actors*, had been quite a success Off-Broadway. It had run for a total of nine months, closing in April of 1987. That same year, I got an agent to produce one other play, *My Four Mothers*, Off-Broadway.

I recently stayed in Cape May at New Jersey's Congress Hall Hotel, introduced nearly 200 years ago in 1816, where a number of Presidents, including Ulysses S. Grant, stayed. "We are definitely not pet friendly," said an otherwise solicitous member of the Congress Hall staff. They would have been put out, to say the least, if they had encountered opera diva Louise Tetrazzini's pet crocodile, which The Savoy accommodated with aplomb. (Turkey Tetrazzini, in case you were wondering, was named after the Tetrazzinis.)

The time is 1933. My father wanted a holiday, one in which he could enjoy theater without writing about it for once. Here's his report, which talks about The Savoy, where he always stayed, and The Savoy Grill, which was virtually an office for many then-famous Broadway players.

London plays seemed better. Or perhaps it was because I was just seeing them, and not seeing them to write about them. I was taking a leave of absence from *The Sun* and it was my first time abroad without copy to write. For the New York playgoer, wandering about the stalls of West End, things have to be awfully just-so, if he is to like the London theater at all. It's much easier to take if you're relaxed. *The Lake*, as played by such people as Marie Nye and May Whitty, appeared to be good drama. Raymond Massey gave a strong performance in a spurious war piece called *The Ace*. Gielgud was in the beautiful but ponderous *Richard of Bordeaux*. Mary Ellis, with something of a West End following, was trying *Music in the Air* and Ivor Novello, as prolific as Noël Coward, but without Noël 's talent, was doing his latest comedy. I've forgotten the title. That, in itself, is significant. It must have been no play at all. For I have always thought that I could remember the title of every play, the name of every actor; that I could, without a miss, go through the personnel of the Daniel Frohman Lyceum stock company or the full roster of the original theater in John Street.

Gilbert Miller, who is a polished producer as well as a linguist and an aviator, and who is becoming, more and more, a showman of the London theater with a branch office in New York, was seldom out of the Savoy Grill during that London week. Neither was Kitty Miller, nor Francine Larrimore, Adrianne Allen, Guy Bolton, Florence Britton, Romney Brent, Basil Sidney. Or Dennis King, my old friend from the Utah airways. Marc Connelly, whose stock as a dramatist took a sharp rise with the writing of the beautiful *Green Pastures*, gave the best of the week's parties, an affair for Ray Massey held in the Pinafore room of The Savoy. Massey was congratulated on his work in *The Ace*. "Great!" everybody said. But he wasn't happy about it. He knew it wasn't much of a play and he didn't feel that he was giving anything beyond a routine performance. He was really getting discouraged about acting anyway. He'd begun to think that he'd have to go in for direction entirely. Some of his friends had been urging him to do Shakespeare; there were others who thought he ought to play Abraham Lincoln, realizing that he could look like Lincoln and that he'd had life-long interest in Lincoln as a character. But how was Ray Massey then to know that Robert E. Sherwood was to come along five years later with a play that would give him the great rôle of his career?

I bade Marc Connelly goodbye after that Pinafore room party, and told him I'd see him in New York. Two days later we found ourselves at adjoining tables in The Ritz bar, Paris. These Americans do get around!

In the 1940's my father wrote my mother from The Savoy.

"Darling: Here's a check which you can probably use. I've some dough in that bank if Frank has been depositing the weekly checks – the first not due until June 7. Call him and ask him, will you? And I hope you took care of the MP. That's very important. I'm writing everything I do in the pieces from London and you've probably been keeping up with me that way. I may be getting back earlier than I thought, coming by air. They've taken off the escort vessels, meaning destroyers, etc. and now it's a case of returning via air or troop ship. Better not write any more after getting this but you might send me the news by deferred cable. I'd like to know how the hell they're liking the copy. I'll bring back the list of London managers; maybe the Bulletin would like to try for some subscriptions here.

"I may be going to Paris this Thursday for a day and to Germany (Bremen) early next week. But will probably be leaving here by ship or plane for NY around the 18th. I haven't run out of dough yet but The Savoy costs! Noël called at 9 a.m. this morning: we have a lunch date for Monday. I haven't the damnedest notion where I'll be staying when I get back. Have you? I wish I could have shown this town to you, but you'll see it yet. xxxx"

My father's life at The Savoy was a continuation of his in New York regardless whether Caruso sang here years earlier or the Johann Strauss orchestra played its waltzes for American million-aires, or that Pêche Melba was created for singing star, Nellie Melba. This was my father's home abroad in London. The castle on the bank of the Thames, on the site that Peter of Savoy, a rel-ative of Henry III, built his "finest manor in England," was where he could figuratively let his hair down. So, too, my father here became not a critic, columnist but a husband and in love.

"Darling, I love you terribly much and so wish I were back in our house. Couldn't we please be nice to each other from now on – and I mean wonderfully nice? I think you're pretty and exciting and fun and I want to have the place in London with you and everything else.

"What I meant was that I'll be back by October even if I have to swim and that I'll have roses and all and that I love you more than anything I know and sometimes wonder how you feel. W."

For my father, London was The Savoy and *vice versa*. But if The Savoy was ever personified by someone, it was Noël Coward.

My father would later write that there was a period in World War II during which Coward, "the world's jack-of-all-entertainment, gave his friends cause for alarm. He came dangerously near pomposity.

"He said goodbye to the theater, proclaiming with a most unbecoming solemnity that he was through with it for the duration. He began dabbling in international politics and was forever being whisked away on missions that were mysteriously official. He took his martinis in Government Houses and took himself seriously while sipping them. He became something of a self-appointed High Ambassador to Practically Everything, filling a war-time role not unlike that which had belonged in former years to the Prince of Wales.

"Fortunately, however – fortunately indeed for bored, restless and entertainment-hungry Allied troops on ever-alerted but inactive fronts – Noël recovered. With a twitch of his impudent and expressive eyebrows and a Cowardesque grimace or two, he got hold of himself, laughed convulsively at himself, begged the drama's forgiveness for his neglect, and returned forthwith to the only job he knew, the combined job of performing and writing. He visited bases, hospitals and troop concentrations here, there and everywhere giving his one-man show – songs in his fashion, and at whatever piano they had around; stories in his clipped, laconic and amusingly venomous manner, never avoiding impish malice when it could be used to humorous advantage. He gave autographs by the thousands, and always to the accompaniment of his own crisp chatter, his delayed and quivering smile, his cruel-lipped and darting twists of speech.

"He gave his concerts, as he called them, throughout the British Isles and the vast Mediterranean area. He appeared in such Near East cities as Teheran and Baghdad, that dusty and over-glamourized metropolis beside the mighty Tigris. He was the theater's, and his country's, royal fun-maker in Australia and

South Africa. He dropped out of the skies to do his highly specialized act for the maimed and the wounded in scores of hospitals, always finding himself greatly moved by the courage and
cheerfulness of the shattered young men of modern war, and
never failing to become somewhat apologetic by his own non-
combatant status. As a government emissary he had been actually stuffy and was probably the first to become aware of it. As a
troops entertainer, paying impromptu calls upon fighting men in
remote corners of the world, he was in his own métier, and he
contributed vitally to the war effort.

"I've known Noël for a quarter of a century and have found
him to be a man of poise, reserve, dignity, humor, generosity and
a devastating charm. And cynical wit, always. Since his preco-
cious child–actor days he has always had a positive passion for
work. He has generally been much more excited over what he
was going to write tomorrow than in what he completed yesterday. He has always been fascinated by Charles the Second and
wants to play him on the stage. He has never been overwhelmed
by a desire to play Hamlet and for this his many friends are
thankful. 'But it would never surprise us,' one of them remarked
recently, 'to find him turning to the serious plays of Galsworthy or
coming forth as Peer Gynt or King Lear.'

"And then he added: 'You see, Noël Coward is a man who
likes having a good time. He likes garden parties. He can even
take cocktail parties. He likes swimming and yachting and lying
on the beach or on a rock in the sun. But he enjoys himself most
when he is acting. He has been acting, off stage as well as on, for
just about all of his life.'"

The Noël Coward Society holds some of its best events at the
National Arts Club and while it is a long way from the Thames to
Manhattan's Gramercy Park, where the National Arts Club resides,
I felt somehow as if I was in the presence of both the mother-
ing/motherly Savoy and Coward.

In the early years of The Savoy extravagance took center
stage at The Savoy just as it did in the early days of the original
Waldorf–Astoria or The Plaza. Champagne millionaire and Wall
Street financier, George Kessler, gave what was one of the most
glittering extravaganzas at The Savoy: the Gondola Dinner. It was
then the summer of 1905, a year before The Ritz and two years
before New York's Plaza Hotel opened. Venice was recreated in
the old forecourt, lit by 400 Venetian lamps. There were some 400

Venetian lamps. You count them! And then a silk-lined gondola decorated with 12,000 fresh carnations, a baby elephant, a five-foot birthday cake and arias sung by Enrico Caruso, who was paid the then-king's ransom sum of £450.

In 1920 the two Savoy dance bands, The Savoy Orpheans and The Savoy Havana Band, became the first to broadcast regularly from a hotel. The BBC's Dance Music from The Savoy Hotel in London was broadcast to millions worldwide. In the Ballroom Gershwin gave London its first performance of "Rhapsody in Blue" in 1925, and Carroll Gibbons played nightly.

Marilyn Monroe had a press conference at The Savoy in the mid-1950s when she came to Britain to make *The Prince and the Showgirl* with Laurence Olivier. The venue brought memories back for Olivier, as it was here that he first espied Vivien Leigh dining in the late 1930s.

F. Scott Fitzgerald readers savored some of The Savoy Hotel in "Two Wrongs" which his agent, Harold Ober, told Fitzgerald was "one of the best things you have ever done." Here's an excerpt from this story:

> Two men sat in the Savoy Grill in London, waiting for the Fourth of July. It was already late in May. "Is he nice?" asked Hubbel. "Very nice," answered Brancusi; "Very nice, very handsome, very popular." After a moment, he added: "I want to get him to come home."
>
> "That's what I don't get about him.," said Hubbel. "Show business over here is nothing compared to home. What does he want to stay here for?"
>
> "He goes around with a lot of dukes and ladies."
>
> "Oh?"
>
> "Last week when I met him he was with three ladies – Lady this, Lady that, Lady the other thing."
>
> "I thought he was married."
>
> "Married three years," said Brancusi, "got a fine child. . . ."
>
> He broke off as McChesney came in, his very American face staring about boldly over the collar of a box-shouldered topcoat.

He wrote that in 1930 when, indeed, London was not exactly "nothing compared to home," but nevertheless didn't approach

Broadway or the more than sixty Broadway theaters that then housed shows – at least before the October 1929 stock market crash.

The Savoy, at that time, was also at the epicenter of the West End: both the Savoy Grill and the Terrace Restaurant as well as the fabulous suites overlooking the Thames River. Today, although Broadway boasted forty-three new productions in the 2008-2009 season, many more than previous years, some veteran theater pundits are convinced that London has eclipsed Broadway in originality as well as glamour. After all, weren't the Elton John *Billy Elliott* and *Mary Stewart* first staged in the West End?

"In "Jacob's Ladder," Fitzgerald's story of a well-to-do man who falls for a younger woman he helps make a film star, he says that Jacob lives even "more deeply on her youth and future than he had lived as himself for years."

Novelist Sinclair Lewis stayed at The Savoy Hotel just before his marriage to writer Dorothy Thompson. They had met at a party in Berlin in 1927, and in 1928 London was alive with some of the greatest theatrical talent of the 20th century. Lewis wrote Thompson from The Savoy that the night he arrived at the hotel he went to Bayard Veiller's *The Case of Mary Duggan* – "so damn good that I was sorrier than ever at the thought of his not having gone through with the dramatization of Gantry [Lewis' novel *Elmer Gantry*]. . . . Sitting down here in the grill, I saw Noël Coward. He leapt up, introduced himself, says Elmer is the greatest of the century, asked me to sit down . . . we'll see Coward's review when you come, and perhaps see him."

Composer Joseph Stein told me, "I've stayed at The Savoy." "We also stayed at Brown's once," Mrs. Stein chimed in.

Michael Shepard, former general manager of The Savoy, said actress Elaine Stritch pushed the limits of his cordiality. "Elaine Stritch used to keep her food in her suite. She had at least one, if not two, fridges," he told me. "On one occasion she called me down to the office and said, 'Mr. Shepard, it's appalling – there are mice in my suite!' So I went up there and I said, 'Elaine, darling, you have food all over the place!'

"'Don't touch those. I have these types of cereal.' She was very particular about her food.

"I said, 'Unless you clean up your act in your suite, we're not going to get rid of these little, furry friends. If you feed them, I can't get rid of them.'"

"Richard Harris was a permanent guest of The Savoy, and I got to know him quite well."

"He'd pay in cash?"

"When he had cash," said Michael. "He used to run up his bill, and when he was working, there was absolutely no problem. But there would be six- or twelve-month periods when he didn't have any work, and I used to have to go to the pub next door called 'The Coal Hole' and I'd say, 'Mr. Harris!' 'Yes, Mr. Shepard. Have a Guinness.'

"'No, Mr. Harris. I haven't got time for a Guinness. I need to talk to you, Mr. Harris, about your bill.'

"'I'll only talk to you if you have a Guinness.' So I had a Guinness in front of me – and I wouldn't touch it.

"'Mr. Harris, you owe us a lot of money – when are you going to pay?' That's the only way I could get through and get his bills paid.

"On the last occasion I saw him, he had a heart attack in his suite. We called the emergency services, and they were very supportive and resuscitated him and got him into the special chair that we can take people down in the lift.

"And he was in the lobby, half reclined in this chair, with the blue light of the ambulance flashing outside, ready to take him to the hospital. He turned around and I was standing ten to fifteen feet away from him as he was going out the door, and with this wicked eye, and he used to catch my eye, and said 'Mr. Shepard, blame the food! Blame the food! And that was the last I ever heard from him. He was in the hospital a couple days and then he passed on.

"Many restaurants have dress codes, and he used to wear this very long, tatty overcoat with sneaker shoes. When he would come into The Savoy Grill, people had to wear a tie as part of the dress code, and he used to mock that we would give him a selection of ties. Dear old Mr. Moresco, who was the manager of the Grille Room, who said, 'The only way we'll let you in, Mr. Harris, is by putting you in the corner,' and they'd put a screen around him so none of the other guests would see him and he thought this was terribly funny."

"The Savoy Grill's probably about the most famous restaurant in London as you know – but it was two years ago they said we're going to change it, and it made the national press!" Susan Scott, archivist for The Savoy, told me. "It made the – I don't mean on the hotel page, you know, they got articles, there were famous actors writing in and saying 'how dare they!' you know, touch our Savoy Grill and, you know. And in the end, it's wonderful in a way that people feel so proprietorial about it but, on the other end, you say, 'I haven't decorated the Grill since the 1980's. Do you know? It's just a restaurant. We're just decorating. *Trust* us! Luckily they did and now, of course, she did it very well. It was an American designer, Barbara Barrington. It's very subtle . . . they like it afterward. People are just resistant to change."

"When he [Richard Harris] was doing the Harry Potter films, then he would pay on time because there was plenty of money," Michael Shepard told me. "That's not true that he used to pay in cash. He had an agent who used to handle all his money. Thank goodness for that. But when he didn't have money, he didn't have money. We hosted at least three of the premier Harry Potter after-show parties, which were wonderful affairs. Absolutely wonderful affairs. And I'd always be around to greet the great film stars and personalities from Harry Potter films. There was a long line of beautifully dressed people, and suddenly Richard would come to the top of the stairs, in sneakers in his long, filthy coat and his long hair and he'd see me at the bottom and he'd say, 'Mr. Shepard, the service here is appalling!' . . . And he had this sort of love–hate relationship. I would always acknowledge, 'Yes, Mr. Harris. No, Mr. Harris' . . . But to him life was just a theater and I was part of it on the stage. We just used to get along like that. . . . That's what a hotelier does: we have to change our spots for every guest."

During the filming of *The Wild Geese*, in South Africa, which costarred Richard Burton, Harris played his recurring off–screen role as practical joker.

"I knew Harris was up to something one evening," Roger Moore wrote in his autobiography *My Word is My Bond*. "I returned to my house and could hear a lot of giggling between him and his wife. I looked around and at the foot of my bed lay a snake – a rubber one.

"I pulled the sheets off the bed and there lay a tarantula – again, rubber. Aha! Harris is up for some fun, I thought. I didn't scream or react in any way whatsoever, which must have annoyed him no end.

"However there were loud screams the next night, from the Harris household, as he went to put on his boots and discovered snakes in them – real snakes."

Just as Michael Shepard needed a sense of humor in dealing with Richard Harris, so did one Savoy employee need it when film great Charlie Chaplin and his family checked in. In his 1994 book, *Hotel Reservations*, Derek Picot, who became Regional General Manager of the Jumeirah Carlton Tower, writes about welcoming film icon Charlie Chaplin to The Savoy. After being as solicitous as possible, Picot writes, "As I closed the door the light went out. It slowly dawned on me that I was not in the sitting room, but that I had taken the wrong door and was between the communicating doors to the next suite along. In the tradition of the establishment, I didn't panic. I had all the hotel master keys and resolved that, under no circumstances, would I re-enter the suite to receive the full blast of assembled Chaplin cold air. I carefully extracted the hefty bunch and proceeded to feel for the pass key to the intercommunicating door.

"Having taken twenty or so seconds to find it, I then fumbled for the keyhole. There was none. I fumbled again. There was still none. I took a step back and in the darkness hit my head on a movable object. It swung back and hit me again. It was then that I realized that if *that* was a coat hanger, then *this* must be the wardrobe.

"Not a small amount of time had passed (at least half a minute) and the problem I had then was to decide how long I was going to stay in the wardrobe before getting out or being discovered. Had the Chaplins actually noticed where I had gone? I was sure Sir C. had, because he waved at me from his chair – and I had politely waved back again.

"I decided to give it a full minute before getting out. The absence of any noise from the bedroom led me to believe that they must already have gone into the sitting room. I watched the luminous dial of my watch as the second hand swept slowly round. Bravely, I inched open the door to check the room was vacant.

"To my horror they all were gathered, as if for a sitting for a family portrait, around the wheelchair. Their faces swiveled towards the wardrobe door with a unified expression: the nearest verbal equivalent would be: 'You incompetent cretin.'

"I did the polite thing and uttered the first words that came to mind, my voice trailing off as I left the assembled crowd, this time via the sitting room door.

"'Just checking,' I mumbled."

On one of Chaplin's stays at The Ritz London, he needed forty policemen just to escort him into the hotel through cheering and clamorous fans.

"He had a suite at the top of The Savoy," Aeronwy Thomas, Dylan Thomas' daughter, told me. "Someone was going to take me to the Savoy Grill. I was looking forward to that. I said to him, 'You don't have to spend all that money because in January they were refurbishing. I went to a literary dinner. And he said to me he would take me out in January. Brilliant timing!! There's Simpson's on the Strand. . . . Basically Dylan Thomas left Swansea and went to London because he needed to have his poems published. And then he went back to Swansea in Wales all the time. And then the next time he spent a long time in London was when he worked during the Second World War for the Ministry of Information writing film scripts. He tended to live in Wales, or in Oxford, and he would travel up, and work for the third program in those days, the BBC. It's all in the biographies.

"But I was born during the war under the bombs because my father was working for the Ministry (of Information), writing basically propaganda films. So my mother and he were there in London Chelsea and that's when I was born. But the bombing became so hard in 1944 that my mother took me to New Key. My father then spent time in New Key in Wales because he could still write scripts there and bring them back to London."

"Shakin' it at The Savoy" was not a song but the job of Harry Craddock, also called the "first mixologist." An American who fled prohibition in the U.S., he joined The Savoy in 1925 and practiced his art. Craddock led The Savoy in introducing cocktails or "mixed drinks." He created new cocktails for special occasions including "The White Lady" and the "Queen's Cocktail." He also compiled his most celebrated creations into a book, *The Savoy Cocktail Book*, which is still a definitive work.

But, you ask, does The Savoy also have afternoon tea? Does the Queen have jewels? In fact, they have something they call "Theatre Tea." I dug up this old press release which tells you all about it:

◊◊◊

HIGH TIME FOR A THEATRE TEA

The Savoy Reinvents a Classic Favourite For the Perfect Pre-Theatre Meal

London – February 2005:

From 1st April 2005, between 5pm and 7.30pm, The Savoy will be offering guests the perfect meal to enjoy in the early evening before visiting the theatre, cinema or concert hall – The Savoy Theatre Tea.

A cross between the dainty sandwiches, scones and pastries of the classic English afternoon tea and the more substantial hot dishes that constitute a British "high tea," usually served later in the day, the Theatre Tea offers the best of both.

The Theatre Tea is served on a three–tiered cake stand and includes: English beef Tea, Mulligatawny or London Particular en Demi Tasse, Leek and Stilton Quiche, Miniature Cornish Pasty, Steak and Ale Pie with Yorkshire Pudding Crust, Welsh Rarebits with English Mustard and Potted Morecombe Bay Shrimps with Toast.

For dessert, Red Leicester Scones with Fig and Apple relish and Saffron Yoghurt, Bread and Butter Pudding, Apple and Sultana Crumble Spiced with Nutmeg, Savoy Sherry Trifle with Crème Chantilly, Cinnamon flavoured Carrot and Orange Cake and After Eight Chocolate Crumpets with Mint Jelly.

The Theatre Tea is light and easy to eat and has been specially designed for that "pre–entertainment early evening time." The Theatre Tea costs £28 per person and reservations can be made by telephoning 020 7420 2669.

◊◊◊

Not quite sure if that telephone number is still in effect, but the tea sounds scrumptious, no?

The Savoy can be forgiven for blowing its own horn from time to time. It is justly proud of its long, distinguished history. It has also been the site of many an innovation in the hotel industry. In fact, they composed a list of these, too. I won't bend your ear with all one hundred of those here, but I will regale you with a handful of the more noteworthy entries:

◊ First hotel to generate its own electricity supply, with the aid of steam generators. So much power was produced that The Savoy actually provided electricity for parts of the surrounding area around The Strand. The hotel was entirely lit by electricity, instead of the more dangerous gas.

◊ First hotel to provide the majority of its rooms with private, *en suite* bathrooms. What's more, the facilities were lavishly appointed in marble.

◊ First hotel to provide constant hot and cold running water in each bedroom.

◊ First 24-hour room service.

◊ The Savoy was the first hotel to provide music while guests dined. The idea, said Ritz, was to "cover the silence which hangs like a pall over an English dining table."

◊ The first hydraulically raised dance floor was installed at The Savoy in 1929.

◊ First hotel to install air-conditioning, steam-heating and soundproofed windows.

◊ First outlet for an electric toothbrush was installed for General Eisenhower.

"The unexpected is always routine in a cosmopolitan hotel,"

Stanley Jackson writes in his book, *The Savoy*.

Jack Dempsey loved The Savoy but maybe not as much as women loved Jack Dempsey. "Women mobbed him and tried to steal kisses which infuriated Marconi who complained that the noise was disturbing his experiments," Stanley Jackson wrote in *The Savoy*. "High above The Thames the champion . . . clowned and sparred with some delighted pageboys. . . . " Hotelier Conrad Hilton was particularly impressed by the floor service," Jackson writes. "At one time he contemplated some scheme to buy The Savoy but, needless to say, the directors were unenthusiastic."

Writing from The Savoy in the mid 1940's my father seemed loath to give up hotel life, but my mother, who had lived at The Plaza and other hotels with him, had found an apartment for $175 a month, I think a large one-bedroom. The same today would be $3,000 if not more.

9 a.m.
Friday, June 15

Darling: Here's a little present from Paris – and it was $6.75! Your letters have been nice. I guess I was glad when I read about the apartment and I'm willing to try it, and I hope it's a good place. But I don't see how it could be nice enough at $175. I'd have felt better if it had been $300.00. Anyway, I'll go to the Algonquin and collect my stuff and stay there maybe a day or two and then – do I just come on over?

I'm cabling you about the phone. If there's not one in the apartment for god's sake get after it. Willie can get it done through George Wellbaum. I got a note from Sherry, and very pleasant. He's been reading the stuff. Willie has written the office and Cluck news and June, copy girl, clipped the *Cosmopolitan* piece. I was pleased about the *Variety* and *Billboard* box score stuff.

Now, as I'm saying in a cable today, expect to be returning late next week by ship and will probably be arriving around June 29. But I don't know. The plan now is to sail from Scotland via the Queen Mary or Elizabeth. I had the choice of going by plane but thought the sea trip would be good to get me in condition for NY.

I've thought about your Situation a good deal and don't know how in Christ I'll fit into it, but I did, of course, detest that goddam one room at the Algonquin and we'll just see. I've been okay over here and have done good copy, I think, and I was damned enterprising to get to Paris and to Germany.

Now, will you do this – call John Martin at the Algonquin and ask him to put me down for a two-room suite just for a couple of days. For around the 29th. You can tell him about the apartment. Tell Willie and Frank to hold everything there. I'm going with Dick Aldrich, who has been wonderful, in a Navy car to Southern England, and we'll be seeing Clare Luce in "Antony and Cleopatra" at Stratford tonight. Then Cornwall and Plymouth and back to London Sunday or Monday. The plays are still lousy.

I've heard from the Kents but not FCS. I've written the 1,000 islands and even sent another check on the damn boat. The *London Evening Standard* has asked to reprint a couple of my pieces to NY and have offered me $80 each which will be okay if I get it. I have a bottle of perfume for FCS but nothing for W. P. . . . Could we arrange it so that the next time I come this way I won't be coming back to a Situation? God! But I'll be glad to see you. And be sure about the telephone, in my name or ours, and that the place is slicked up nice. XXXX

Baby, ask John Martin to make it 505 if he has it . . . or one of the [5]'s.

Founded in 1889, The Savoy is, at the time of this writing, undergoing the kind of once-in-a-lifetime renovation that The Plaza underwent in 2006–2007. The marble splendor of the two-story front hall, the river-front suites facing The River Thames, and of course, The Savoy Grille, run in recent years by the incomparable Gordon Ramsay, had little if any need of renovation and polishing.

Appearing at the Savoy Theatre in early 2009 was a revival of *Carousel* with Alexandra Silber, a young American actress who had taken the West End by storm. I had drinks with her near The Savoy one night and she told me how she had been plucked from an acting school in Scotland to appear on the West End. At 25, she had everything The Savoy Theatre and Hotel were about: looks, success, gentleness. She not only inspired awe; she inspired hope that anyone – with quite a lot of talent to be sure – could be plucked not only from obscurity but through a positive attitude could attain one's dreams.

The Savoy's voluminous index card system keeps even minute tabs on guests' wants and whereabouts. When someone died a simple red line was drawn through their names. Benito Mussolini's card had the words "elected President National Socialist Party of Italy 1935' and the entry ended with "Lynched Rome Square 1944" with the customary line in red.

Susan Scott looks after the hotel's history as if she were a mother hen with its chicks. It is, really her hotel as well as having been a Fairmont Hotel.

Let's listen to her talk – or, rather, swoon – about the hotel's origins and renovation plans: "Well, they're going to begin next year. I don't have an exact start but, yes. We've already put together some model rooms. We're doing 117 [170?] . . . which is two-thirds of our room stock, anyway, we're doing. And twenty-seven-odd suites. So obviously we want to make sure we get it right before we roll the program out so we've done two sample rooms and two sample suites. The area I'm most looking forward to is the heart of the hotel, this area we're sitting in now. As you can see, it's a mixture of styles: the ceiling was 1953 for the Coronation Ball, the mirrors are listed Art Deco from the Twenties although we have no more information on them sadly, but we're very proud of those. The paintings are by an American artist called Lincoln Taber. Now, what's going to go and what's going to stay apart from, as I say, the mirrors, I don't know, but as it sort of defines the hotel – it's the central hub of it so . . . These paintings are from the Seventies, I think. And so we've got the Fifties; we've got the Twenties; we've got the Seventies.

"But it's going to be completely renovated so I mean it's going to be given – well, we obviously have to work with the English heritage within those guidelines, you know. . . . It's like, people come along and say, 'you can't possibly change that!' Like when we did The Savoy Grill.

"You can't remain in the past. Otherwise we'd be sitting here in our hotel built in 1889, you know, and looking at Victorian decorations. So I mean it moves on all the time. Every generation's allowed to make their changes, I think. We're sympathetic to changes.

"Richard Harris took great pleasure in flouting the dress code, and a few years ago – you realize now The Savoy Grill has been taken over by Marcus Wareing – but before that the then-manager of the Grill was so strict on the dress code, you wouldn't have been allowed here – no tie. Perfectly respectable, very smart, you know, don't care! No tie! He turned away Prince

Andrew, but one day Mr. Harris made so much fuss, and he said 'I'm going into the place!' so he walked in and sat down at a table and the manager got a screen and put it round him in the corner, so nobody could see him!"

There is obviously a lure at The Savoy that has crossed generations. "Afternoon tea, especially. What I like about this is you'll see people here doing completely diverse range of things, I mean, everything from the family over there having tea to businessmen. You see businessmen having meetings over tea. We see people having wedding reception tea. Yesterday I was delighted to see two women over there complete with Japanese kimonos! And that looked incongruous, you know, having an English tea in a Japanese – we have a lot of celebration teas. A lot of people take the champagne and they're celebrating a special occasion. We even have a school here. We use The Savoy tea to teach etiquette to the children where they're given a special treat and you'll see them, you know, when the little girls go to the lady's cloakroom, the little boys stand up. It's so sweet."

"My favorite hotel in London is The Savoy!" said Fred Winship, renowned critic–at–large for United Press International, almost with boorish glee. "Is that in your book?"

"Yes."

"Okay! I look forward to it."

"You know," another well-known New Yorker, Louise Kerz Hirschfeld, not too long ago told me, "when I first went to London I arrived at a hotel theater now being redone, as the one right near Joe Allen's, The Savoy. I stayed there with my first husband, Leo Kerz who was there negotiating the play he was producing, *Rhinocerous*, for me, and we stayed at The Savoy and I will never forget, there were Australians there . . . they were singing the famous 'Down Under' song. And we're all in the lobby and it was a wonderful experience. There was a feeling of great elegance, which matched the building, and the architecture.

"Al very much loved London," Louise then recollects of second husband Al Hirschfeld, the great theater illustrator of *The New York Times* for over half a century. "He had a guest friend named Roger Furse, who was Olivier's stage designer, and he used to stay with him and he always went to London and we just had a great time. . . . We stayed for two weeks at a time in an apartment."

According to a 1998 Brand Republic report, in 1993 Julia Record, "while working as an account director for the travel P.R.

company Paramount Publicity, handled media relations for a then little-known charity for people with disabilities, MacIntyre Care. One of its patrons, Sarah Ferguson, the Duchess of York, had volunteered to part-climb Mount Everest to help raise funds. The event received mass TV coverage and more than 1,000 press cuttings. 'I have had thoughts about working in the voluntary sector, but I love travel and hotels,' she says. 'I could sit in a hotel lobby watching people all day – it is like sitting in a mini-theatre.' She will lead a five strong team at The Savoy Group, which owns five London hotels, including Claridge's, The Berkeley and The Connaught. Bought by U.S. investment group Blackstone in April, 2008. for 520 million pounds, the group also owns restaurant Simpson's-in-the-Strand, The Savoy Theatre and Worcestershire hotel the Lygon Arms."

In the winter of 2007-8 The Savoy sold much of its furnishings, including a yellow and gray sofa from Rroom 415 where Katharine Hepburn stayed; the bedside tables from 209, a room Oscar Wilde had; and Claude Monet prints from Ssuites 512-513 where Monet painted *Waterloo Bridge*.

"We were established, I think, at the beginning by Richard D'Oyly Carte as a theater-hotel and I think they realized hotels are theater, aren't they?" Savoy archivist Susan Scott told went on to tell me. "A changing cast of players, stage sets all on show all the time so, yes, I think that's what defines The Savoy, the actual locality, and we're within walking distance of both London and . . . over those years, you do accumulate an enormous amount of stories, you know. We were talking about your father being here. We've always been incredibly popular with American correspondents, so, especially during the war years, and, of course, we were lucky enough to have Walter Cronkite here the other day making a return visit. Walking into the American Bar and saying 'that was my seat forty years ago!' That's amazing. . . . It was a privilege to meet him and we were all standing there being quite thrilled and even the younger people here, and I thought they won't remember – they won't know – and I said, I made the booking, and I said Walter Cronkite and quite a young woman said 'Walter Cronkite!'" I said 'do you know Walter Cronkite?' 'Yes!' she said. 'He's the voice at the Epcot Center now when you go to that!' . . . Perhaps not quite how he'd like to be remembered but . . . they're making a documentary about his life. They shuttled him all over London, visiting all the places he'd been to."

"Was he actually here during the war," I asked. "And did he stay here?"

"Yes, but sadly – we have an archive here but the only – we employ the only archivist, we think – trained archivist – in the world. But sadly it's incomplete. It wasn't set up until the Seventies, so lots of things went missing before that, and we have no trace of his actual guest card.

"I'm just about to finish seventeen years at The Savoy. A long time! I've seen an enormous number of changes, met an enormous number of very exciting people, but, you know, so I'm very fond of the place. I always think it has a magic about it and a *huge* amount of stories."

Michael Shepard, former General Manager of the London Hilton Park Lane and former manager of The Savoy told me, regarding The Savoy's massive renovation plans, that, "The Savoy is a complicated building. A building of that age you need to close it down and start again from scratch. The challenge comes in trying to regain your loyal customers. . . . So it will take another three or four years after it is reopened to build up its reputation.

"At the same time, when the Connaught closed down for its renovation, general manager Anthony Lee and its owners kept on paying the entire staff at full pay because they realized the hotel, despite its glorious renovation, is really only as good as its employees.

"If you look at The Savoy, it's really more than just a hotel – It's it's a bit like the London Hilton. It's a destination with a number of different businesses going on . . . destination restaurants: Galvin's on the top floor, Trader Vic's downstairs, the Whiskey Mist. All of those, along with the banqueting, are independent businesses.

"I'm sure they will try and maintain many of the historical elements but bring it up to the 21st century, and then it becomes relevant for today. It shouldn't be a museum. Then it becomes irrelevant." Michael and I were conversing over over breakfast at the London Hilton Park Lane.

According to the *Forbes* magazine fifteenth annual list of the world's richest people (2001), Alsaud, Prince Alwaleed Bin Talal, 44, a nephew of King Fahd of Saudi Arabia, has been the sixth best off with a net worth of $20 billion. (Bill Gates leads the list with

$60 billion, followed by three other Americans, including Warren Buffett, and then a German family, Theo and Karl Albrecht.) The Prince, who is married with two children, is based in the royal palace in Riyadh, Saudi Arabia, and his $9.6 billion stake in Citigroup is his largest holding. For fun, he told me "he relaxes in Europe" and, according to Forbes, he "takes long walks near his weekend desert retreat."

In January 2001, Chairman Kwek and HRH Prince Alwaleed bought out the remaining 12 percent of The Plaza that Citibank had owned, Chairman Kwek told me. "At the time of purchase [in 1995], the prince and CDL Hotels were negotiating for a 50 percent stake each in the ownership of The Plaza Hotel. However, both parties managed to secure only 41.6 percent each with the banks holding the balance. It was agreed with the banks that should they wish to sell their stake the prince and CDL Hotels have the right of first refusal. The prince and CDL Hotels now own 50 percent each in The Plaza Hotel."

I interviewed Prince Alwaleed personally in early April 2000, and found him to be not only articulate but someone with unabashed affection for The Plaza. He also lavished praise on his partner and co-owner of The Plaza, Chairman Kwek, with whom, he revealed, he is very comfortable co-overseeing the management of The Plaza.

"Mr. Kwek is an incredible partner and I like him a lot. I leave in his hands completely the management of The Plaza," the prince explained.

The *London Evening Standard* reported in April 2009 that "The Savoy Hotel may soon be put up for sale because of huge losses suffered by its billionaire Arab owner." I quote: "Industry sources say that Prince Alwaleed of Saudi Arabia is looking for a buyer for London's most famous hotel, which could be worth more than £200 million.

"The Prince, who is ranked 22nd on the Forbes magazine list of billionaires, has suffered huge falls in the value of his investments since the start of the credit crunch.

"His personal wealth is said to have gone from $21 billion to $13 billion in the past year. The most painful loss came on his five percent stake in American banking giant Citigroup, which has collapsed in value by more than 90 percent.

"The 54-year-old-prince – dubbed the Warren Buffet of the Gulf because of what were seen as astute investments – also has big holdings in Songbird Estates, the majority owner of Canary Wharf, Euro Disney and News Corporation.

"News of a possible sale comes as a £100 million refurbishment of the 120–year–old Strand institution approaches completion. The 268–room hotel is expected to reopen towards the end of the summer after an eighteen–month refit."

I was amazed by the reverence with which some London hoteliers held The Savoy. It was, and is, to them more than an icon or wife. More like a child. Albeit one in maturity with history galore, but as they fervently wished it would go on doing what it has been doing since 1889: being the grand dame of hotels for London – and the world. I talked to Simon Hirst, formerly General Manager of One Aldwych, now heading up Gordon Campbell Gray's London–based hotel empire that includes Dukes. It's what makes some hotels great, this desire to preserve the best. Here's our interview on the subject, talking about the renovation of The Savoy. He began, "You need to be pretty careful you get it right because that can get you into a lot of trouble, and so I think that's a very difficult thing to achieve, to take on a graceful old lady, give her the facelifts and the nip and the tuck, and keep her looking handsome and beautiful but yet change a few joints, change a few hips and keep her moving forward into the future." He told me, "It's a very subjective exercise. ... I think they're out to spend £30 million or something – £20 million. [It reputedly will end up being £100 million.] That's impossible and still have people stay there. You know, in terms of our industry, that is a true icon. I mean, these days everything is an icon; you know, this second rate movie star, this third–rate artist – everything's an icon. But that's a real icon. That's kind of a Winston Churchill, Theodore Roosevelt – that hotel is a real icon. And it's – you know the Mandarin in Hong Kong was modeled in terms of its service, its style, its attention to detail, it was modeled on The Savoy. So a lot of us have come through that training school. But like everything, everything has to move on and it's how you do that – it's very difficult to do. ... There's so much unwritten history, unwritten knowledge. That is a very good point. I mean, the Mandarin Hong Kong, my alma mater, they have just shut that for a year because they have been putting it off and putting it off and putting it off for probably ten years. And now they decide to close it. ... There comes a point where you have to say, 'we have to close this hotel for a year. We'll make the money back because the rates will be better, the occupancy will be better. But we have to close it for a year and just fix it! But it takes courage, it takes courage to do that, . You know, political courage in terms of the company and the way it's run."

Hirst was not happy The Savoy was leasing out The Savoy Grill. "And on one side it seems to make, it probably does make, economic sense. They charge a rent, they have a lease, it's guaranteed, there's no headaches for The Savoy. Gordon Ramsay is a sensational chef. He's got good business practice. He puts these chefs in charge of these restaurants and they deliver the product. And yet at the same time, it's such a shame that a hotel like The Savoy with all its resources, all its experience, has to do that. It's almost like an abdication, I mean, our current feeling, and always has been, we haven't kind of wavered, but our feeling here has always been we would never give up. This is what we do. If we can't run a hotel and find the people to run the restaurant really well and make it successful, which we definitely are, then it's almost like, 'well, we should probably be doing something else.'"

In order to turn to The Savoy of the future, I turned to The Savoy website of the present. As of June 2009, the site notes that:

Paying homage to its original Edwardian and Art Deco design, The Savoy will once again lay claim to its long-standing status as London's premier social destination when it unveils the culmination of a circa £100 million restoration programme in early 2010 – the most expensive hotel refurbishment in London's history.

Encompassing the entire building from the courtyard and famed American Bar to the public areas and 268 guestrooms, the responsibility for this extensive restoration is being handled by the renowned designer, Yves Rochon, who has earned special recognition for his work on other landmark hotels such as the George V in Paris and the Hermitage in Monaco. The programme heralds a number of notable highlights including the addition of a luxurious new two-bedroom Royal Suite, the complete remodel of the legendary River Restaurant and the re-launch of the fifty-eight River Suites with their iconic views over the River Thames.

In addition, The Savoy Grill will return again under the operation of Gordon Ramsay Holdings. New to the hotel will be The Beaufort Bar and Savoy Tea Shop, the first an opulent new venue to enjoy champagne and cocktails and the latter, a bijou teashop selling Savoy branded tea products, patisserie and other goodies. Within the Thames Foyer, the re-introduction of a stunning winter garden gazebo beneath an ornate glass dome will provide the perfect ambiance for afternoon tea. For those who wish to continue their fitness regime on the road, there will be a contemporary, glass-enclosed fitness gallery and rooftop swimming pool – one of only two in the city.

Room rates at The Savoy will start from around £350 per room per night. . . . A leader in the global hospitality industry, Fairmont Hotels & Resorts is an extraordinary collection of luxury hotels, which includes iconic landmarks like Fairmont Le Château Frontenac in Québec City, Fairmont The Norfolk, Nairobi and London's The Savoy, reopening in 2010. Fairmont hotels are one-of-a-kind properties where sophisticated travelers can discover culturally rich experiences that are authentic to the destination. Situated in some of the most exclusive and pristine areas in the world, Fairmont is committed to responsible tourism and is an industry leader in sustainable hotel management with its award-winning Green Partnership programme. Fairmont's portfolio includes fifty-six distinctive hotels, with plans to develop over twenty-five new properties in the coming years in destinations as diverse as Shanghai, Morocco and Anguilla.

Fairmont is owned by Fairmont Raffles Hotels International, a leading global hotel company with ninety-one hotels worldwide under the Raffles, Fairmont and Swissôtel brands. The company also owns Fairmont and Raffles branded Residences, Estates and luxury private residence club properties.

In June 2009, The Savoy's General Manager, updated us all on the progress of the renovation:

> Things are at last hotting up around here and I'm not just talking about the temperature in our temporary office! The ninth floor corridor ceilings are up (always a reassuring sign to see those pipes and wires disappear!) and the first run of Art deco guestrooms are nearing completion, ready for snagging. Such a critical juncture as it establishes the standard of finish that will be accepted here on out.
>
> Downstairs the public areas seem to be a different story as progress appears painfully slow. Talk amongst

the team is how the programme hinges on the impending arrival of the new glass dome for the Thames Foyer, after which work on other key elements of the interior design can rapidly move forward.

Chef Mayer's a happy chap as his kitchens are progressing well and he seems to think that it won't be too long before he dons his chefs whites once again!

For those passing by Savoy Court lately, they may have seen Sir Howard Robertson's 1929 iconic steel canopy coming down as it undergoes restoration, and over the coming weeks beautiful granite pavers will replace the bitumen road surface, a befitting upgrade for such a famous road.

Much has been written in the press recently speculating about The Savoy. No idea where these rumours came from as our owners continue to be totally committed and supportive to the successful reopening of The Savoy.

The design will combine the two aesthetics of the original – the Edwardian style of the buildings, opened in 1889 and added to in 1904 by the architect Thomas Collcutt, and the Art Deco style that was introduced in the late Twenties and Thirties designed by Sir Howard Robertson.

Thus the new Savoy will retain the traditional Edwardian influence for the lobby and public spaces including the Thames Foyer, while Art Deco will inspire treatments of the entrance, the new Beaufort Bar and the River Restaurant.

Michael Shepard had one more thing to add on The Savoy, "I remember on one occasion I met with Nancy Sinatra, the daughter of Frank, and I was showing her up to the suite and I was telling her about the suite. This is where Frank used to stay and the piano in the ballroom where he used to go and practice, and I opened the door and the sun was shining through and you had the view over the Thames, and I said 'this is where he used to stay. He used to sit and dine and write his notes here at the desk.' And she turned to the table and she saw this wonderful arrangement of white lilies and she said, 'Oh, just like daddy would have ordered! Thank you so much!' And that put goosebumps on the back of my neck. That was really wonderful."

The entire hotel world has been waiting with baited breath for the grand reopening of this great institution in 2010. What surprises will the "new" Savoy have in store for its clientele? What will the critics say? It's been like a great cliff-hanger serial.

Alas, the £100million restoration of The Savoy Hotel has evidently hit a number of delays. The 120-year-old hotel was due to reopen in May but the grand reopening has now been pushed back to autumn. Fairmont, the Canadian company which manages The Savoy, began the 18-month project – the most expensive renovation in British hotel history – in December 2007. The hotel will partially reopen with 160 rooms, the front hall, The Savoy Grill and the largely unchanged American Bar, in the summer. A Fairmont spokeswoman offered: "I don't think there is one specific reason for the delay, it is just one of those things that happens with projects of this size."

To come full circle, my last Savoy story brings my father back onstage. As a war correspondent based partly in London during the Second World War, my father and U.S. Army General Terry Allen rented a penthouse suite at The Savoy. "Here, during a bizarre week end, Terry Allen and I shared a royal suite," my father wrote in his book *Just the Other Day – From Yellow Pines to Broadway.* "We entertained prodigally. Military friends came in to see the General; nonmilitary friends, all of the theater, were my visitors. Room-service waiters were forever bringing in trays and rolling in tables. . . . There was a colonel in for dinner one evening and also a major, who had served, as a private, with the General in the St.-Mihiel offensive during World War I. There was a female star of the London stage . . . and a celebrated actor who had played Iago in New York . . . also a dark-haired and vital young woman who played the Ophelia to John Barrymore's Hamlet. There was war talk, army talk, theater talk . . . flowers, floor waiters . . . When the revelry subside, when the week end ended, when the Battle of The Savoy was fought and lost, and when the General decided that he would have to get on back to camp, and in a hurry, we called the cashier and asked that the bill be sent up to the suite. We blinked as we looked it over. It all seemed so much Arabic but down in the corner was the total in pounds, which, when translated, came to some around $466. The General's shock was obviously greater than mine. As he wrote out his part of the check his only comment, and a quiet one, was 'Hell, Ward, I never thought it would be this high. We people in the Army can't live like you correspondents!'"

The Savoy may or may not reopen soon, but, in the meantime, one is never at a loss for other great luxury hotels in this great city to patronize, such as our next destination, the somewhat exotic Mandarin Oriental.

Chapter 9

The Mandarin Oriental Hyde Park Hotel

In the late 1920's Rudolph Valentino raised the temperature in the Grille Room several degrees. At the height of his silent screen fame he came to London with wife Natasha Ramboua. His animal magnetism was such that the dark green Verdi and Sicilian white marble visibly paled by comparison and smoke seemed to emanate from his eyes and the contours of his sensual lips, as they did in "Son of the Sheik."

Fast forward to today and the Mandarin Oriental hotel brand; the Mandarin Oriental Hyde Park has its same glorious views overlooking Hyde Park. Every time I see it I think of Ginger Rogers and Fred Astaire dancing to *Isn't It a Lovely Day to Be Out in the Rain?* It's an illusion, of course. But the parade of celebrities that have stayed in the Mandarin Oriental is far greater than the countless Horse Guards, in all their red–vested glory, clip–clopping past the hotel from Knightsbridge Barracks.

Think of yourself ascending the plush–carpeted marble steps past forests of flowers and you are a changed man or woman which also brings me right back to that major theory I have about truly luxurious hotels. I've always thought, as a life–long journalist who has been fortunate to stay in and interview people in some of the world's preeminent hotels, that even ambling through a grand hotel you find yourself somehow transformed, elevated perhaps only momentarily, to a different outlook on life.

You certainly may not be King George VI and Queen Elizabeth (the Queen Mum, remember, not QEII) celebrating their silver wedding anniversary at the Hyde Park Hotel but a stay at this fairy tale of a hotel is almost guaranteed to make you feel like you're king or queen of something, even if it's only your own fantasies.

Or are you Fred Astaire and Ginger Rogers at the hotel dancing at Hyde Park gazebo, which is just as real, even today, as in your imagination and singing "Isn't It a Nice Day to Be Out in the Rain!" For my part, I have never felt so cared for – from the attitude of the front desk staff who greeted me as if I were a long lost relative, or lover, to the huge bouquet of roses to the king–sized bathroom that may at one time, unlike most king–sized items, have actually been used by a king. I wanted immediately to marry the front desk manager, who was a cross between a raven-haired Vivien Leigh, golden–tressed Gwyneth Paltrow with a touch of flame–haired Gina Lollobrigida. Unfortunately, I don't recall her name – I was a little too dazzled to remember to ask – but her warmth and beauty come in a graceful thought.

The Mandarin Oriental Hyde Park, 66 Knightsbridge, domi-nates the Knightsbridge area as well as Hyde Park which, in a way, is its own private park. No "Royal" park, of course, can be private but as its "terrace step," with a single, narrow road separating it from the hotel, a road which is closed on Sundays, by the way, it might as well be its private park, complete with heavily forested nooks and standings of trees. Sherwood Forest comes to mind.

And yet, The Mandarin Oriental Hyde Park is about a lot more than the gorgeous white orchids I'm looking at as I write these lines; more than the black–bordered octagonal rug framed by the hardwood floor on the eight–windowed tower suite I'm in, one of two such suites on the ninth floor. It's about innocence revisited; about a child's Christmas in London, seeing the roof lights of Harrod's lit up year round as a celebratory of Christmas; all of Robin Hood's evergreen Sherwood Forest; more than the 900 pound–per–night cost of the suites; more than walking around the outside perimeter of the octagonal room. As Holly Johnstone, public relations manager, said, "The Mandarin Oriental reminds me of the Darling residence in 'Peter Pan,' which housed the children whom Peter taught to fly off to Neverland. And, for a moment, as the lights poured – not sunlight mind you – down over Big Ben and Westminster Abby, somewhere more solid than Windsor Castle to the west, I thought I espied Peter and Wendy flying interference for our lost innocence. Telling us all that they know and have found a place "Where Dreams Are Made," as the Julie Stein–Adolph Green–Betty Comden song goes in part.

To be sure, only a few privileged might stay in the turreted rooms of the Mandarin Oriental but the spirit of James Barrie's immortal Peter is speaking to everyone . . . "A Place Where Dreams Are Made and Time Is Never Planned," as the song from the 1954 Broadway musical, "Peter Pan," goes. I got this notice of kinship with Peter Pan from Arabella Huddart, a beautiful English woman and mother of four children, and who I'd invited up to the suite for a drink and some laughter, *sans* romance of course, and *sans* the four children as well.

As you may have noticed heretofore, on this trip I took to the habit of recording notes about my experiences in individual hotels with a tape recorder. Just wandering around the gorgeous grounds or sauntering through the sumptuous rooms of these marvelous edifices, I'd just switch on my recorder and voice my impressions, stream-of-consciousness-style. Here are some observations I recorded in a hotel I'm certain Fred Astaire and Ginger Rogers would have been right at home in:

Bar has live jazz in the evenings . . . my suite probably in the £900 range . . . I'm in a round, actually octagonal, room, at the Oriental Hyde Park. Ironically it has a beautiful print of the new theater Haymarket at its opening on July 4, 1821; the Royal interior at it appeared on the night of the opening published 1823 by R Wilkinson; round room one of two on the ninth floor, four windows, on the right facing is Harrod's beautiful night lights and, as if it's perpetual Christmas, on the left is the Millennium Eye and Big Ben – quite spectacular. Good trivia question for next party – what's the name of the building that houses Big Ben? Saint Stephen's Tower. . . . Berkeley is down the street. Terraced penthouse looks like a little cabana on top of the Berkeley. Can see Westminster, distant hills beyond the Thames, financial district. . . .

Pretty, pixyish and yet as professional a publicist as you'll find on either side of the Atlantic, Holly and I had lunch at the hotel over-looking Hyde Park.

"I don't think I could ever stay in a hotel and relax again because I'm always thinking, 'what needs to be changed!'" she said.

The Hyde Park became the Mandarin Oriental Hotel in 1996. After a £56 million renovation it opened in 2000 as the Mandarin Oriental Hyde Park. World renowned designer Adam Tahani did the interior design of the rooms and public spaces. One Hyde Park, modern, new residences, will open in 2010 in 198 residences, including 25 suites.

"Our original entrance was on the Hyde Park side of the hotel, and there was to be no advertising it at all in Hyde Park because that's where property is 'Royal parkland.' They're very, very strict on what they do and don't allow, so we moved the new entrance across to the other side of the building. . . . We hosted Margaret Thatcher's eightieth in our ballroom, which was a fantastic event. We also use our ballroom for the Royal Black Dance.

. . . We now have royal permission to use the former front entrance for weddings and things like that. Any heads of state, people of that stature who come to the hotel, they always use that entry."

Holly took a bite of her salad and continued. "It's nice for me to be on property because I was at an agency before, and having a relationship with your brand is just so great. . . . We have our agencies and they do a fantastic job, but we want to make sure that when VIP's and guests come to the hotel that they're well looked after, so that's important to us.

Turning to the topic of room rates Holly said, "we have different categories of rent. You've got courtyard rooms that face inwards. Because if you look down on the hotel from the bird's eye view, it's more in an "H" shape, so you've got the courtyards facing in. They're our lowest category. They're best for sort of business travelers, things like that. They're very quiet. Then prices are going to go up. On the Knightsbridge side, you've got the view over the whole of Knightsbridge, and the most expensive would be on the Hyde Park side of the hotel, obviously, for the views. But there are fantastic packages that we always do, and actually booking on the Internet itself, you can get amazing rates. And people often forget that over Christmas rates go right down and people can really get some amazing, amazing rates."

"Less than £300 for a room?"

"Yes. Not much below, but you can do it."

"But still, you're staying at one of the top, say, five hotels in London."

"Exactly. And if you think about one of our packages at the moment is for Easter and it is just over the Easter weekend, you can get a room, two rooms – so all our rooms are interconnecting – once you get one room for £275, you get the interconnecting room free. And a bottle of champagne in your room.

"If you want five-star service, it is going to cost, but it's what you get for it – the whole experience – I personally think it's incredibly worthwhile because it's the attention, five stars, you'd hope it's the attention to detail; it's those little requests that they just remember, and at least here, there's a fantastic service where if a guest has stayed at one of the hotels and they stay at another one, and they have their favorite drink, it will be placed in their room on arrival. Things like that. And they make a difference.

"You know, we never want to do anything that's too promotional," Holly continued. "We just really want to sell what the hotel's got going for it. So something like the spa, which we're very famous for, the holistic spa, you'll never find us doing sort of trendy caviar facials or anything like that because that's not what it's about. What it is, is there's a whole philosophy behind it. You step into the spa and sort of step away from real life, and you take off your shoes and you have these aromatic, holistic treatments. And that's in keeping with Mandarin Orientals throughout the world. If we suddenly started doing something that was different than that, I don't think our clients or our guests would really like it. They know what to expect."

The Spa at Mandarin Oriental has been awarded Condé Nast *Traveller's* 'Favorite Hotel Spa' in the United Kingdom, ranking eighth best spa in the world.

Accolades for Foliage as well as the Mandarin Oriental are seemingly endless. The *Telegraph* says "London's best-sited five-star hotel," while Brides' Hot Venues in the U.K., 2008, points out "This Knightsbridge institution isn't just one of the city's finest hotels but one of the best in the world. Your guests will be blown away." "If service is the hallmark of a first-rate hotel, the Mandarin Oriental is top of the class," says *Image* magazine. "The new Terrace restaurant surveys the most immaculate lawn outside Centre Court." The *Telegraph* includes it in their Top 50 Summer Restaurants of 2008. Frommer's mentions, "No other bar in London showcases the art of the cocktail as beautifully as this one." "This is a delightful restaurant. . . . Chef Chris Staines is accomplished and as inventive with modern ingredients as he is at ease with luxury ones," says the Tatler Restaurant Guide, 2008. Foliage Under the Stars, as of July 2009, pairs an exquisite menu from the award-winning Foliage restaurant with special Moët et Chandon vintage champagnes below the starry sky of The Park Terrace. The menu is priced at £120 per person and includes a champagne and canapé reception, four courses and all accompanying champagnes and digestifs.

Foliage's fantastic interior is the brainchild of internationally renowned designer, Adam Tihany (creator of Le Cirque 2000, Manhattan). The restaurant's great views and convenient proximity to Hyde Park were a natural starting point for Tihany as he strove to "bring the park into the restaurant." Clean lines and geometric shapes, perfectly illuminated by soft lighting and lush fabrics provide a sense the good life in an otherwise cozy setting. The restaurant's raised floor ensures all diners can enjoy looking out over the park.

Over coffee, Holly shifted back to the origin of the Mandarin Oriental in London. "In 2000, when it became a Mandarin Oriental hotel after the big £56 million refurb, it was overseen by Adam Tahani, who's actually from New York," she said. The adjoining apartment complex, she said, "will be serviced by Mandarin Oriental so they'll have all of our services. We'll get a swimming pool, hopefully!" The architecture is completely different. The hotel is an old, historic building and the new residence is very modern, glass–paned on the outside.

Another New Yorker, Woody Allen, stayed at the Mandarin Oriental when filming a movie not too long ago, although before Holly joined the company. Not to worry. When you work at the Mandarin Oriental, you're bound to see your share of world famous names stroll by sooner rather than later. It's one of those magical places where, even if, like me, you're definitely not a household name, on either side of the Atlantic, you will get a palpable taste of what it's like to be one.

It's time now, though, to leave Holly, the Mandarin and the park behind. Like Alice's famous white rabbit, we have to be scooting along to our next appointment, which is at The Hilton Waldorf.

Chapter 10

Hilton Waldorf Hotel

I treated myself to afternoon tea in the Homage Patisserie of the Hilton Waldorf where once upon a time stage door Johnnies and earls, well-to-do and not, waited for the Gaiety Girls after their show at the Gaiety Theatre next door.

Ruby Miller, one of these girls, talked this way about the dandies who waited to woo them in her autobiography, "Resplendent young men in their tails, their opera hats and cloaks lined with satin, carrying tall ebony canes with gold knobs and gardenias in their buttonholes."

Some of the girls found properly upper class and even titled husbands, much to the chagrin of those who pampered and prepared them for stardom.

Gaiety manager George Edwards was quoted in *London Town* in 1929 as angrily complaining about one of his stars, "Bluebell," who married her way out of show business. "It's ingratitude. Sheer ingratitude! I've done everything for her – taught her to pick up her aitches, clean her fingernails, had her teeth looked at, her appendix removed, her hair dyed, dressed her from her underclothes to her boots and now, when she looks like making good, she marries!"

Queen Victoria and William Waldorf Astor were the variegated team to bring The Waldorf Hotel into being a *grands frais*. Now called the Hilton Waldorf, the hotel opened in 1908, two years before the Tango first burst upon London society at the Gaiety Theatre next door.

The Queen was "not amused" by the acres of slums, gin mills and bordellos she rode through in her carriage on her way to Buckingham Palace. Something had to be done. Thus commenced one of the largest clearance projects since the great fire of 1666. By the time it was completed, the Queen had shuffled off this mortal coil, but King Edward VII opened Aldwych and Kingsway Streets several blocks from the even then venerable Savoy Hotel (which had opened in 1889) in 1905, and the hotel opened with a glittering champagne reception on January 28, 1908.

Astor, who had built the new wing of New York's Waldorf Hotel, named The Astoria, to become The Waldorf Astoria on the site of where the Empire State Building now stands, advanced a fairly large part of the 700,000 pounds needed to underwrite the new hotel. Developer and theater owner Edward Sanders was so grateful for Waldorf's help he named the hotel after him.

The hotel "contains nearly 400 bedrooms, and the number of bathrooms is said to be proportionately larger that in any other hotel in the world," *The Times* of London would proclaim on January 8, 1908. "The rooms have been so planned as to make it possible to convert many of them into suites for the use of guests using the hotel as a permanent residence. Throughout the building the style of decoration is Louis XVII, which has been employed with discrimination, and the appearance of the rooms is both elegant and refined. . . . There is a magnificent palm lounge, which is decorated in pale green and white."

That Palm Court Lounge, which society flocked to for tea dances and weddings for a hundred years, still has periodic "Tango Teas." The first Argentine tango, as I say, was in 1910 at the Gaiety Theatre and it quickly spread next door to The Waldorf. Dancing was interrupted in 1939 at the start of World War II when a bomb exploded in the street, shattering the glass ceiling of the Palm Court.

The Twenties witnessed a fierce rivalry between The Savoy and The Waldorf about which hotel could sell the most albums of its radio broadcasts. The Waldorf's Howard Godfrey (Howard – not Arthur, the American radio and T.V. personality) and the "Waldorfions" (yes, there was such a group!) recorded such hits as "In Heaven" and "Sweeping the Clouds Away." "My Canary Has Circles Under His Eyes" was a favorite of the time; the saucy tune goes, in part, something like this:

> Since making whoopee became all the rage,
> It's even got to the old birdcage.
> My canary has circles under his eyes.
> His only pals are the yellow lark and just a tiny sparrow,
> But I am scared when he's in the park,
> He leaves the straight and narrow

In a small souvenir book on the London Waldorf, Lisa Kirk, appearing in a West End show at the time, is quoted ordering orange juice and eggs at noon. "I am sorry, madam," the room service waiter replied. "We are serving only lunch now."

"Oh, really!" Kirk retorted. "Then I'll have orange juice, soft boiled eggs, toast, coffee and jam – for lunch!"

"At once, madam!" the voice on the phone snapped.

The late Lord Charles Forte, one of the world's greatest hoteliers, felt that his acquisition of London's Waldorf Hotel really set the stage for his global hotel empire. (See the chapter on Brown's Hotel for more on Charles and his son, Sir Rocco Forte.)

"In 1958 we involved ourselves in what was perhaps our most significant venture so far. It was made possible by a fortunate conjunction of events," he writes in *The Autobiography of Charles Forte*.

"The Waldorf was a respectable upper–middle–grade hotel with its own freehold site, part of Frederick Hotels Ltd, an old-established hotel company which was controlled and directed by Sir Stuart Goodwin. Stuart was also chairman of the Neeps End Steel Corporation. He was in fact more of an industrialist than a hotelier, hence his reasons for making the sale.

"Forte's [his then current London venture] was then concerned solely with catering and entertainment. I was intrigued by the hotel business. I wanted to broaden the character of our activities and indeed I believed we could apply the methods which worked so well for us in our current business to the running of hotels. I also felt that the addition of a hotel would make us a better balanced concern, although I knew nothing about the running of hotels at that time. My only experience was limited to staying in them.

"I do not know how my name and activities had come to the notice of Sir Stuart, but it was probably through the press. He invited me up to his Sheffield home. I remember that this was not a luxurious residence, but comfortable and nicely appointed. He was a modest, straightforward man with a most agreeable personality.

"He came straight to the point: 'I would like to sell The Waldorf. I have already made up my mind about the price I want. I am not going to put it up for auction and I do not want to bargain about figures. If you agree to the price, you can have the hotel.'

"The price he named was £600,000. It was a wonderful opportunity. There were many companies and individuals who would have been glad to have paid that for The Waldorf and I am still mystified as to why I was his choice. My company did not have the capacity to borrow £600,000, the equivalent probably of about £5 million today."

Fortunately, some fast, fortuitous financial transactions with a fellow London businessman gave him access to the vast funds he needed.

"I could hardly believe my good fortune. This transaction would realize all but £100,000 of the purchase price of The Waldorf. I knew that I could raise the balance of the money and, indeed, more money than I needed to refurbish The Waldorf on a sale and lease-back arrangement, which I quickly managed to achieve with the Prudential Assurance, who bought the freehold from me and granted me a ninety-nine-year lease. And so I acquired my first hotel. . . .

"The Waldorf was the precursor of more than eight hundred hotels that we later owned, leased, or managed, and its purchase opened a whole new chapter in our lives. My first priority was to obtain a top-class manager. After due inquiry I engaged John Lee, who had been the general manager of the Dorchester. He was the complete hotelier and I learnt a lot from him."

The Hilton Waldorf Hotel remains a lively stepping-stone from the past to the present, from 1908 when it opened to now, with the Novello Theatre on its left and the Gaiety Theatre on its right, although the Gaiety Girls are long gone. (All married off, no doubt.) The Waldorf name remains a symbol of elegance and stability in London as in New York.

Are there any more Hilton hotels on our itinerary? Well, we'll just have to wait and see. Onward – for now, to that legendary establishment of song and story, The Ritz.

Chapter 11

The Ritz

"I love jewels," agreed Percy enthusiastically. "Of course I wouldn't want any one at school to know about it, but I've got quite a collection myself. I used to collect them instead of stamps."

"And diamonds," continued John eagerly. "The Schnlitzer–Murphys had diamonds as big as walnuts–"

"That's nothing." Percy had leaned forward and dropped his voice to a low whisper. "That's nothing at all. My father has a diamond bigger than the Ritz–Carlton Hotel."

– "The Diamond as Big as the Ritz"
by F. Scott Fitzgerald

Ever wonder what it's like to live inside a life–sized gold pocket watch? Maybe not, but try The London Ritz, the gilded Louis XVI chateau overlooking Green Park, for sheer elegance, comfort and high glamour. But The Ritz is a lot more than tall mirror reflections, pink lobster curtains, Cinderella's castle. It is finding a boyfriend for a girl you had once hoped might be yours; it is a petit fours completeness. No wants, no past, future. Now. The rarity of now. How many times in our lives could we have said to ourselves, "Stop time. I have what I have always wanted." You, too can perhaps feel F. Scott Fitzgerald's fast–fleeting sense of well–being when he wrote to his friend and editor, Max Perkins, in 1926 that, "In fact, with the play [the dramatization of *Gatsby*] going well and my new novel growing absorbing and with my being back in a nice villa on my beloved Riviera, I'm happier than I've been for years. It's one of the strange, precious, and all too transitory moments when everything in one's life seems to be going well." Spend an hour at the Rivoli Bar or go for afternoon tea or dinner at The Ritz, and you may feel like F. Scott did at this moment.

In fact, when F. Scott was of a mind to write a tall tale drenched in the greatest luxury he could possibly imagine, what's the one word he thought of to convey that idea? "Ritz." F. Scott Fitzgerald said of his story that it "was designed utterly for my own amusement. I was in a mood characterized by a perfect craving for luxury, and the story began as an attempt to feed that craving on imaginary foods." Well, you don't have to imagine the Ritz. It's still here, still big and very real. And yet, in all its storied elegance, a bit unreal as well.

Of course, Fitzgerald was referring, probably, to the Ritz in Boston, or perhaps to one in Manhattan on Madison Avenue that has long since closed, but it's all in the family, as even today the New York and London Ritzes are what they call "partner" hotels. Perhaps we're getting too technical here. It's really the name "Ritz" which conveys the richness. Fitzgerald knew it. Irving Berlin knew it, when he penned that little ditty, "Puttin' on the Ritz." The word has for many decades now been shorthand the world over for the best.

For every hotel aficionado, however, there are only two Ritz hotels in the world: The Ritz London and The Ritz Paris. For sheer grandeur, as well as attention to detail, it's hard for any hotel to compete with the oracle of opulence that was Céesar Ritz's fantasy and reality.

Before there was The Ritz, there was The Ritzy Old White Horse, one of the most celebrated "coaching inns" in England. The inn, in 1805, had "a pleasant coffee room passengers can wait for any of the stages and travelers in general are well accommodated with beds." The inn was replaced by the red-brick Walsingham Hotel, built by Lord Walsingham, which at least in photos of the time seemed to resemble the Mandarin Oriental Hyde Park in its turrets and gables if not in actual height.

The Ritz was designed by Charles Mewes, who worked with Céèsar Ritz on his Paris property, and Joseph Davis, who lived in Brussels as a boy and studied architecture at the Godefroy. Judging from photos of the Walsingham House, which opened in 1887, which replaced the Old White Horse which was a favorite stopover of stage coach drivers and their passengers, The Ritz' designers took some of their inspiration from the design of the Walsingham. Only The Ritz became more palatial and less like the old Hyde Park, now the Mandarin-Oriental Hyde Park.

When the hotel first opened in 1906, several attendants were on duty on all seven guest floors to take dispatches sent in pneumatic tubes, from business cards to letters, and rocketed them to and from guest rooms.

I've stayed at The Ritz several times, once in a suite over-looking Green Park. But the most unusual time was in the same room with a rock singer. Perhaps I should explain that. Now when I say "nothing happened" between us, I really mean nothing happened. I was her public relations representative and friend. I slept in the bed, my friend on the floor with a "barrier" between us (shades of Colbert and Gable in "It Happened One Night"), a kind of walled city for herself behind a chair and some pillows – those she didn't sleep on. She was in town to appear at a corporate event near Covent Garden. But the defining moment of our visit to The Ritz came during a ten-course dinner in the fabulous dining room of the hotel. We were on the last course when we spotted (she was probably first) a tall, blonde, incredibly handsome Englishman dancing with a young girl who turned out to be his niece.

"Go up and ask him to dance," I suggested, probably echo-ing her silent thoughts.

So she and the young man danced and danced. And I watched, feeling pride at being a matchmaker but a twinge of the loneliness of the odd, and in my case, older man out. He left with his family who were in town at The Ritz and they exchanged emails.

When we came back to London from an "In and Out" singing date, where my son did a wonderful job selling CD's, they got together. This time we were staying at The Savoy in different rooms and I saw the young man coming out of her room and breaking a bit of my heart as he walked, I thought a bit sheep-ishly, down the corridor for some ice or who knows what! Well, what began at The Ritz ended in The Savoy. But the singer and her British beau continued to see each other in England and New York. He became a correspondent for a leading newspaper.

In January 2002, The Ritz London was awarded a Royal Warrant for Banqueting and Catering Services from His Royal Highness the Prince of Wales. The Ritz is the first, and only, hotel to have been honored with this prestigious award. (The Prince seems to have a real fondness for the hotel, which may explain why his Mutton Renaissance project supplies them with mutton – see the chapter on The Metropolitan.)

In November 2006 The Ritz opened William Kent House, also Grade II* listed, at No. 22 Arlington Street. (The asterisk counts as part of the listing: roughly it breaks down as: Grade I buildings are of exceptional interest;   Grade II* are particularly important buildings of more than special interest; Grade II are of special interest, warranting every effort to preserve them.) Green Park adjoins the hotel. It reminded me of a smaller version of Spencer House, several houses down this illustrious Green Park block. And here Gerri Pitt, The Ritz's indefatiguable public relations person, talks about it:

"Designed in the 1740's by the 18th century architect William Kent, from whom the house now takes its name, the historic mansion was known as Wimborne House when The Ritz opened in 1906. Acquired by the owners of The Ritz in 2005, almost a hundred years after Céesar Ritz first tried to purchase the house and was rebuffed by Lord Wimborne, William Kent House underwent an extensive period of restoration and refurbishment immediately prior to the re-opening of its magnificent new reception rooms. In keeping with the guidelines set down by English Heritage, the exquisite collection of lavishly decorated private dining rooms and residential suites have been retained in their original Italian Renaissance style décor and the majesty of the William Kent House interiors are now resplendently reborn."

To many, Marie Antoinette is the essence of extravagance, overindulgence (although recent writings put her in a much more sympathetic light); to Charles Mewes, she was deserving of having a private dining room, off the main dining room, named after her. "Here is an opportunity to drink in the whole elegant, decorative vocabulary of the Louis Seize style," writes Marcus Binney in his book *The Ritz Hotel, London*. But more than the gilded, floral swags in arches and around ovals, there is a life here without a party going on. Yes, marble, marble and gilt. But there is more here, like the love between two lonely people who have never even kissed each other. They just know. Maybe Shakespeare said it best in his sonnet:

> Not marble, nor the gilded monuments
> Of Princes, shall outlive this powerful rhyme;
> But you shall shine more bright in these contents,
> Than unswept stone besmear'd with sluttish time.

"I have a feeling nothing short of the end of the world can change what goes on here," novelist Louis Bromfield once said

about The Ritz in Paris. The same could be said of the London
Ritz, although some of the staff and guests never were in the kinds
of danger as their counterparts in the Paris Ritz under Nazi occupation.

Paris once had its own Claridge's on the Champs–Elysees
and it is no longer a hotel. Cole Porter wrote this Claridge into *La
Revue des Ambassadors*. It goes:

> That building there upon the right,
> Is the famous Hotel Claridge.
> It's where ladies go at night
> When they're fed up with marriage.

He worked The Ritz into his song, "Let's Do It":

> The world admits
> Even the bears in pits do it.
> Even the Pekinese in The Ritz do it.
> Let's do it, let's fall in love.

During World War II, "Life at the Top" in London hotels was
characterized by wary, watchful waiting. Ground floor rooms
were always in demand as they were furthest from aerial harm's
way. In Paris, however, as Samuel Marx writes in *Queen of The Ritz*,
the real fear of arrest was added to tensions. "In the summer of
1942, the elegance was dead, almost destroyed by stiff restrictions
and short rations. Nobody would live at the top, eat well, drink
well, order well. Fashion was nonexistent," he wrote.

Queen of The Ritz is the story of Blanche Rubenstein, who was
married to the owner of the Paris Ritz. She barely survived the
war, having been severely interrogated a number of times, and
miraculously escaped death.

Yet, after Allied Forces marched into Paris, "Blanche wasted
no time in shaking off the hardship of war." Marx wrote.

Marx has a wonderful description of Céesar Ritz, after whom
both the London and Paris Ritz Hotels were named. Many, Marx
says, were "in awe of Ritz's regal manners, his insatiable search for
perfection . . . he sported thirty business suits, forty-two fancy
waistcoats . . . three hundred ties . . . "

The 18th century William Kent townhouse next door is used
for private functions including lavish weddings. Its ornate "music

room" with a vaulted ceiling seats up to 60 guests for luncheon or dinner or 120 for a reception. The Italian Renaissance styled William Kent room, with views overlooking Green Park, is adorned with trompe d'oeil paneling and a breathtaking gilded barrel ceiling. The Queen Elizabeth Room next to it also has a sweeping view of Green Park. The Wimborne Room next to it also has floor-to-nearly-ceiling windows overlooking the Park.

One of the several best dinners I've had in my life was at The Ritz London. John Williams, the hotel's Executive Chef, prepared a meal (not personally, maybe) that was fit for Queen Elizabeth who sometimes dines here. His goal as executive chef is to run the finest hotel, restaurant and banqueting in England.

"I have always had a great love for The Ritz and its time-honored traditions and culinary history," he told me. "Escoffier and his forward thinking methods have influenced my career significantly and it is a pleasure and an honor . . . "

The Ritz is not an imitation nor can it be imitated. It is an original whose origins stem from decades if not centuries of hospitality.

Hazel Sloan, a noted watercolorist, who taught painting to Andrew Lowe, managing director of The Ritz Club, has an interesting thing to say about painting and imitation. Usually one thinks of painting as an imitation of life. In the case of a hotel, the hotel is an imitation, reflection of the people who love and frequent it. But Sloan told The Ritz Magazine that the subject of a painting, a flower, teacup, person, whatever "is only important insofar as it is the source of inspiration. A painting lives independently from its subject; it is a new creation, not a re-creation, of something that already exists. Watercolor is not used to paint a rose, but a rose is used to paint a watercolor."

Speaking of art, no hotel does the art of afternoon tea better than The Ritz. Here I'll let The Ritz's Pitt have center-stage: "Afternoon Tea at The Ritz is served daily in The Palm Court Restaurant. Popular since the hotel first opened and enjoyed by a wide varied audience, Afternoon Tea devotees through the years have included King Edward VII, Charlie Chaplin, Sir Winston Churchill, General De Gaulle, Noël Coward and Judy Garland.

"In keeping with the beautiful surroundings of The Palm Court, tea is served on fine Limoges china decorated in an exclusive design of gold, pale green and rose colors to perfectly complement the charm of the room. Tea is served in silver teapots with silver milk jugs and tea strainers. The Ritz Traditional English Tea is offered together with an extensive selection of some seventeen teas, including China Oolong, Lapsang Souchong, Earl Grey, Ceylon Orange Pekoe, Darjeeling and Jasmine tea. Freshly cut sandwiches with traditional fillings include smoked salmon on brown bread, roast ham, cucumber and cream cheese and egg mayonnaise with cress on white bread. Finger sandwiches are served on a three-tier stand together with freshly baked raisin and apple scones with organic strawberry preserve and clotted Devonshire cream, and a selection of afternoon tea pastries and fresh cream cakes.

"The Ritz London is a member of the Tea Council's prestigious Tea Guild and was the proud holder of the Tea Council's 2004 Top London Afternoon Tea Award, being described as the 'perfect venue for afternoon tea.'"

Only England would have a Tea Council! America has its politically charged "Boston Tea Parties" but London still cherishes that most elegant of non-alcoholic beverages.

"Afternoon Tea at The Ritz is priced at £34.00 per person," Mr. Pitt continues.   "Reservations are required and it is recommended that they be made well in advance. To avoid inconvenience, guests are offered the choice of five daily sittings – 11:30 am, 1:30 pm, 3:30 pm, 5:30 pm and at 7:30 pm for Champagne Tea. Guests are respectfully asked to observe a formal dress code in the Palm Court which requires gentlemen to wear a jacket and tie while jeans and sportswear shoes are not permitted."

Pitt also waxed eloquent on The Palm Court: "To the left of the Long Gallery, between the hotel lobby and The Ritz Restaurant, lies the Palm Court. Originally known as the Winter Garden, it was designed as a dramatic stage set to delight those entering from the Piccadilly entrance. The Palm Court makes imaginative use of a mirrored backdrop reflecting the impressive marble columns which flank the entrance to the restaurant. Much of the appeal lies in the charming centrally focused fountain sculpture of a reclining female figure wrought in gilded lead.

"Light streams from a central glazed roof, lifting the mood on a dull day and ensuring the glass is not black at night. Two decorative shell windows skirt the central roof-light where a pair of wrought iron chandeliers, reminiscent of fanciful birdcages, are entwined with painted metal flowers. The gilded trellis, which is composed almost entirely of simple geometric motifs, lends a soft golden sheen to the room."

Where does the tradition of afternoon tea come from? One story is that late in the 1700's Anna, Seventh Duchess of Bedford, asked her butler for a light afternoon meal. The Grosvenor Park Room named its tea "Anna's Tea," in her honor. I'm often asked, what's the best place to have tea in London. For one thing it's in hotels. For another, it's anytime you like.

Perhaps the most ornate tea is at The London Ritz, where its tea became so popular that the first afternoon tea seating actually starts at 11:30 a.m.! (I suppose it's always afternoon somewhere in the world.) And the last seating has been as late as 5:30 p.m.! Other favorites are teas at The Connaught and The Lanesborough. I had a delightful tea with Anthony Lee, general manager of the Connaught in February, 2009, made more delightful by the presence of Anthony Lee himself who, along with many friends I have gotten to cherish, London's ultimate innkeeper. After tea, we embarked on a tour of rooms and suites including the then-as-yet-unfinished penthouse suite.

Michael de Coza, Head Hallporter, who has been welcoming guests for thirty years, even made a cameo appearance in the movie *Notting Hill*! But, truly, one of his greatest joys, he says, is having "formed friendships with families (who have stayed in the hotel) that span generations."

Broadway actor Jim Dale, the epitome of an English gentleman, stays at The Ritz in London even though he says he doesn't know the city as he once did. "Don't forget I left London in 1979 to come to live over here . . . apart from going back rushing around seeing children, grandchildren, I haven't really explored London for the last twenty-five years," he told me at an after-party for the New York Drama Desk Awards in 2009.

But he does still have a few favorite hotels. "I went over for this," he said, pointing to a lapel pin. "The MBE. And our children and grandchildren came to see us on Green Park. The Ritz was really beautiful. I really enjoyed it." He is slated to star in the Broadway-bound musical "Busker Alley." "One day it will go on, whether I'm in it or not. I don't know. There comes a time when you can't play it any longer. You just get a bit too older for that – dancing around!

"I'm looking forward to the revival or a play where I'm in a wheelchair – with dancing nurses or something like that! There are certain roles later in life you don't attempt because it's okay for one or two nights, but not eight times a week. The best thing I did which tore me to pieces was 'Christmas Carol.'" He played the role of Scrooge in the musical version of "A Christmas Carol" at Madison Square Garden's Paramount Theatre.

In Anita Loos' *Gentlemen Prefer Blondes* (the book not the Howard Hawks movie musical) Lorelei and her friend, Dorothy, are wined and dined by gentlemen callers who ply them with diamonds as well as champagne. They travel from one Ritz in one country to another in another country. In London, Lorelei, who is also the narrator of the story, says she is very happy to be "staying at The Ritz. We are very happy here because there are a lot of Americans in the hotel. I love trips round Europe because you can always meet Americans," who buy dinners!

Bayard Veiller, who wrote "The Trial of Mary Dugan" and other hit plays in the formative years of the last century, stayed at the London Ritz Hotel. His suite overlooked Green Park and had "plenty of windows and sun." But he was nonplussed. "Frankly, I liked the rooms. They were all right – nothing to write home about. I said, however, that they would do very nicely. And the clerk said he was glad of that, because that's what President (Woodrow) Wilson had said when he occupied them. This was his suite!

"Then he told me about some of the other people on the same floor with us – princes and dukes, and I think there was a king from somewhere. And I still think it was extremely rude of my wife to giggle at that point. She said afterward it was the first time she had ever seen me with a purple face. Well, there we were in President Wilson's suite on the sixth floor of The Ritz looking out on London, and just under our windows the roar of traffic in Piccadilly. Only a stone's throw away there was Berkeley Square, and a short stroll away was Buckingham Palace and in another direction St. James's, and right around the corner was Pall Mall.

"A. H. Woods was there ahead of us at the Piccadilly Hotel, he had sent agents to meet us on arrival and see that our baggage got through without difficulty, and he bustled in to see us."

This was the same Al Woods whose "theatrical empire was soon to begin falling apart" in the early 1930's, as my father once wrote of a conversation the two of them had had. "Sweetheart," he told my father, "show business is lousy. . . . 'Grand Hotel' was mine for eighteen months. Paid $1,500 advance and then let it slip away . . . things are bound to get better, sucker."

"We went to the Haymarket Theatre [now next to the Haymarket Hotel] and I had a surprise there," Veiller continues. "I had forgotten in watching the play that I, too, had had a show at the Haymarket. *Within the Law* ran there for nearly three years, way back in 1914 and '15. Between acts I wandered into the smoking room for a cigar, and nearly all of one wall of this walnut-paneled room was covered with photographs of scenes in my play. I am willing to admit there was a little bit of strut in my walk as I went back into the main lobby of the theatre.

"On another night in London, during an entr'acte, I ran into Michael Arlen. I had met him in America. We chatted. With a funny little twisted grin he asked me what time it was. So I drew out my watch – a paper-thin, platinum watch with the bevel entirely encrusted with diamonds – a gift from Al Woods.

"'I wonder if my time agrees with yours,' said Arlen. And from his white waistcoat pocket he pulled out a watch, paper-thin, platinum, and the bevel of his watch was all encrusted with diamonds, also a gift from Al Woods. Those were the days when Al knew nothing about money, and I have an idea that he bought these watches by the gross. Then I showed Mike my cuff links and he had cuff links to match. It was amusing. I've always liked Arlen. I like his wit, I like the way he tells stories. And I think he won't mind if I repeat something that Noël Coward once said about him – not that it reflects against Arlen but it gives a very good indication of the cruel streak which underlies nearly all of Coward's retorts. Coward said: 'I like Arlen. He's every other inch a gentleman.'"

Back at The Ritz, Stephen Boxall was appointed General Manager of the 133-room Ritz London in September 2003, after a ten year tenure at the legendary grand deluxe hotel as The Ritz Restaurant manager. All told, he had twenty-three years in the hospitality industry. "This is an exciting and challenging time for The Ritz London," he said in 2005. "As we approach the landmark celebration of the centenary of The Ritz next year, we continue to invest in the restoration and traditions of this legendary hotel and look forward to many more years of 'Putting on The Ritz'!"

Ritz, Savoy. Savoy, Ritz. Two very different places. Yet Céesar Ritz, who grew up in Niederwald, a remote village in the Swiss Alps, would first turn The Savoy into London's finest hotel more than a dozen years before his namesake hotel opened on Green Park. But Ritz and his master chef, August Escoffier, were later sacked by The Savoy's board for, among other things, developing other hotels and projects at, the directors claimed, the expense of The Savoy. Court action was also taken with Ritz agreeing to repay the cost of "certain wine supplies" that were either missing or unaccounted for.

John Williams joined The Ritz after being Maitre Chef des Cuisines at Claridge's. As Executive Chef for The Ritz, Williams oversees some fifty-four chefs and is responsible for the menus in The Ritz Restaurant, The Palm Court, The Rivoli Bar, Room Service and the private dining rooms at the 133-room grand luxe hotel.

I had Dover Sole, filleted by the waiter at the table. The smoked salmon appetizer was also sliced in front of my guest and me. As for the salad, it was, and always is, tossed in a bowl and freshly served at the table as well.

Of Céesar Ritz himself, Samuel Marx says in *Queen of The Ritz* (the queen being Blanche Auzello, who helped her husband Claude Auzello run the Hotel Paris Ritz) that, "He was a gallant, chivalrous fellow who named each new creation for singers and actresses of his acquaintance. His menus listed Salade Rejane, Coupe Melba and Toast Melba, Poires Mary Garden, Coupe Yvette, Consommé Bernhardt, Poularde Adelina Patti. Crêpes Suzette, one of his most lasting triumphs was never identified. Suzette was believed to be one of Edward VII's roommates at The Ritz, but Escoffier refused to confirm it."

Blanche Auzello, by the way, had originally left the States with her friend, Pearl White, silent screen star of "The Perils of Pauline," for Paris in the mid Twenties. During the Second World War, Nazi commanders lived at The Ritz. Blanche was accused of helping the Resistance, was arrested and sent to prison. She was released before American troops marched into Paris in victory.

On Valentine's Day night, I attended a party at the Chelsea Arts Club, a transatlantic sister club to the National Arts Club where I've been a long-time member. Here I danced with half a dozen women, and spoke to another half dozen. One was an Arabella Hardart who, after a few emails, agreed to meet me for dinner. We decided on The Ritz but I really wasn't sure who this Arabella was among those I had talked to or danced with. Was she the short, Italian girl who stuffed her face with hamburgers?

I asked the concierge if there was someone waiting for someone me. I checked the bar. No one I recognized there. One concierge then pointed to a lady reading a newspaper in the lounge outside the Rivoli Bar and suddenly, possibly hearing us talk, Arabella, a tall, statuesque strawberry blonde I had danced with, smiled at me, the concierge smiled at us both, and we were off for a delicious five-course dinner at The Grosvenor House.

The concierge's satisfaction in making the connection hints at the satisfaction staff gets from assisting guests. I talked to Linda Zaggaria, a prominent and hard-working member of New York's fabulous National Arts Club about her stay in June 2009. "The Ritz has become our hotel of choice in London," she told me.

"We came to this realization after checking into another hotel that had been recommended. We arrived later than we had expected on a Monday evening in June, rather tired after a drive from the Cotswolds, which included a stop at Blenheim Palace and a visit to Oxford. I won't go into detail, save to say that neither our room nor the hotel met our standard. We decided to stay the night (we were too exhausted to go through the hassle of moving) and agreed to see if The Ritz – where we enjoyed a lovely stay on our previous trip to London and was located just down the road a bit – could take us.

"It just so happened that we dined that evening at the Wolseley, which is directly across Arlington Street from The Ritz. After dinner we crossed the street to The Ritz to ascertain room availability; we were in luck. Honestly, if all the rooms had been booked, I believe they would have found a spot to carve one out for us – that is how the staff aims to please. The affable desk clerk clearly and carefully presented our options and we chose a room. Upon arrival at the hotel's entrance on Tuesday morning, we were greeted graciously by a gentleman in handsome livery and escorted inside to the reception desk. The reception manager extended a warm welcome, addressing us *by name*! During the check-in procedure, she thoroughly explained the services and amenities and stressed that if there was anything re required it was merely a phone call away.

"The room was divine. Two spacious closets accommodated our overpacking; the bed, an extra-large king, boasted the most sumptuous pillows a head could ever hope for; the décor – historically chic. A generously sized double sink and restorative shower highlighted the beautiful marble bath.

"On the way out to visit the sights we stopped to chat with Michael, the concierge, whom we had met on our previous stay. He informed us that an underground strike was scheduled to begin at 7:00 p.m. Oh, dear – how would we reach our evening's destination; even if we planned to take a taxi, would we be able to find one? Not to worry: Michael would arrange for a car to take us. At that time he also secured theatre tickets for the following evening.

"At 6:15 we went down to meet the car. We were squired into a Rolls-Royce that awaited to take us to St. Martin-in-the-Fields for a candlelight concert. If you must be stuck in London traffic, let it be in a Rolls! After a delightful evening we returned to The Ritz and decided to have a nightcap in the Rivoli Bar. What an Art Deco jewel! The Rivoli Bar must be the most magnificent Art Deco space on the planet. A sleek, modern, glittering work of art, the room exudes elegance and sparkle. And the staff matches the décor. We were welcomed royally (this is London) and made to feel extremely comfortable. Talk about being transported to a golden era – we felt as though we had stepped into a stylish Thirties film. This scene repeated itself each evening during our entire stay.

"After a delicious night's sleep, we opted for coffee in the room. I tried to use the laptop but couldn't seem to get it to work. A technician was sent up immediately and fixed the problem (it was I who had done something wrong). Throughout our stay, everything was superb. The laundry we sent out was returned meticulously laundered and wrapped. Any calls to the desk were dealt with immediately. Any assistance we required was provided promptly and cheerfully. We hated to leave. But, alas, the time came to bid a fond goodbye. Checkout was smooth and efficient – friendships had been formed. As the doorman sent us off in a taxi, we vowed that our next stay in London would be at The Ritz. Why go anywhere else?"

Well, of course that is in part the subject of this book, but I can certainly sympathize. The Ritz is indeed very spoiling. For Tony Award-winning Broadway producer, theater owner Stewart F. Lane, just to take one recent example, the London Ritz "is my new favorite hotel. They gave us a suite overlooking Green Park and treated us like a king (and queen)!"

Despite the strong convictions of many, however, there *are* other fabulous places to spend the night in London, such as at our next stop, and British secret agent 007's, Dukes.

Chapter 12

Dukes Hotel

Dukes is your own private London townhouse or, as someone once said, your own "baby grand hotel." If you can't afford the townhouse next to the London Ritz Hotel, which is available for thousands of pounds a night complete with formal dining room and expansive views of Green Park and Buckingham Palace, try Dukes. Walk from Piccadilly down to St. James Street and look for a narrow cobbled street called St. James's Place. The former home of Barbara Villiers, Duchess of Cleveland, a mistress of Charles II, she bore him two children. The hotel is as close as a lot of inveterate travelers will get to heaven – in a hotel. With 90 "units" which include suites that range upward of £625 a night. Mary Fox Linton, along with owner Gordon Campbell Gray, who has become legendary for his charity as well as his extraordinary hotels, designed all of the suites and rooms.

Turn-of-the-century gas lamps throw fireflies of light on the flower-filled courtyard leading to Dukes. The hotel known as Dukes opened in 1908. But in the courtyard around which Dukes spreads its gilded, brick wings there is a special hush. Even the purr of Rolls-Royces and Bentleys fades. Charles II, King of France, visited his mistress, Barbara Villiers, in the townhouses that once stood where the courtyard is.

Hear that? No, not the whoosh of a martini being stirred, but the incandescent notes of composer Sir Edward Elgar who lived at Dukes, stalking the air like Hamlet's "flights of angels." Frederic Chopin once lived some cobblestones away. Inside, Mary [Fox Linton] in collaboration with owner Gordon Campbell Gray, redesigned Dukes ninety suites and rooms. New, stylish fabrics and carpets, and state-of-the-art technologies vie for attention along with the gas lit courtyard.

Dukes feels most like a discreet gentleman's club. The lobby area has a mahogany concierge desk. The hotel is set back from the main surrounding areas and is cozily situated in a no-through road, which ensures a privacy that not too many London hotels can claim. The hotel is home to its own collection of portraits, drawings and antique furniture. Each room at the Dukes Hotel has a classic contemporary style.

Amenities include guest controlled air–conditioning, private writing desk, Wi-Fi internet access, en–suite marble bathrooms, private bar, armchair, room safe, satellite flat screen television (with on demand movies) and two line telephones with data port and voice mail. Perhaps my own personal favorite Dukes perk is the free newspaper and shoe shine. It's the little things that make you realize you're living it up.

There's a small complimentary health club for guests. It includes an Italian marble steam room and a modern, well-equipped gym, as well as high–tech cardiovascular equipment. If you're more of an outdoorsman when it comes to personal health, nearby Green Park is perfect for a stroll or a run.

"Its peaceful courtyard location and sense of tradition has always made Dukes a special place," explains Gordon Campbell Gray. "I believe we have brought the hotel into the 21st century in a sensitive way, without losing its quintessential charm."

I stand mesmerized watching the lead barman at Dukes Hotel making the ultimate martini, trying to visualize author Ian Fleming, of 007 James Bond fame, in the wood paneled bar drinking his favourite martini. The bar at Dukes whether you have the late Ian Fleming's penchant for cocktails or not, is one of the very coziest rooms in all of London. I spent a fascinating couple of hours observing bar manager Alessandro Palazzi making martinis. In fact, the word 'making' doesn't capture his artistry. Like a great chef, such as Paul Gayler, executive chef of The Lanesborough, he makes a martini the way Tiger Woods hits a golf ball or the way Paul prepares one of his signature sauces.

"The distinct home of the perfect martini," writer Jordan MacKay proclaimed Dukes in "T", *The New York Times'* Style Magazine.

Ian Fleming, the creator of James Bond everything, loved to spend time in Dukes bar. One of the location scenes for "Live and Let Die" was in Ocho Rios, Jamaica, where Fleming had a home. Roger Moore wrote in his autobiography that he was reminded of Noël Coward's remark when he saw "Goldeneye," the Fleming house, which was a sprawling hospital–white bungalow. "It's very golden eye, ears, nose and throat!" Moore remembered Coward saying.

Dukes website explains how its signature martini is made: "It is prepared table-side by the Dukes bartenders. The ritual begins as extra dry vermouth is sprayed from a crystal atomizer into a chilled martini glass. Next the rim is swiped with a fresh-ly cut lemon peel and the frozen vodka or gin of choice is poured. Guests appreciate this attention which harks back to the days when hotel restaurants triumphantly made dishes at tableside such as . . . crêpes Suzette." As Mr. Palazzi explains, "A martini is very easy to make but like all simple things, it's also easy to get wrong." But he is quick to add that despite accolades, he doesn't regard himself as a celebrity barman. "The guest is the star; not us."

Was Ian Fleming using some of his time in Dukes Bar to hatch new plots for his James Bond series of books? I don't know. I do know he was worried about running out of new plots. Ian Fleming told Roy Newquist in an interview published in Newquist's book on writers and writing, *Counterpoint*, that "It is a matter of running out of inventiveness. One can't go on forever having blondes and guns and so forth in the same old mixture. . . . I hate the idea of short-weighing my public by giving them the same jazz all over again. In fact, I'd be too bored to write it myself."

Most people nowadays are familiar with James Bond through the blockbuster movies, but Mr. Fleming's books are quite a different experience. Fleming was himself a world famous traveler and bon vivant, who poured all of his hard-won expert-ise in luxurious, tasteful living into his books. He even once penned a travel book himself, *Thrilling Cities*, wherein he revealed of all his favorite haunts, both high-toned and risquerisqué, in all of his favorite cities. Reading it is a bit like going on vacation with Mr. Bond.

Aside from the martini, Dukes is also famous for its rare vin-tage cognac such as Bignon 1800. Some of these cost £200 a shot, and I thought that was high until I stayed at The Lanesborough and one cognac there was £4,000 a shot! And if I ever found I'd spent four grand on a single drink, I would shoot myself.

With 38 single rooms and fourteen suites, Dukes, set like a gilded dream amid majestic Royal residences, the cozy clothing retailers of Jermyn Street, high-octane Bond Street, Dukes has lit-tle in common with Fleming's "Moonraker," let alone "Casino Royale." But Fleming took to its elegant, secluded cocktail bar the way James Bond did beautiful women. When I was given a tour of the hotel's splendid penthouse suite, with its spacious yet almost secret terrace overlooking Green Park, I thought it would suit Fleming, who "tended to solitariness" as biographer Andrew Lycett says, perfectly.

In February 2007 I stayed at Dukes and interviewed Michael Voight, the then-general manager; although he's no longer there, his remarks bespeak Dukes extraordinary quality. Regarding a Hundredth Anniversary Party in May, commemorating Fleming's birth, he told me "we have a big support from the Fleming family because there is obviously that link to us which is also recorded from Ian Fleming so they can see there is a genuine connection between the two of us. So we had the Fleming Collection, which is in Mayfair, approach us already and we want to do something with them. And there is an exhibition all about spies in London. They have approached us as well, so I think it's going to be an interesting year for us. . . . We have created a package called 'Bond About Town' which is an overnight stay. It is, we call it 'Moneypenny Manicure' and then Truefit & Hill is just literally three minutes walk from here – the oldest barber in London. You get a wet shave from Truefit & Hill, then you come back and have a martini master class so our barman explains how to do the perfect martini for either two people or one or ten; it doesn't really make any difference. And then you have dinner in the restaurant."

"Are your rates better in January and February?" I asked, forever on the lookout for a bargain.

"On weekends, but we are surprisingly busy even midweek in January and February which we all thought maybe this was going to be a kind of wobbly year, but, you know, it's not so wobbly as we thought. But I have to say our main, our big clients are doing very well. Christie's, the auction house is next door, and Sotheby's – because there's big diamond sales and modern art sales on – so basically all their clients and auctioneers are staying here, and we'll be full during the week. On the weekends you will always be able to get a special arrangement – you can get a room here for £200 a night."

"That's four hundred American dollars, basically," I said. (This was in early 2008 when the pound was worth vastly more than the dollar.)

"Yes. On weekends, so rates then go up to $600, $700 during

the week, but on weekends. We have it in the brochure printed, and we try to promote the weekends a little more. When the location is so wonderful because you've got Bond Street and Jermyn Street and you have everything here in terms of shopping – Fortnum & Mason – so the location's very good."

"That's fabulous. Now, one thing you were talking about, the Connaught, being similar in style and some of the guests have similar desires and needs, but what about The Savoy where you worked?"

"At The Savoy there was always something happening, you know," he began. "When you were duty manager at The Savoy, you would have a fire on the fourth floor, and a bomb alarm in the lobby and you would have a suicide on the seventh – there was always something happening because it's such a big hotel. You learn how to be stretched, really. I think it's the times, really, that have changed the whole business because at The Savoy and at the Connaught, at the time, we had the big arrivals which would stay for two or three months, with their luggage which would arrive a week ahead of the arrival of the guest and then everything had to be pressed and be sent to the dry cleaners and furniture had to be changed. Because people stayed for the season and, I think, that is really more the time that changed the big, grand arrival. Because The Savoy before it closed, you know, you walk through the lobby and it's corporate travelers, their average stay is 1.2 nights and it – all the grand arrival experience has disappeared."

"Right. Like in the Grand Hotel – in the film, *Grand Hotel* – with Greta Garbo."

"Yes, yes. So I think it's more the time which really has changed, because I know from the Bristol in Paris and I worked at the Hotel Palais in Biarritz, which is also a lovely hotel, and it's really because this is all sort of ten, twelve or fifteen years ago, with time things have changed, even at the Connaught when I worked there. These big arrivals became rare, more and more rare, and then people stayed for one night or two nights only. They were traveling for business rather than for these big leisure stays where people arrive for the Chelsea Flower Show and they left just after Wimbledon. . . . with our package. The package itself [the Ian Fleming package] is priced at £400 with the overnight stay and the wet shave and the manicure and the dinner for two. So, it's also available on weekends and also during the week. The price changes slightly during the week. . . .

"Dukes – someone described it quite sweetly as a baby grand hotel which I think is a good description . . . we will never be The Ritz, we will never be the Dorchester or Claridge's but we don't really want to be – these grand hotels – but I think we can be a nice baby grand where people sincerely care and the service is there. I have a lot of people here having worked in wonderful places around the world. So I had concierges from the Connaught who've been there fifteen years and we have a lot of staff from the Bower in Venice, from The Ritz in Paris, and from Antigua . . . which are all leading hotels of the world. So lots of staff here know what service is all about. It's not that – I think that the quality of people being here – they know what grand hotels are really all about and this was the basis of getting this hotel back up to what it used to be because we've been trying to raise the profile.

"We started with refurbishment and since I have taken over we were able to employ quite a lot of additional staff to bring the service levels up to what it used to be. I know we will get there. We already are well on the way, and the letters I'm getting on a daily basis are people who really enjoy it. Very well traveled people who really enjoyed – it's the biggest compliment for us all, I think. I'm very grateful to have such a caring team and I'm very grateful to have people with such a lot of experience in grand hotels. And that's really what makes all the difference."

"I see. So that experience can be put to use here to make this what it was and it can be – what it should be," I said.

"Yes, but it's the people, I think. I love the Holiday Inn – but if the hotel was run by staff which had experienced the really grand hotels and what guests can actually expect in a grand hotel and not compromise with anything and 'no' is not a word which is usually used at the Connaught. We never use 'no' because we had to find a way somehow. You know, Anthony Lee would cancel his flight – I can quite easily see that, that he would cancel his flight just to say goodbye to Lauren Bacall on departure. But you worked around this somehow because the guests at the time weren't used to hearing 'no.' And you try to work around this as well, but it's nice to have such a lot of people who worked in larger grand hotels with a huge reputation, to have them here as a base to train everybody else to get up the standard we are expecting. So I am very grateful to have such a nice team."

"Did you go to hotel school in Europe?" I asked.

"I did my apprenticeship at the Schlosshotel Kronberg near Frankfurt and I went to hotel school there and afterward was at the Bristol and the Berkeley and The Savoy and the Connaught and a hotel in Biarritz and I've done a master degree at Cornell University. I've done a two-year master degree. And that really helped me . . .

"It's the essence of a hotel group to be able to greet your guests or to meet them at least once during their visit. Because at the end of the day, you are the host of the building, and you would never consider yourself being in someone's home without having met the host. . . . Or with Anthony Lee or Simon Hurst – every general manager tries to meet as many guests as possible. That's just in my breeding, you know, and I feel completely frustrated if I have a day of budget meetings and I can't see – or if I'm outside the hotel. It is so unnatural and it comes very natural if you've been bred into this meeting and greeting guests which is the most important thing really."

Listening to him, I began to think of a hotel manager as the director of a vast play or musical with guests as actors and audience!

I pressed him about great hotels that he himself liked to patronize. In New York he stayed at the Carlyle which "I liked a lot. But I have to say the New York Palace was a very well run hotel. It's very slick and the room service breakfast was on time and the porridge was hot . But there are little things which you think, wow, how do they do it with almost a thousand bedrooms. I was very impressed about the systems in place there, and I take my hat off to the person who leads the two thousand employees there and makes it all happen. The wake-up call was on time. We stayed there eleven nights; it was a long stay. There was not one error during the visit, so I was very impressed by this. Obviously it's nothing to do with the traditional upbringing I had in terms of these more traditional hotels and to me it's very – hard work is very important but manners is very important to me as well. All the staff, I make sure they have the manners and we try to recruit people with manners, obviously, as part of . . . and it helps when their parents and grandparents had good manners and have given it to their children and you can sense it and feel it when you interview people and see, hmm, do they have the right attitude, of course, but also the manners to work in such a place.

"There are pictures of Princess Diana leaving Dukes often so she was quite a regular here before the marriage to Prince Charles. She was quite close and it was a discreet place where they could meet at the bar and there are sort of official pictures. But yes, we do have lovely people staying. We do have a few resident guests as well. They stay here for the year. . . . Sometimes we have to rein them in [and if they're royals does one rather "reign" them in?] . . . they know the hotel so well that sometimes they know the way to the kitchen and sometimes you see them in their slippers and bathrobes, open the fridges downstairs because they know exactly where things are. And then you have to say, "right back. We'll do that for you!"

So much to see, so much to learn. I must refer to my notes to slip in a few "snapshot" items before I forget:

No coffee machines in rooms because hotel staff want to serve it. Just press the buzzer and people do it for you. . . . When refurbishment was down (this is the manager relating another story), lift broke down and all the mattresses had to be carried up to the first floor all weekend, and I can now tell you how much a king-size mattress weighs because I had to help . . . you have to show the staff you'll do anything and are involved . . . which reminds me of the story I did on Hershey's, which does great charity work for kids . . . founder Milton Hershey had no kids of his own, showed everyone how to give . . . talking about somebody who gives to charity; Gordon-Campbell does the same. . . . try to use organic and local things like English smoked salmon and lamb; seasonal local vegetables and fruits . . . lots of ethical thought goes into purchases . . . many profits go to charity . . . staff quite proud of this . . . back to Hersey's giving back to children of the world . . . Stafford now owned by a brewery, private family . . . Ritz owned by Berkeley bros. . . . smart-casual dress code on main floor . . .

"I remember at the Connaught we had jacket-and-tie for breakfast, and if you didn't wear jacket and tie, you know, Herbert von Karajan would walk in in his polo neck and the head waiter would say, 'Sorry, Mr. Von Karajan, you can't have breakfast without a jacket!'" Here's a man who spends half his working life in white tie and tails leading the Vienna Philharmonic, then he goes on vacation at long last and he learns he has to dress up for breakfast! . . . We had one guest staying here, he'd taken his wife to The Ritz for afternoon tea and he forgot to take a tie, literally, and he didn't bring a tie at all and so our concierge, Ian, who is our head concierge now who has spent fifteen years at the Connaught, took his tie off and said, "Here you go! Off you go!" because his wife was already there . . . I was a little surprised to see Ian without a tie, then, behind the concierge desk but then we managed to get him one as well.

"Getting back to Charles II, would he come to visit here?" I asked.

Charles II, it should be noted, son of Charles I, who was beheaded by the Puritans, was another famous high liver, a la Ian Fleming. Only Fleming was a boy scout compared to the 17th century king whose court was the epicenter of the raucous Restoration period. I personally am very interested to see how Prince Charles will behave if and when he ever becomes Charles III! Will the Charlesian legacy for wildness live on? Stay tuned, anglophiles.

"That's a good question," replied the general manager, with an intriguingly coy smile, at least for a general manager. "I'm not quite sure. He would probably come here." Good heavens, did he still feel obliged to keep mum on royal secrets after the elapse of three centuries? "It should be pointed out that the house his mistress lived in stood in what is now a Dukes courtyard and has been demolished."

The most famous mistress of Charles II, of course, was Nell Gwyn, one of the first female actresses to grace a London stage. And that is not redundant. Before that, all actresses, by law, were played by boys. Acting was not considered a proper profession for women. Not that the bawdy Ms. Gwyn did much to change that perspective! But I am interrupting the general manager yet again.

"The queen, she has been here for dinner and for lunch. There is a side entrance to the restaurant so she's been here before."

This, somewhat peculiarly, led to a very serious discussion about lemons. When you're the manager of a great London hotel, you find yourself intensely interested in all sorts of otherwise mundane subjects.

"I had an argument with our head barman because he said the lemons have to come from Sicily because they're especially oily and they're organic and the lemon is just more intense in its flavor but they cost seven times more than any lemon you can buy in this country, so he convinced me in a very dramatic Italian way that if I get rid of the lemons he's using currently, then the martinis will just not be the same. Of course, I said "I'm sure you're right" and we continued with lemons from Sicily! The same with our olives. They come from somewhere in Italy and they're delicious olives and everybody comments on the olives, so he's right. But it's quite funny in how protective people are about their little things. It makes all the difference, I have to say. Because we tried the martini with the different lemon and it just didn't taste the same. It has to be *that* tree in Sicily, you know, with *that* particular lemon and then it makes our Dukes martini.

" . . . at The Savoy with the Piccadilly Dance Orchestra which was sixteen people playing with the old microphone. This lady was – and she had this wonderful hairstyle – and she would, without moving an eyelid, sing "the bluebirds over the white cliffs of Dover" and then the whole sixteen-piece band would play. It was the most wonderful experience you could have, and that doesn't exist any more. Which is a shame really. Because there is no other place you can have an experience like that. The Ritz does dinner-dance; that must be the last place where on Friday and Saturday you can go for a dinner-dance, but, you know London on a Friday and Saturday evening changes as well."

If you've ever stayed at a hotel and gotten a lemon of a martini, now you know why. It requires almost fanatical attention to detail to make a grand hotel run smoothly. There are hundreds of little elves running around like mad behind the curtain to make sure that you get exactly what you want, when you want it, and without really having to think about it. When you stop and ask yourself, Gee, just what am I getting for my four hundred pounds a night? This is it. You're getting service that you simply cannot get anywhere else for any price. I'm not saying it's priceless, necessarily, but it don't come cheap either.

If Ian Fleming, the man behind the fictional James Bond 007, loved martinis, Dukes and The Savoy, he also harbored a soft spot for many hotels. His wife, Ann, once said that he would, according to Andrew Lycett's biography, *Ian Fleming*, "make a hotel room bedroom into a home in ten minutes."

"He would," Lycett quotes Ann Fleming as saying, "first unpack what he called 'traveler's joy,' which was a large bottle of bourbon. Then he would put out his typewriter and the books he had chosen to read. He would ring the bell for some ice, and he would be as happy and relaxed as other people feel in their homes." He sounds like, and much more than sounds like, a man after my own heart.

In December 2009, Dukes got a new general manager, Debrah Dhugga. With all those capital "D"'s aligning, that must mean good luck for the establishment.

"It's a tremendous little hidden gem," Ms. Dhugga enthuses about her new charge. "One of the things I have liked about Duke's is people calling and saying, 'Where are you!? I can't find you!'"

"I have one practice – treating everyone with great passion. It doesn't matter the name of the guest. But you need to treat everyone the same."

She also strongly feels employees must be cherished as well as guests. "To make it a great place to stay you must make it a great place to work. I say to the staff, 'Think of this as your home.' That's just what a hotel is, isn't it, a big house?"

Years ago, as an up–and–coming hotelier, Debrah says she "used to come to work for almost nothing. I was paying a nanny. But I was doing it for the long term and not the short term."

What, I asked her, can women bring to the hospitality industry that men can't? "Women," she began, "have tremendous attention to detail.

"Having initially been faced with some skepticism when I joined the hotel management industry, I soon found that hard work and perseverance earned me the respect to continue and succeed in a more predominately male orientated sector.

"The one thing I think women in business should learn is that if a company board gives you power, you should take ownership. A university professor once told me to remember that 'Ginger Rogers did everything Fred Astaire did, but backwards in high heels!'

"At Dukes I try and encourage the philosophy that women and men will both receive the same impeccable and hospitable service and can appreciate the atmosphere.

"I think that managing a hotel is a difficult and complex job; however, it does not compare to the pain of childbirth. Having had two children, I would say it makes running a hotel look easy!

"I think it is refreshing to have a woman at the top of a business, as it brings different skills to the table and can promote creativity.

"Every woman I have met in a similar role to mine throughout Europe, has been a genuine leader, innovator or outstanding businessperson in their own right. They have been determined to use the recognition they've received to help them and other women achieve more.

"I believe Dukes offers the simple touches and details to the highest standards, such as: a unique experience in a quintessentially classic English hotel; a warm, genuine, sincere welcome, and key knowledge of repeat guests' preferences; a home for the duration of the stay – you are at home when you stay with us; attentive yet discreet service that exceeds expectations; and a fantastic team who are dedicated and focused on attention to detail.

"Dukes is a classic, elegant hotel and one that compares to the likes of a classic British brand such as Chanel."

Some of my own last minute notes on a tour of Dukes: *penthouse has windows all around . . . can see St. James' Palace and Princess Diana's family house . . . changing room, bathroom, courtyard, charming with balcony (have several rooms with balconies) . . . Ian Fleming write* Chitty Chitty Bang Bang *as well as the James Bond stories* . . .

And now, like Mr. Bond's famous martini, we must shake ourselves loose of the comforts of home at Dukes and bestir ourselves to move on to the next purveyor of incredible hospitality. Let me just stow that bottle of bourbon and I'll be right with you. We're bound for the One Aldwych, you know.

WELCOME

To London's Most Fabulous
Hostelries and the
Transatlantic Celebrities
Who Love to Stay at Them

Previous page: The magnificent Mandarin Oriental's cupula. Above, Virgin's Sir Richard Branson. Right, "41"'s reception area. Below left, actress Christina Ricci; right, actor Alan Cumming.

Above, the entrance to the Connaught Hotel caught spectacularly at dusk. Below, Meryl Streep steps out on the town. Right, the majestic entrance to the Lanesborough Hotel.

Above, the Milestone's groovy Conservatory. Right, stage great Rosemary Harris. Far right, musician Sean Lennon. Opposite page top, the oh-so-English garden eatery at the Ritz. Opposite page, bottom, the resplendent Millennium Mayfair.

Above, the stylish spa at the May Fair. Right, the Fernando Botero cat sculpture at Firmdale's SoHo hotel. Opposite page, top, more Firmdale avant-gardism in the Haymarket's lobby. Opposite page bottom, a touch of the exotic in the Milestone's safari-themed suite.

It doesn't get any more English than at, opposite page top, the Brown's Hotel English tearoom, and opposite page bottom, the Claridge's tearoom. You can taste the scones already. This page, above, the Ritz sits right in the busy heart of it all. This page, right, author Ward Morehouse III (on right) with London and world hotelier extraordinaire, Chairman Kwek Leng Beng.

This page, above, the botanically splendid entrance to Claridge's. This page, right, the homey inglenook of the lounge of "41." You expect Sherlock to wander in any moment. Opposite page, top, the towny entrance to Firmdale's Haymarket Hotel. Opposite page bottom left, film actress Sigourney Weaver and friend. Bottom right, a 5-star bathroom at Brown's Hotel.

CELEBRITY PHOTOS: ROSE BILLINGS

The Mandarin Oriental's outdoor dining spot is a picture-perfect English garden, this page above. Tony Bennett, this page left, can do more than just sing about the good life. Oppostie page, top, the lofty lobby at Bailey's hotel. Opposite page, bottom, the classical reception area of the Chesterfield Hotel.

You never know who you'll run into at a great London hotel. This page, above left, General David Petraeus, and above right, actor Ian McKellan. This page left, the distinctive silhouette of One Aldwych. Opposite page top, the entrance-way of Brown's Hotel. Opposite page, bottom, get in some laps of luxury in the Berkeley roof pool.

Above, the May Fair Hotel's deco-ish lobby. Near right, stage and screen legend, Angela Lansbury escorted by Broadway producer extraordinaire, Stewart F. Lane. Far right, actors Johnny Miller and Jude Law.

Chapter 13

One Aldwych

Charles Mewes and his associate, Arthur Davis, designed One Aldwych for the *Morning Post*. Now as a hotel its modern interior diverges almost as much from that of The Ritz, Claridge's or The Lanesborough as the 19th century coaching inn did from The Ritz which replaced it.

"Half a decade on from its launch, One Aldwych remains a benchmark which other hotels can only aspire to," *Sleeper* magazine" founding editor Paul Day said. Day talked to Gordon Campbell Gray, One Aldwych's owner who was what could only be called brutally honest.

"If the hotel industry was a more Machiavellian environment, someone would probably have had Gordon Campbell Gray shot by now," Day wrote. "Not simply out of envy for the extravagant success of One Aldwych, nor out of concern for his renewed expansionist vigor. More likely it would be because Gordon has an agenda that makes pointedly awkward reading for the major players in this industry. Moreover, he has put his principles to the test and dammit if they haven't passed with flying colors. And while he might identify fault in all corners of the industry, the Lausanne School – whose alumni all but control the global hotel business – recognize enough sense in his words to offer him a very public platform from which to reiterate them. When I met Gordon, he was preparing for a speech there in front of 800 people. 'My message will be that you can be a good guy and be successful. We're the proof. Being ruthless is not a prerequisite to being successful, I will not buy into that.'

"One Aldwych houses, according to *The Sunday Times*, one of the ten best hotel rooms in the world. The list of awards it has won cover two A4 pages without any need for the compiler to grub about filling the space. At one point the words 'Runner Up' jump out, only for further reading to reveal that this is an award bestowed across the Atlantic in the 'Best Boutique Hotel in the World' Category. So we can forgive them that. I am not going to review One Aldwych for you. If you are not already aware of it, you really shouldn't be reading this magazine.

"The five-year birthday aside, our meeting with Gordon was well timed. One Aldwych was probably only a year old when the speculation began about his next move. Amsterdam? America? Everyone wanted to know when One Aldwych Two would open. It's just that they had not made allowances for the sort of man Gordon is. They had presumed he was the same as the rest of us, even if what he had achieved with One Aldwych demonstrated that he clearly wasn't. One Aldwych, lest we forget was a trail-blazer among hotels. Five years might not seem so long ago but every hotel you have ever seen reviewed in *sleeper* followed in its wake. *Sleeper*, you see, opened its metaphorical doors a few months after Gordon.

"Here is a passage from a One Aldwych press release, part of a simple, one page pen-portrait of Gordon Campbell Gray: 'Gordon cares greatly about the environment, politics and individuality. He has a deep dislike and distrust of most large corporations and institutions and believes passionately that it is the power of the individual which can – and will – make change for the better.' The profile concludes with 'he regrets that he has left it too late to be called "an angry young man."'

"I asked if, looking back across those five years, he would have done anything differently? 'No, I think I can put my hand on heart and say I would do it exactly the same again. The way we are developing can only be evolutionary and for me the creation of Pure Products, the desire to be as organic as we can, the desire to buy everything we possibly can, best practice . . . this is all part of the natural evolution of the hotel and it's the way the world is going. . . . If someone told me that a genetically modified tomato was fine, I'd say 'I'm sorry, I don't believe you.' If someone told me that the chemicals in cosmetics and deodorants and shampoos are fine, I'd say 'I'm sorry, I don't believe you.' I think we have to make an enormous stand in what we do here. It's what you do with the power of leadership that really matters. I gave quite an aggressive speech in Berlin . . . the Hotel Investment Forum . . . and it was to remind people of the absolute necessity for honesty and integrity in private life, in the workplace, but particularly in the boardroom.

"I love my staff," Gray also told Day, "and to have a successful business you must love your staff. I'm often quite shocked by how many people in positions of power don't love their staff. They see them as an unavoidable cost, they don't see it as a pleasure to have a team that is motivated and as good as it possibly can be. Why would I not want everyone to love to come to work? Why would I not want them to love going for lunch? Why would I not want them to eat well?   Because that's what I want for myself. I don't want a room attendant cleaning the bath with toxic material, so we are currently developing our own cleaning range. What's good for the front of house should be good enough for the back of house, I would be equally if not more upset if someone told me they'd had a bad lunch in the staff canteen than a bad meal in Indigo [one of the hotel's two restaurants]. One cannot supersede the other. Our philosophy was always to create a snob-free zone. Snob free amongst the guests and snob-free towards the staff and I can say that we've really achieved that. Treating everyone the same is not rocket science but it is a powerful thing. It is easy to have a company where politics and egos creep in but I am the politics and ego police. The minute I sense it, I sort it out because the 'me, me, me' manager is a killer. And it is staggering what the lack of politics does to an environment."

He also likes to think of One Aldwych, his hotel which is located in the historic old Morning Post building, "as a modern classic. It has gravitas whilst at the same time it feels truly cutting edge, exciting and fun."

The sleek, sophisticated hotel is really about "'stealth wealth,'" he continued, "rather than the 'dripping deluxe' that is traditionally associated with grand hotels. We wanted to pare back the superfluous trappings of luxury, which now seem dated and unnecessary, and concentrate on what really makes a hotel work – that is, highly professional service and great comfort. In fact our guiding philosophy is 'It's all about service.'

"In essence his vision for the interior he says is 'One Aldwych is subtle because I was determined to avoid the design clichés of the predictable "international deluxe" style and to resist the temptation to be relentlessly fashionable. Nothing is so dull as standardization and nothing dates so quickly as trendy. One Aldwych is contemporary, but definitely not trendy, nor is its look purely of the moment. The interior is interesting and different – but comfort and function have not been sacrificed to design.'"

Howard Rombough is Public Relations Director for One Aldwych and other Campbell Gray Hotels. Howard told me that

Campbell Gray's first property was the 80-suite luxury resort Carlisle Bay in Antigua, West Indies, launched in late 2003.

Simon Hirst was manager of One Aldwych when I stayed there.   On his personally signed card he wrote "Dear Mr. Morehouse, a very warm welcome from us all. I look forward to meeting you on Tue. or Wed. Simon Hirst."

I talked to Hirst specifically about One Aldwych. But he had also a lot to say about The Savoy, much of it fascinating, when I saw him a year later. The Savoy is a couple stones' throws from One Aldwych.

"I've worked in Mayfair," he began.   "I was at the Four Seasons in the late Eighties, early Nineties; I was the number two there – and I didn't know this part of town particularly well," he said. "I thought it had been like this for even hundreds of years, but, actually, this whole development shape here with the crescent shape of Aldwych and King's Way which goes up to the north just down here; that was only all built around 1900, and before that this area was a bit of a mess. It was kind of, you know, gin holes and brothels and open sewers. It was a bit of a dump, really. And then you had all the expensive houses down on the river, on the Strand. But up here, this was where all the poor people lived, and St. Martin's in the Fields was in the fields, and all that. This was all rebuilt around 1900, and there was a building, this building actually used to be a rectangle as opposed to this triangle that it is now, and it faced directly towards the river. And it was actually just new, the building was there second, sort of, they rebuilt their original headquarters. This was around 1895, something like that, and when the London County Council decided to build Aldwych, and they said, 'bad news, we're going to cut off the corner of your new building because we need to put this street in, so they had to knock it down and this was the third, actually the third quarters. So the newspaper went out of business in 1937 and then it was sold on and used – this was a banking hall for a long time for a Lloyd's bank. So it's been through quite a few metamorphoses over the years.

"This area, I suppose, was considered to be, other than The Savoy which has always been a bit rich and rare, this is a more earthy kind of London in terms that there's theater land, it's restaurants, it's street buskers. Whereas Mayfair is quite sort of refined and smart and all that, but I wouldn't say chic. I don't think – I think chic brings a certain element to it, a fashion trend, you know, youthful progressive approach to it. . . . And even twenty years ago, apart from the odd townhouse places, there was really one type of five-star hotel which was the big, sort of modern, grand place. And I think as wealth has become redistributed, people have got younger, it isn't just one – five-star has niched up now into a whole range of different styles.

"Gordon Campbell Gray, of course, . . . describes it as a sort of modern classic or a five-star hotel sort of slightly in disguise because our sort of culture and our philosophy here is we want to do everything beautifully but we're 'now,' without this kind of being wrapped up in this sort of blanket of pretentiousness and snobbishness and ostentation, we want the lobby to be a vibrant, enjoyable place. Not overpowering but we don't want a library in the lobby, we don't want a hushed environment. We can talk more about the service if you have time but we want our service here to be, I sort of call it normal."

"Was your dad a hotelier?" I asked.

"No, he wasn't, actually. He was a civil servant."

"And where did you start in the hotel business?"

"I started – I was actually abroad. My father worked for the government in Hong Kong, and I was at school in this country; there weren't really good schools over there. And I went out there at the end of my sort of basic schooling before I went to college. I went out there on a sort of a year off, you know, what we call a 'gap year' in this country, where you take a year before university or college. Anyway, I sort of went out to Hong Kong and I sort of never came back! And I joined a hotel which was run by a company called Trust House Forte which is the old Excelsior Hotel which was very new then. Huge. In Hong Kong. It's a one-thousand room hotel. . . . I fell into it by accident. I had no designs on the hotel business, and I got a summer job. I literally, you know, worked in the kitchens doing chopping vegetables and then around that time, Trust House Forte set up a management training program and they invited me to join this thing and I said, 'fine.' I had a bit of fight with my parents because they wanted me to come back to college in London and either way, I decided I would give that a go. So I stayed with them about three years. Then the hotel, Trust House Forte pulled out so it was taken over by Mandarin Oriental which was just chance, you know. Although the parent company of Mandarin owned the building as a management contract so we all sort of became Mandarin employees overnight. Which I suppose, because I stayed with Mandarin for another twelve years. And I moved around in Hong Kong, two or three different hotels that were affiliated with obviously the Mandarin twice doing room stuff, and food and beverage stuff. They trained me and developed me; they were brilliant. I went – they moved me to San Francisco around in '86, '87, '88, and I opened the Mandarin in San Francisco as well in '92 so that was a fantastic experience.

"I applied for a job in London and got the number two job here at the Four Seasons. I was here for three years. That was sort of '88 to '91, and then went back to Hong Kong to rejoin Mandarin for three years to '94. And then I joined Four Seasons after they bought Regents, after they hooked up with Regent. And I went to Northern Thailand and opened the Four Seasons in Chiang Mai in north Thailand. I had a brilliant experience up there, wonderful time. But then my kids had come along in the meantime and we were in the straws and so I joined this project in '97 from Chiang Mai. But now we're just hoping to develop this company now. We've opened our second hotel two years in Antigua, the Caribbean. And we've got two more that we're working on at the moment in Beirut and Iman, and we got a couple more in England that we're negotiating on to be the management company."

"Are you thinking about New York as well?" I interjected.

"Gordon's looked at a couple of projects in New York over the past three or four years but either the economics got in the way of it or it wasn't the right size or the right hotel or the right physical property. In fact, we looked at Paris; we looked at New York. I think those experiences that actually we felt the way forward was to look at interesting destinations that have got either the potential to develop, whatever. And then places like Beirut that have either faded or had a civil war and is sort of now returning. There's going to be ups and downs obviously in that part of the world, but thinking five to ten years ahead someplace like Beirut could be a stunning success if we get in early enough and Four Seasons are opening there about six months after us. Grand Hyatt are opening there. Who's the designer? I think, Philipe Starck is doing a project there. So Beirut is going to come back. So we're really looking – Antigua is a good example. Antigua is a place that used to be quite glamorous but then it kind of went off the radar for ten or fifteen years and now it's coming back. The

Caribbean is coming back, especially with some of the political issues that are going on in the world. It's seen as a relatively safe haven. And so, of course, Antigua is a very natural British market. It's been a big British market for many years, so to do a hotel there under our management that we could promote to our database in and around London and overseas for that matter. It's a great kind of four to five day stopover for New Yorkers, for example. It actually made good business sense, although it seems a bit of left field in other ways. It actually has a good synergy from New York and London to go there. It's eight hours. It's seven or eight hours and it's a very easy trip from London."

"I've read about your hotel there."

"I didn't really know the Caribbean at all until we got involved in this project, but it's been a very interesting experience. Difficult – very difficult on occasions, but very, very interesting."

"And Antigua has an interesting history, too."

"Absolutely."

"What you've done here at One Aldwych is marvelous because it's deceptively spacious but you have the amenities, the pool – in New York it would be unheard of to have a pool so it shows what you can do with a little bit of planning."

"I totally agree. When Gordon was designing this space in the hotel I think he made some very astute decisions, because would we have still done well without a pool, without a screening room, you know, probably reasonably well. We could have made the gym bigger and so on. But what I think was a significant amount of money but relative to the whole project as manageable, you create a tremendous sort of marketing tool and the old statistics about 80 percent of people want a pool, and 10 percent of people use a pool and so on. It still has, I think actually that gap is closing by the way, but it still – you have to divide that cost by the number of rooms that you sell. You don't look at it as £2 million. You say it's £2 million spread over 105 rooms spread over ten years. That's how you look at it. And actually the cost is infinitesimal. And what do you end up with? You end up with a fabulous thing, saying 'look what we've got!'"

"Do you also have a membership in the pool, outside of guests in the hotel."

"Yeah. We have a little membership but we keep it around 200 – 180 to 200 – and the vast majority of those people are what we call personal training memberships who come in by appointment. You don't get a flood at seven in the morning and a flood at six in the evening. So you never have more than five or ten people in the gym or people in the pool. These are the sort of people that come in nine-ten-eleven in the morning. They're dealers; they're trading on different markets, and so on. It works very well. We're never going to make a huge amount of money with a facility like that because it's so expensive, from labor to capital requirements to –"

"Insurance?"

"Yes, insurance. So it pays for itself, and that's all we want. And I keep it in tip-top condition."

"If you could name one hotel that you really like, just for fun, that you stay in?"

"I'll tell you where I was quite pleasantly surprised the other day; I went to the Soho Hotel in Soho which is pretty new. It's part of the Firmdale Group, and they've got your Covent Garden, Charlotte Street, the Soho, and they're doing another one in the Haymarket called The Haymarket. And I thought that was very well done. It's a little more, I don't know if the word is – maybe the word isn't 'edgy' – but it's a little more extreme than we are here in design, a little more 'in your face.' But I felt that it was not silly, it wasn't overdone, it wasn't wild for the sake of being wild. It had a sense of purpose to it. I mean, they've all copied our screening room down there. We were the first one to put the screening room in, and now they all come along and say, 'Hey, guess what, we've put a screening room in,' and actually you saw it here first. But that's the way it goes. I liked that."

"What about as far as the old, grand hotels?"

"The old, grand hotels? I'm not much of a grand hotel person really. I quite like the Berkeley. I think the Berkeley has a lot to recommend it. I think that's very chic – the Berkeley. It's got a great location; it's a good sized hotel; it's got good facilities. I think it's a hotel that probably meets its potential."

Once again we confront that modern London hotel dichotomy – the "old" or traditional vying with the "new" or trendy. Although I know a lot of hotel managers who would shudder at the word "trendy." In the Sixties they'd have called it "mod." Whatever you call it, there's now a definite split in the London hotel world. There's The Savoy-Ritz contingent, all those old private mansions transformed into gorgeous wedding-cake trimmed brick and stone edifices (with Wi-Fi, of course), and then

there's the new Firmdale and COMO approach. Bring in a fabulous young designer and create something no one's ever seen
before. With a screening room (and Wi-Fi, of course). Well, it's
your choice. But I can tell you from personal experience, it can be
a very difficult choice. On the other hand you could do it the way
I'm doing it – stay at them all! In fact, we're due at our next stop
any minute now, the Stafford.

Chapter 14

The Stafford Hotel

If part of staying at a great hotel is a feeling of security as well as ultimate comfort, then The Stafford, physically, lends itself to this premise perfectly. Picture yourself in The Stafford Hotel's inner courtyard, tucked between the hotel's elegant main town-houses and the two-story Carriage House – putting you at least in the mood of the Cotswolds if not physically there. Tables and chairs dot the terrace of the courtyard. But it's not the tables and chairs nor the sculpted busts but the clear air of security, the way Henry VIII must have felt in the Tower of London. Then there are the 380-year-old vaulted wine cellars below the cobbled mews and hotel and stables. Venturing deep into the darkness, where the cellars are the remains of what seems like a World War I fox-hole right out of the classic war play, "What Price Glory?" In fact, it is where some American intelligence officers were stationed during World War II and the London Blitz.

The 350-year-old wine cellars of The Stafford, in a 19th century mansion at 16–18 St. James' Place, are said to have originally belonged to St. James's Palace, the nearby medieval castle where King Henry VIII lived when in town. The hotel's adjoining 17th century carriage house has also been turned into rooms . . . Windsor Castle it's not, but then Windsor can get a bit drafty. Speaking of the monarchy, the late Queen Mother used to dine at The Stafford every now and then. The hotel named a dish after one of her homes – called it Castle Mey.

As I've said, one of the great things about the top London hotels that luxury hotels elsewhere in the world have a tough time matching is the great history. The Wine Cellars at the Stafford are a particularly good example of this. Any hotel can spend a ton of money outfitting itself, but you cannot buy history at any price. The Stafford's fabled wine cellars are 350 years old, but that's only the beginning of the story. Lord Francis Godolphin built the cellars in the 1600's beneath what a hundred or so years later would become Blue Ball Yard, a stable yard that at that time formed part of the Royal Mews. Finally, in the 19th century, another hundred years later, the whole deal became the property of a private London wine merchant, who a hundred years after that is still in business in the same locale.

Madame Prunier was a legendary expert–in–residence in the Cellars for a long time but she has been replaced by the equally expert Gino Nardella, who is a longtime vet of The Stafford. As Master Sommelier, Mr. Nardella is in full charge of the Cellars' vast and rapidly rotating inventory – somewhere between 18,000 and 20,000 bottles. Gino does double duty in the hotel's restaurant, helping those oenophile–challenged among us with our wine selections and histories. Listening to Gino is a bit like going to a college that encourages you to drink up in class.

You won't be surprised to learn that The Stafford boasts one of the most complete cellars in town. They also conveniently offer half bottles of this vast treasure for those of us whose left elbow is a bit rusty. You can even sample many of their great wines. For instance, the Château Lafite Rothschild 1961 and 1976 or Ducru Beaucaillou 1978 are both available by the half bottle. They also have what's called an imperial–sized offering. The Château Leoville Poyferre 1978, I'm told, is a good choice there. If you get to the end of your meal and your throat's still a bit dry, Gino can tell you about his vintage cognacs or Armagnac, which is a mature malt, or maybe some vintage port wine. Just skip dessert and you'll have enough room.

As if Gino's day and list of responsibilities aren't long enough, he also cheerfully conducts tours of his renowned Cellars. If you're a wine lover, this is a must. The charming candlelit trip winds its way through the whole of the million–dollar collection of fine vintages. Moreover, Gino will happily answer your questions – on wine related topics, that is. Although I suppose you could try him on other areas. Frankly, Gino is not only a wine expert and wine enthusiast, he's also a bit of a show–off – I mean, showman. Many of those who take the tour, Gino says, are simply awed by the Stafford's Cellars, the space as well as the contents.

Upstairs, the American Bar itself has been thus dubbed because in the Thirties, many West End hotels began catering to an increasingly large contingent of Americans – as crossing the Atlantic by steamship became easier, and safer. That was the era of the cocktail craze in America's drinkeries, the wilder and more colorful the better, and the Yanks of course brought their drink lists and recipes to London with them. Manhattans, Martinis and Sidecars were just the tip of the iceberg. Who remembers the Vanderbilt Cocktail and the Waldorf? The English themselves were a tad slow on the pickup. For them, an exotic drink was a Pink Gin. But when they did catch on, every West End hotel named its bar "The American Bar" to broadcast the idea that they served the latest and coolest cocktails. Since then, many hotels have renamed their bars, but The Stafford, The Savoy and The Connaught have stuck by the original name.

You know how it is when bar patrons start imbibing – they get up to all kinds of shenanigans. At The Stafford's American Bar, a tradition began in the early Seventies of the customers providing most of the furnishings. When Terry Holmes got to The Stafford in 1972, the bar had only two lonely paintings adorning the walls. Both had been painted by the hotel's managing director – who then took the paintings with him when he left the hotel's employ. Now all the bar had was two naked nails on the walls. So Terry talked an art dealer friend into loaning the bar a couple of paintings to hide the nails. That began the avalanche.

The assistant barman at this time was a fellow by the name of Charles Guano. Honest. One American patron gave Mr. Guano a bald eagle figurine wood carving. Not too long after, not to be outdone, a Canadian patron, offered a scale-model Eskimo figure. Shortly after, an Australian donated a miniature kangaroo. You get the idea. It all sounds like the intro to a long bar joke, but it's true. Eventually, wealthier visitors began giving burgees from their yacht clubs, then photographs of the yachts themselves, and then of their horses. The floodgates were wide open at this point.

Among the more interesting artifacts in this horde are the items from World War II. The hotel was a favorite stopover for the Free French, the American Eagle Squadron and Canadian fliers, among others, during the war years. They all deposited their war mementos in the bar. Many of these gents have since returned on holiday, with their families.

If you prefer celebs to war heroes, over by the bay window is a collection of photos of famous stars of stage and screen, all of whom have at one time or other stayed at The Stafford. Out in the corridor, you'll find the paintings by Richard Downer that have supplied the images for the hotel's Christmas cards over the years. Of more recent vintage, there is the copy of the photo of the New

York Fire Department raising the American flag at ground zero on 9/11. The photo first had been placed on an easel in the hotel's lobby right after the tragedy.

But wait, the tour's not quite over yet. Just to the left of the FDNY picture you'll find a collage of photos of holders of the Victoria Cross – all donated when those depicted were still with us. There was a reunion of sorts of these brave fellows at The Stafford in July of 1995. Or perhaps you'd be more interested in the bar's collection of glasses used by members of the Royal family? Apparently, every time a new royal enjoyed a drink at the bar, his or her empty glass was whisked away to be wrapped in cling wrap and then placed in the case of honor. Sort of like a forensics team swinging into action after a crime. If future scientists ever need the DNA sample of a 20th century British Royal, they'll have a ready supply to choose from at The Stafford.

Did I mention that, as you first enter the bar, there are three photographs of the highest decorated woman of the Second World War? Nancy Wake first arrived at The Stafford in 1946. Back then the hotel was the domain of the famous Louis Burdet, who himself had been a leader of the French Resistance, code-named "White Rabbit." Ms. Wake met Mr. Burdet when she worked with the Resistance, code name "White Mouse." Nancy herself graced the bar, sitting at her favorite corner seat, holding court and reliving those exciting days of war and espionage.

The bar's collection is quite remarkable by now, and quite extensive. Just a few more quick highlights to whet your appetite: A photo of the famous Spitfire MK IX, signed by three British air aces who flew it, as well as by General Adolf Galland of the Luftwaffe! Indeed, the American Bar at the Stafford must be a congenial place if those fellows learned to get along. Also on display, a photo of the good ship *USS Stafford* and one of Margaret Thatcher, Britain's first woman PM, who liked to stop in from time to time. Of more arcane interest are the various animal artifacts on display, including a crocodile head, a rattlesnake skin and a set of shark's jaws. The model airplanes hanging from the ceiling were donated by the manufacturers of the real thing or by pilots who flew them.

The key factor here is that every single one of these often singular items has been donated by a devotee of the bar. It all adds up to an engaging informal history, as well as a plentiful supply of noble items to toast!

The restored Carriage House suites, with their original rough–hewn wooden beams salvaged from 18th century stables where horses of the nearby St. James Palace were housed, stand in sharp contrast to the antiquarian, elegant and traditional rooms and suites in the main House and the twenty–six suites in The Stafford Mews across from the Carriage House. When I worked for Reuters News Service, I stayed in one of the Carriage House rooms and felt like I was in a coaching inn in the rural Cotswolds. For the Carriage accommodations, like many London hotels, are a world unto themselves. You can almost see a bearded William Shakespeare coming down the wooden stairs from the second floor balcony. "Is that Charles II going to visit his lady at Dukes?" Of course not! But London hotels do set you dreaming, and that's almost the entire point. Dream on!

Stafford General Manager Stuart Proctor started in the hotel business when he was only sixteen, at the same time he was working toward his Hotels & Institutional Management diploma. Following this he became an assistant manager of the Shine Hotel, a family–owned brewery that also owns The Stafford, all when he was still under thirty years of age. The hotel he was managing, the Devonshire Arms Country Home Hotel, received the Country Life Hotel of the Year Award. After being resident manager of The Stafford for three years, he was named General Manager in January, 2006.

Both the Stafford and Dukes are a long stone's throw from London's most magnificent 18th century private palace, Spencer House, which was built for the first Earl Spencer, an ancestor of Diana, Princess of Wales.

Next, however, we'll be visiting the "home" of one of the London hotel world's most enchanting hosts, Jeremy Goring.

Chapter 15

The Goring Hotel

I like to think of The Goring Hotel, 15 Beeston Place, in Belgravia, as one's very own in-town castle with a manicured backyard lawn you'd expect to see in a stately manor house in the Cotswolds let alone nearby Buckingham Palace. But the house the first Goring built in 1910, now run by the fourth Mr. Goring, Jeremy Goring, is the only large hotel in private hands, with nearly 100 suites and single rooms, some fully the size of suites in other hotels. Set foot on the rich, dark blue carpets lapping over the black-and-white marble of the entrance hall and you *are* in your private Buckingham Palace.

In fact, if you are distinguished enough to have one of the Queen's carriages sent for you, The Goring is just opposite the Royal Mews where the Queen's carriages are kept and through which the Queen usually leaves or enters Buckingham Palace.

Otto Richard Goring, who built the Goring, earned his hotel stripes working in one of the best hotels in the Grand Duchy of Saxe-Weimar-Eisenach in his native Germany. It was his early dream to build a truly luxury hotel and he succeeded beyond his dreams and those of his nearest and dearest London competition. The Goring was very possibly the first hotel in the world which had private baths in each bedroom,

The Goring, London's family-owned grand hotel, has welcomed British royalty ever since George VI, in addition to the King and Queen of Norway, Crown Prince Philippe and Crown Princess Mathilde of Belgium, the King and Queen of Bulgaria and King Michael and Queen Ann of Romania as well as England's own of Kent (who were guests in late 2008). Being a family-owned hotel, with a sort of royal line of succession all its own, means the Goring family is involved in everyday matters – and even Jeremy Goring occasionally picks up a mop and joins in to make public rooms all the more spotless.

The Queen has actually paid for her meals at The Goring. "The Windsors can be bought . . . the Windsors came to Palm

Beach and they never paid for anything – they thought it was just their way," one knowledgeable social historian told me. Perhaps they were stung by such criticisms and began at least offering to pay. They still probably don't get handed many bills, though, especially in London.

My own dinner at the Goring was incredible. And for which, acting in my capacity as travel writer, I didn't receive a check, either – this is the single area, I think. where royalty and journalists share the same perk.

During the meal I had the delightful experience of watching a "play" while being in it. It started with a glass of champagne, followed by "Glazed Scottish Lobster Omelette," followed by Beef Wellington served from a silver trolley. I watched one of the assistant head waiters glide around the room looking for a half-filled glass here, a champagne glass yearning to be kissed there. The Goring is not without Beluga caviar on its menu and 100 grams are yours for a mere £400!

And, yet, royalty is only one kind of clientele at The Goring. "It's amazing the type of person who seems to gravitate towards us, here. We do seem to attract the nutcases!" said manager David Morgan–Hewitt, a gentle, large gentleman with a touch of Robert Morley, one touch of Rex Harrison in *My Fair Lady*.

"That can be both a challenge and something that you can be very proud of as well," I responded.

"I just think that it makes our guests feel relaxed. It makes our guests feel a lot more at home, when they know they're dealing with actual human beings. We don't have name badges. When you answer the phone, we don't give you a long sentence you have to say. I just think that means the guests feel that they're not being processed by machine. . . . Because we're small, as well, we don't have to have incredibly overworked systems because David [Morgan–Hewitt, the Managing Director] and myself, we can see what's going on everywhere in this building by just wandering around it for two minutes. For that reason we don't have to have quite the same number of checks and balances that you do in those huge great resorts."

He continued, explaining that he is bothered a bit at being categorized as a "boutique hotel." (Clearly, he hears this adjective applied to his beloved hotel a bit too often.) "There is this trend that has emerged, well emerged some time ago, that has caught on for this disgusting word – boutique – but for boutique or small hotels, and I think it's wonderful. But some of these hotels are so small that you really feel uncomfortable because you're almost walking in somebody else's living room – it's that small. And you walk into the lobby and you can't sort of hide away from anybody because it's the size of one bedroom at home and the floor boards are creaking and you don't feel that you're having an experience. You've got a lovely, comfortable room and it's great, you do feel sort of at home. But sometimes you don't feel there's any buzz or atmosphere. You just think, 'well, I pay all this money. I want to get an experience as well.' If I go to Paris, I like arriving – not me personally – I would like to arrive at the Maurice, into that lobby, where there's a piano playing somewhere in the distance and I really feel, Gordon Bennett, I've arrived. And it *should* be a little bit of an experience, not just a comfortable bed and a pretty sort of lobby. It should actually feel different to being at home. You shouldn't actually feel just like you're in your own home. You should feel *as comfortable* as you do in your own home but you shouldn't actually feel that you *are* in your own home."

At first glance, Jeremy Goring with his Errol Flynn good looks, his great grandfather having first opened the Goring in 1910, would seem to be more at home on a West End stage than at the last major family–owned hotel in London. "The secret of our success," he says "has been our understanding of what our guests expect: luxurious comfort, good food and drink and the most attentive service. For us, the most important of these is service."

The Goring. Its name may not rank up there on the international fame meter with The Ritz, Claridge's, Brown's or The Connaught, but the story of the only grand luxury hotel to remain in private hands is as colorful and exciting as its more well known counterparts. I caught up with Jeremy in the quintessentially English drawing room of The Goring. I give you some of his words, albeit in a stream of consciousness form:

"Dinner last night was delicious and service great . . . restaurant full of Londoners – place has to pass test for locals rather than being tourist trap . . . seeing in restaurant ladies in their grand hats and men with their morning suits and possibly a few medals is great for the hotel guest's experience . . . Belgravia now most expensive area in Europe . . . every once in a while a black sheep goes missing – they're custom made by a chap and guests are directed to him if they want one . . . favorite restaurants, Scotts (near Connaught) for the

atmosphere, several Chinese restaurants, affordable neighborhood place called Chez Bruce ... occupancy rates running ahead of competition in current environment ... New York prices make London look amateur ... loves the Montage in Laguna – worth a visit ... Goring's future is to continue improving, have it's own 'heyday' ... Dad retired five years ago and has 'gone off on his horse' ... way is to always try to improve a tiny bit on each of a hundred things rather than a lot on one large thing ... "

Stream of consciousness was popularized as a literary device by James Joyce, an Irishman and a bit of a bon vivant and dandy himself. In fact, I very much suspect James Joyce would have loved staying at the Goring, and gotten a huge kick out of Jeremy Goring.

Famed director Stephen Daldry, who directed Elton John's "Billy Elliott" on Broadway, told me that "we have a hotel near the Victoria Palace where 'Billy Elliott' is playing in London called The Goring. It's one of the only family-owned hotels and I love it. And the people when you stay there, they look after you and they know you when you come back. I prefer it to The Dorchester – or what I call the 'chain hotels.' ... Who knows what, in the end, The Savoy will turn out to be ... I love The Goring."

Getting back to David Morgan-Hewitt, we discuss a friend of mine legitimately telling her butler at Claridge's, "I'm waiting for my husband," and him replying," yes, Madame." David said, "The standard line is 'I'm just waiting for my wife,' and the response is 'Aren't we all?!'"

The Goring is a hotel you don't have to ask for things twice at. "We have lots of clients who come in and say, 'Can I have this? Can I have that?' David offered. "Most of the time we know what they want. Because, you know, people are creatures of habit. We do a lobster omelet here. It's a signature dish and absolutely gorgeous. ... We have people coming in, we know they are going to have a lobster omelet. Dover sole, raspberry ice cream. A very famous person always has that. Because we're creatures of habit. A lot of men will have liver and bacon because these were what was cooked at home."

Some celebrities feel like they own the place. "We did Richard Harris's funeral; after the funeral they all came here. He didn't stay here," Michael said. "It was his wife, ex-wife, who used to come here. And she arranged the funeral meal here. There were quite a few celebs at that. I had to come and sort of ask Russell Crowe to get off the bar. He was actually *on* the bar.

Russell Crowe had just been in a [film] with Richard Harris. I actually had to say, 'Come on, now, off the bar! That's not how we do things at The Goring!'"

Mr. Crowe does seem to get up to all kinds of shenanigans in hotels the world over, doesn't he? He might be one person who actually feels a bit *too* much at home in hotels.

"We have a lot of characters who are our guests. He asked [Crowe] to stay here. But I felt we didn't have any suites big enough ... Our guests are very subdued; they've arrived. They've been here a long time. And they become friends. Like Christopher Plummer. He still sends Christmas cards every year. He sends *us* a Christmas card ... we have Christmas trees all over the place.

"For our centenary next year, we've actually commissioned another chapter of our book on The Goring.

"We're a five star – top of the tree. Interestingly enough, we have two bodies that award stars. One is the AA, the other is the British Tourist Authority. They come in unannounced ... I talked to this chap who said, 'We've just done an inspection on you.' I said, 'Oh, great!' I said I didn't have much time because I'm going from one apartment to another. 'Well,' he said. 'All I have to say is I've stayed in every five-star hotel in the city and you are the best.'"

I got this personal note from David when I arrived: "Dear Ward, Welcome to the hotel. We are delighted to have you with us and hope you have a wonderful stay. David."

Although "names have been changed to protect the guilty," "A Very Special Place: Tales from the Goring Hotel" reveals a few instances where the hotel's watchful eye was evaded. Here's a sampling: Monday the 17th, Room 110, Single Occupancy. "Female arrived to see this gentleman and asked to visit his room. Refused. Guest informed and came down. They sat in the bar for ten minutes and then tried to make a break for the lift – in vain ... and both left the hotel together ... Mr. ... arrived back looking rather tired!"

David commissioned a list of Goring "firsts" and I give it to you:

The Goring – Firsts:
    Vacuums – pumped debris into main sewer
    Communication system to actual "desk"

Garden – alone in London hoteldom. Of course, The Ritz has Green Park.

And here's the history of the Goring borrowed from their press archives.

1910 – *Founding*
Grand Opening of The Goring by founder Otto Richard Goring – the last hotel built in the reign of King Emperor Edward VII. Each bedroom has 'en-suite' bathrooms – the first in the World.
Price of a room – 7s 6d (37p)
(As far as I can make out, in the old currency that's 7 shillings (s) and 6 pence (d), or about a third of a pound sterling. In today's money that would be – I have no idea, but thank God they switched to a decimal system.)

1914 – *War*
Outbreak of first World War. Hotel becomes command center for Chief of Allied Forces. Direct telephone link between General Pershing and President Wilson. The Allied War Effort is being run from The Goring Kitchen. Goring staff from France and Germany are evacuated, famously walking arm in arm to Victoria station singing each other's national anthems.
(The first transatlantic cable was in place on the ocean floor in 1866, but that was for telegraph, of course. Somehow I can't picture Pershing and Wilson tapping out their messages to each other, so it's good they got that phone working.)

1919
Lady Randolph Churchill comes to live at The Goring and is visited frequently by her son, Mr. Winston Churchill. (Winston's mom, by the way, was a Yankee, so he was sort of transatlantic himself.)

1919 – *Peace*
"Air-conditioning invented!" O. R. Goring installs enormous fan on roof, piped to every room. Vacuum cleaners are attached via outlets in skirting board – underwear

sucked out into the air, blowing across London.

Price of a room – 25d (1.25 pounds)

(Not sure if that's right. 25d is actually a little over 2s, or two shillings, which would be about a tenth of a pound. Of course a pound back then was like a hundred dollar bill today, so – oh, to heck with it. It was a good bargain, trust me.)

1920–1925

The Hon. Violet d'Arcy comes to live at The Goring while she is Lady in Waiting to Queen Mary. The Queen often comes to take tea with her at The Goring.

1926

The General Strike.   Opening of the new wing and Restaurant.

(Uh, the two events were not related, of course.)

1930

Novelist Anthony Powell is inspired to invent his heroine The Hon. Angela Goring for his epic series of novels "A Dance to the Music of Time" over tea at the hotel.

1937

Coronation of King George VI.   Visit of the Norwegian Crown Prince, who explains his fondness for the hotel by saying "at Buckingham Palace I have to share a bath with five people! Here I have one to myself."

1938

Leslie Nicol, switchboard operator, witnesses Churchill lifting the French Prime Minister Daladier off the floor by his lapels, with Chamberlain looking on.

Price of a room – 1.37 pounds

(Chamberlain was prime minister but both he and Churchill were vying for leadership of the Conservative party; 1938, of course, was the year of the disastrous Munich Agreement with Hitler. Everyone in England was probably a little on edge.)

1939 – *War again*

Outbreak of the second World War. Occupancy down to 6 percent. 150 Polish officers accommodated.

(When Poland and then France were blitzkrieged by the Nazis, both of their military commands moved to London.)

1944
The first ever color footage of WWII is made. The Fox film crew stay at The Goring on their way to board landing craft for the D–Day Invasion.

"Mrs. Goring's Salad" invented. To beat rationing, Edna Goring invents a special dish from "whatever we can find," including, hare, whale, and on one occasion, an antelope shot by an officer in the Western Desert campaign. No rabbit is safe in the Goring garden!

1945
Peace declared. Election of Labour Government and the austerity years. The King and Queen come to the Goring for sausages and scrambled eggs with the Princesses.

1948 – *Lasting Peace*
Christening of Prince Charles, with Christening Cake supplied by the Escoffier–trained Goring pastry chefs.

1953
Coronation of Queen Elizabeth II (Her father, King George VI, had died the year before). Vast influx of foreign royalty come to stay at the Goring, which becomes an annex to Buckingham Palace.

1960
Fiftieth Birthday. The Swinging Sixties. Jean Shrimpton causes consternation at The Goring by appearing in one of the first miniskirts.

Price of a room – 4 pounds

Seventies and Eighties – *Modern times*
Annual visits from Queen Elizabeth the Queen Mother as Patron of the Injured Jockeys Fund.

Price of a room in 1970 – 4.50 pounds

(Elizabeth Bowes-Lyon, the Queen Mum, was Queen Elizabeth II's mother and wife of George VI; I know, it can get confusing.)

1990
George Goring accepts an O.B.E. from HRH The Queen at Buckingham Palace for 'Services to the Hotel Industry'.

2005
Acquisition of the gardens from the Duke of Westminster. Retirement of Mr. George Goring on March 22nd after 43 years at the helm.   Appointment of fourth generation Jeremy Goring.

Opening of the new Dining Room, designed by David Linley. The Dining Room voted best British Restaurant by ITV Carlton TV, in front of five million viewers.

The Goring voted number one hotel in London by readers of *Travel & Leisure Magazine*.

2006
The Goring is the only family owned and run 5-star deluxe hotel in London.

Again voted by best hotel in London by readers of *Travel & Leisure Magazine*.

2010
The Goring Centenary.
(Can't wait to see the cake for that one!)

In matters of redecorating the Bar and Lounge, the Goring painstakingly tries to "make it look like we never refurbished," designer Tim Gosling was instructed.

Mayfair & St. James's Life put it this way about The Goring's facelift: "The Dining Room at The Goring, London's oldest 5 Star de Luxe hotel, has had a makeover from world-famous designer and cabinetmaker, David Linley.

"The new Dining Room combines state-of-the-art modernity with timeless, classical elegance. The colors are in shades of meringue, biscuit and toffee, and three amazing Swarovski chandeliers float above the diners.

"'When you have an enormously popular Dining Room that

needs refurbishment, it is the most terrifying situation'" Jeremy Goring told the magazine. "'You have so much to lose. When William [Cowpe, MD], David [Morgan–Hewitt, General Manager] and I looked at the options, and the name Linley came up, we just knew: he was the only one that could give us the absolute elegance we were looking for. The fact that he had never designed a commercial restaurant before only whetted our appetites further. Six months later, all I can say is that we are bowled over by the result, and quite relieved that our guests seem to agree with us!'"

Having dinner in the David Linley–designed dining room of the Goring was like being in the thick of musicians playing Gershwin's "Rhapsody in Blue," with the captain and waiters attending tables, filling water glasses, like they were playing many instruments.

"We have our own unique way of doing things here. It's very much led by what our guests want," owner, Jeremy Goring told me. It's evolved over quite a long period of time, and it's certainly not a textbook thing. It's very much do we allow our staff to be themselves. We don't give them *too* much direction in terms of how to do things. We make it clear to them that we want them to make sure all our guests are having a really, really good time."

But, sometimes, not too good a time! How was I to broach this rather delicate subject to Mr. Goring? It's a problem all hotels have to deal with. Oh well, it's now or never . . .

"We're not very good on prostitutes, I'm afraid," Jeremy responded, utterly unruffled. "It's a definite weak point at the Goring. We don't seem to have – we're not the hangout for prossies. I've been in other hotel bars in London that make even *me* feel uncomfortable. . . .

"One time my staff had decided they would have a huge laugh at my expense. There was a chap in charge at this hotel that I won't name, and I was called up to a room and asked whether I would help them get rid of an unregistered guest. So I assumed it was a lady of the night. Off I went. Went into the room with this hall porter chap. And the guy who checked out of the room – I'd seen him leave – very cute little glasses, like this, and he was shorter than me, and I remarked on that because I'm short. He was a very nice mild–mannered man. And lying in this bed from one corner to the other was a six–foot–six, bald, black man! The porters had just stitched me up and sent me up there so I tugged on this big guy's toe and said, 'Excuse me. I think it's time to leave now!' and I just ran out of the room! . . .

There are some things only an owner of a hotel can discuss, because everyone else is too nervous about what the owner might think to say anything. It's such a relief going right to the top.

"But one thing I like about this space is when you come to this bar or you come to the restaurant, it is full of Londoners," Jeremy continued. "And I think a place has to pass a certain test for locals to go eat and drink in it, rather than being classified as a tourist trap. I think our guests appreciate that. On [investiture] days at Buckingham Palace, you'll go in the dining room and see these tables, people wearing their Sunday best, they're wearing their hat and chaps wearing morning suits, probably with some medals on, and for somebody whose not used to it to come and see that very English thing going on in there is actually really, really quite nice. Actually, I think the guests that we have add to the experience of staying here; the experience that other guests have staying here."

I mentioned I had heard that the "toy" sheep, life-sized sheep in some of the rooms, sometimes go missing into a guest's luggage. "Once in a while, a sheep does go for a wander. Hard to know, really, where they go. Every so often they might go for a little stroll and you never see them again."

These are not live sheep, of course. Just models. They won't nibble your toes whilst you're asleep or anything.

Where does Jeremy like to dine? "There's a little restaurant where I live, where I live in Wandsworth. I live near a prison in Wandsworth. All the warders are female and they've all got biceps – I have to go past them on my way to work every morning and I watch them rolling their sleeves up, preparing to wrestle prisoners or whatever it is prison wardens do. But up that street is a place called Chez Bruce, which is a little corner restaurant which happens to have a Michelin star but doesn't charge anything like Michelin star prices. And the result is the place is absolutely packed all the time because people can afford to go there, sort of once a month or whatever. So I really like just corner restaurants. It's one thing I think you have in places like New York, you have these great corner restaurants that don't look anything special but you just feel you could go there every few weeks and feel comfortable and have a great meal."

I got Jeremy to talk also of hotels he likes in the U.S. "The

Bel Air is a wonderful hotel. You never know who you'll bump into. Because it's in its own private jungle. It tends to attract the kind of people who don't want to be seen which is what makes it such a classy joint. The last time I was there I sat down at breakfast, opposite David Crosby. You know the singer from Crosby and Nash and whoever else it was. [Stephen Stills; you're welcome] Young and someone else. [Neil Young, Jeremy. Come on. You're not that old. Crosby, Stills, Nash and Young, a band not a law firm.] And it's that kind of person that just sort of, 'right, I don't want to talk to anybody. I'm going to go stay at the Bel Air!' I love it. I think it's phenomenal."

"Where does the Goring go from here?" I asked. "Does it keep doing the same thing for the sons and grandsons of the people who came here in the past?"

"Well, hopefully, it's a continuing curve of improvement starting ninety-nine years ago and carrying on through today and on into the future. I would like to feel we're different from some of the other established hotels or so-called established hotels that have had a certain heyday, whether it be in the Twenties as is the case of one particular hotel that is being refurbished at the moment [The Savoy], or more recently. And I'd like to think the difference is we haven't actually had our moment of glory yet. And there are certainly no laurels to be rested on and therefore our heyday is yet to come. We certainly I think every five years can genuinely stand in this hotel and go, 'Wow! It is a much better hotel than it was five years ago. My dad could have said that five years ago, and five years before that, and five years before that.'"

For a 99-year-old hotel that's quite a record of improvement.

Eccentrics have had a way of finding longtermlong-term lodging at the Goring, according to the Goring's biographer. One was Rosie Myers who lived at the hotel for decades.

"Short and plump," he writes, "she lived in Room 33, entirely oblivious to bombs, blackouts and food shortages during the war, going out for her daily walks and evening theatre trips wearing, always, one of a selection of enormously wide-brimmed hats in which she resembled, quite unmistakably, a perambulating mushroom. As she grew older so her girth expanded, until the day came when she stuck in her bath. Miss Myers lay like a half-beached whale until at last she heard her breakfast arriving and was able to summon help by shouting through the locked door . . . a valet [was sent] on a precarious journey along a narrow outside balustrade until he was able to gain access through the bathroom window . . . Eventually, three of the housekeeping staff managed to heave her out [of her bath].

"Rosie Myers might have been a trifle eccentric. but she had nothing on another long–term eccentric, Mrs. Violet d'Arcy who dressed entirely in violet . . . One day . . . she electrified a full lunchtime dining room by entering and standing stock–still until her startling appearance slowly silenced the guests. . . . Assured of the full attention of her captive audience, Mrs. d'Arcy spoke: 'This place is full of either witches or bitches! I shall lunch in my room.' Mrs. D'Arcy might have been following the advice of this sign in one Paris hotel elevator: "Please leave your values at the front desk."

In his praise of Robin Rhoderick–Jones's book on the Goring, "A Very Special Place: Tales from the Goring Hotel," The Crown Prince of Norway, said: "I much prefer to stay at the Goring – I don't have a bathroom to myself in Buckingham Palace."

On a much more serious note, great stage and film actor Sir. Michael Redgrave spent his last declining months living at the Goring surrounded that Christmas by some of his adoring family

Think of a cross between Cyril Richard as a quite jolly Captain Hook in "Peter Pan" and author/TV personality Rex Reed and you have approached, but not necessarily captured, the essence of David Morgan–Hewitt, Managing Director of the Goring Hotel. "We have Christmas trees everywhere," he says of The Goring at Christmas, and the sense of wonder and excitement that is Christmas seems a year–round thing at The Goring.

In some ways The Goring reminds me of the formerly family–owned Algonquin Hotel in New York. Ben Bodne, the late owner of New York's Algonquin Hotel, told me my father once told him that he was going to see "Edward, My Son" in London. "I thought Ward was going to see his son. But he was going to see a play called 'Edward, My Son.'

Al Hirschfeld drew Morley when he was appearing in London in a play on Oscar Wilde. This is what Sheridan Morley, the late London drama critic, had to say about Al drawing his father (in *Hirschfeld's British Aisles*, from Glenn Young Books): "Al only ever drew Robert, my father, twice and me once; but (as if anyone really cares) this is the drawing that explains my birth almost 65 years ago. Robert was playing Wilde on Broadway; as an unknown he had created the role (the first actor ever to do so) in a London club theatre, been spotted by an MGM talent scout, gone out to Hollywood to make 'Marie Antoinette' and then repeated his 'Oscar' on Broadway. The actor playing Lord Alfred Douglas, John Buckmaster, asked Pa if on his return to London he would look up his sister Joan. Robert did, married her, and she was my mother, dying at 94 only this year. 'I told you to meet her,' wired Johnnie on their wedding day, 'not necessarily to marry her!'"

Staying at the Goring is not, I suspect, a little unlike going to Buckingham Palace across the street and staying with "the Windsors." At the Goring, no less resplendent and only slightly less historic, you stay with "the Gorings," who boast almost as much family history as the Queen. This is as Londonish, as British, as it gets.

Once again, however, we must push on. Next stop, The May Fair Hotel (and, yes, that's right, spelt with two words not one). I don't suppose a coach-and-six is available from the Royal Mews? No? Too bad. Taxi!

Chapter 16

The May Fair Hotel

"It was a great, great hotel," John Grimaldi, one of New York's top public relations executives in the 20th century told me. "I was coming back from an extended trip to Saudi Arabia in 1980. And I was going through London and I knew I was going to be tired so I had my secretary book a hotel in London. I said, 'Just get me a hotel in London, a good, decent hotel.' So she gets me into a May Fair, all right. I think it was the Mayfair Ramada or something like that. I get a cab and tell the cabdriver where I want to go. You know, in London, you tell your cab driver where you want to go and he takes you there. He doesn't ask you where it is! So we come into town and all I said to him was the May Fair Hotel. So he comes up Berkeley Street and turns on Stratton and there's the May Fair Hotel. I see this is a great-looking hotel and I go to the desk – it's late. And I said I have a reservation.

"The guy at the desk says, 'I'm sorry. There is no reservation.'

"I said, 'I'm certain I have a reservation. My secretary sent me a fax' . . . I showed it to him. He said, 'Oh, you're at the Mayfair Ramada around the corner.' 'But I like it here,' I said.

"And he said, 'Well, allow me to cancel your reservation there and we have room for you here.' He went on to say, 'It'll take a few minutes for your reservation. Meanwhile, why don't you step into the residence bar, which is the Chateau Bar, and you can have a drink while you wait. We'll have your bags taken up to your room.'

"So I walked into the bar and it is jam-packed. I get a drink and I take my drink and go over to where Ian is playing and I compliment him on his performance.

"'Do you have a request?' he said.

"I said, 'play "Melancholy Baby,"' trying to be cute. So he starts playing. Ian can play just about any song every written, an old vaudeville guy. He introduced me to a guy at the bar who is an American who used to come there all the time, and I wound up closing the bar. I got there around 10 p.m. and I didn't get up to my room until about 2:30 or 3 a.m. in the morning. The residence bar had no time limit. Regular bars and pubs had to close at 11 p.m. I was spending a couple days in London so I decided the next night I was going downstairs to have a cocktail and then go out to dinner. So I get to the bar a little late and as I walked through the door, Ian strikes up "Melancholy Baby." That became my theme song for nearly twenty years. Whenever I walked into the Chateau Bar, Ian would start playing "Melancholy Baby." It was just fantastic. He now has retired. . . .

"Back to the May Fair. One night rather late, I had been drinking at the bar – the bar was very tiny. It had four or five stools. One night I happened to be there and there were three people sitting on stools; there was one empty stool. And David, the bartender, pours me a drink and said these guys next to me are from "X" group whose lead singer was a young female. It's 1:30 or 2:00 a.m. in the morning and I think it is Sunday night. One of them gets on the house phone and calls her in her room and she comes down. She stands at the door right behind us and she's wearing a fur coat which she opens and she's stark naked. She steps up to the bar and has a drink with us."

You can sense Mr. Grimaldi's delight. He's talking about another world, a world that he loves. The May Fair, which when I stayed there in February 2009 was in the capable hands of General Manager Charles Oak. He first learned the hotel business from a master – or mistress – with the name of Ivana Trump, the former wife of mega–developer Donald Trump. Ivana ran The Plaza Hotel for Donald jointly with my friend, Richard Wilhelm, one of the most polished and capable hoteliers around anywhere. Ivana told me running the hotel was akin to running her household.

"I became Ivana's "go–fer" (personal assistant) for nine months which was fascinating, Oak began. "It opened up doors of New York that I would have never seen . . . I was in my twenties. First time I ever saw a black marble bathroom . . . I lived there. I lived in a great suite because of my job. I thought they had made a mistake when they allocated the key to me. I thought they thought I was some guest arriving (before 1991).

"History happens now but in a more contemporary context. We have deals going on here. The center of the contemporary art world is now in Mayfair; it was New York. Now it's Mayfair. And this bar is now the center of it. The center of fashion, too.

"For the last fifteen years it wasn't such a hot place to be. But we reinvented it. And it gives back that edge and style and buzz. It has been a hot spot for young and up–and–coming celebrities . . . we attract the edgier, the funkier. We would attract Pink, and The Ritz and the Dorchester would attract Dame Shirley Bassey."

Dame Shirley, for those of you too young to know, is the powerhouse singer of, among other things, the theme songs for the James Bond movies *Goldfinger* and *Diamonds Are Forever*.

"We are 406 rooms," Oak continued.

"Ivana has been here twice. . . . Her daughter, Ivanka, has been here . . . We are trying to be London's friendliest five–star hotel. If you're friendly at the outset, people are going to want to do business with you."

And, sure, The Savoy has the Thames, The Ritz, Green Park, the Dorchester and Hyde Park, and if you crane your neck out of one of the windows on the park, Buckingham Palace. But the May Fair, now part of the Radisson Edwardian Group, has one of the most important things in real estate: location, location, location and then some. Its Park Lane counterparts, like the Grosvenor and Dorchester have Hyde Park, like the Mandarin–Oriental. But the May Fair is tucked just south of Berkeley Square, still fashionable without the nightingale that may have once sung there in the Noël Coward ballad. The rooms at the back of the hotel have wonderful direct views of Berkeley Square.

Green Park Station is next door; and if you work in one of the Mayfair's ultra–fashionable office buildings or shops, what could be more convenient to plop down on a circular bed (in one suite) on Stratton Street and listen to Paul McCartney's latest on the Bang & Olufsen entertainment systems in every one of the 406 bedrooms (including ten suites). Many fans of the hotel cherish memories of visiting the hotel, which served, like The Savoy did for its regular guests, as their home away from home.

Sir Francis Towle said the origin of the hotel's name is derived from the Mayfair district of London. But the district itself was originally called May Fair so the hotel's owners adopted the original spelling as their own. "Modern London has grown accustomed to seeing 'Mayfair' spelled as one word, but the latest Gordon hotel had decided to revive the two–word form, which actually recalls the origin of the name," he wrote.

Gordon Hotels would expand upon the knowledge they

gained from operating The May Fair in building The Dorchester on Park Lane in 1930. Prior to The May Fair, Gordon ran The Grosvenor and Metropole Hotels.

In a special magazine celebrating the hotel's first seventy-five years in 1997, head concierge Paul Keane remembers a time when "no one packed their own bags. The valet would do it. There were fourteen valets including me for the floors, seven during the day, seven at night. Three pageboys were ready to run errands, while a person worked full-time in the parcel room, wrapping and sending parcels all over the world."

The May Fair, like The Savoy, has boasted a theater – a 300-seat jewel box of a theater – which opened in 1963 and had a 25-year run. Ralph Richardson, one of the world's greatest actors, starred there in "Six Characters in Search of an Author." It was the first play by Pirandello to open in London since before the Second World War. Rehearsals were held in a hotel room upstairs, and Sir Ralph told *The Evening Standard* that, "We are rehearsing in a room in the hotel and I wander down to see how it's getting on. And the stage set workmen ask how we are getting on upstairs!"

Among the first-night, star-studded audience was Peter O'Toole, who told *The Daily Mirror*, "I wouldn't miss this one," and "It's a chance to watch other people work!" Jean Simmons and Otto Preminger also turned up. The play, helped enormously by "Sir Ralph's Touch of Magic" as *The Daily Telegraph* called his performance, ran 295 shows until February the following year. It was followed by *Beyond the Fringe*, a review starring Peter Cook and Dudley Moore, later of *Arthur* fame. The review went on to great success on Broadway, as well.

Square-jawed film star Richard Todd starred in the long-running *The Business of Murder* at the May Fair Theatre. At a joint birthday party for the theater, celebrating its 21st year and Todd, 65 years old, and the 1000th performance of *The Business of Murder*, Todd told reporters there was surprise among many folks that the play had lasted as long as it did. "The other day the carpenter working on my country home asked in a broad Lincolnshire accent: "Are you still in that play in London?"

An English midlands accent can be a real challenge, even for the English. Sample phrase: "Aya gorra weeya?" Would you believe that translates to, "Is the wife with you?" Aye, me duck!

"Yes," replied Todd, who was an Oscar nominee in 1949's *The Hasty Heart*, costarring Ronald Reagan.

"What, the same play?"

"Yes."

"Gor," the worker said. "You must know it by heart now!"

Composer Jack Urbont did the music for *Iron Man* and his musical, *All in Love*, was produced in London at the May Fair Theatre. "At the time, they were screening the show for us," Urbont said. "I worked for months. I co-produced the show in New York at the time and we had to cut things . . . they started adding back things I cut. I stayed at the May Fair. The May Fair was owned partially by Eddie [Danziger] who also owned the Monte Carlo. And I saw the ads come out in the papers and around London and my name was not there and Danziger said, 'well, nobody knows you!'

"I said, 'That's the point. It's also in our contract, Eddie!' And because I had the agent call him and say we want Urbont's name on it, he kicked me out of the May Fair Hotel and I went to the Grosvenor House Hotel."

Ian Kerr, the hotel's resident pianist for many years, made art out of his music. "The art is to play songs so that they don't drown out the conversation but so people can catch their favorite melodies. . . . When they suddenly pause (in conversations) and catch my eye, I know that the song is one that means something to them," he said.

One evening Marlon Brando came in with his daughter, who promptly handed a note to Ian. The list didn't include any songs from famous Brando films. But it did include "Winchester Cathedral," "Cherokee," "Small Hotel," "Foggy Day in London Town," and "Manhattan." Maybe they were songs Brando would have liked to sing on stage or on film. He handled himself pretty well (opposite the Chairman of the Board, Mr. Sinatra, himself no less) in the filmization of *Guys and Dolls*, after all.

Another night Stephanie Powers came in and ordered a large brandy. Fred Astaire had just died. Ian said, "I suggested we commemorate him with music, so out came the 'Who Sang What' book and we went through the lot. Stephanie sat beside me at the piano singing every lyric very softly. We kept on until around 3:30 a.m. until we had sung them all. It was a proper tribute."

"At any given time you'd go in there. And you'd be sitting on the couch and there would be a sheik, an international play-boy, a gun runner," John Grimaldi told me. "I met a guy who lit-erally sold guns. He used to come into London; have a suite at the May Fair. Stay there for six months. He would fly on to parts unknown and so on and sell arms. He had a bodyguard who would be standing there packing a gun and he would be sitting there drinking. Packing a gun." Well, it was his trade. If he'd been a brush salesman, you'd have expected him to be carrying a brush.

" . . . There's Peter Turnbridge, the beverage chief of the May Fair who came to look forward to my visits because I helped him to make budget during the months of those occasions. Peter, and Ian, acted sort of as my guardian angels whenever I'd have one or more too many . . . they made sure that my bar bill stayed under 200 pounds per night!" Wow, I've heard of people being able to lift their own weight, but to drink it?

"Sir Hugh Thistlemore, a purveyor of Jaguar and Aston Martin automobiles, has been frequenting the place since long before I showed up the first time . . . he popped in just about every night after work with the rare five-star edition of the *Evening Standard* under his arm. Irving, whose newsstand is at the corner of Berkeley and Stratton, saves it for Sir Hugh who can be found most nights tucked away in the corner of the bar working on the crossword puzzle [one of those screwy British puns and anagram puzzles which I can never figure out] and sipping at one of the two or three double Famous Grouse's he's apt to drink before dinner.

"That blend of scotch must contain a secret ingredient because Sir Hugh is a trim, fit-looking young bachelor in his late forties."

The May Fair had a £75 million facelift in 2007 and every room was changed. All the interiors were done in-house. What's more, the hotel has a theatre again, a 201 seat theatre/cinema/screening room which is used for conferences, press junkets, launches and film premieres. Michael Attenborough was the head of design for the hotel. He created the interior [design] for the whole hotel. The hotel wasn't shuttered. They closed off parts while they were refurbishing it, so they still had the hotel open, and it took, I think, two and a half years before the work was finished.

As far as prices go, as of February 2009, a one-bed signature suite would run you between £1500 and £2000, up to £3000, £3500 for the penthouse; single rooms start at £330. Now that's the "rack rate" rather than necessarily the rate depending on occupancy, time of year and day. The May Fair is very discreet about people staying, but there are names of people who have stayed here who are in the public domain.

Charles, the General Manager, will sit down with some celebrities and interview them in one of the suites. These interviews are shown on the hotel's in-house TV channel.

The color pink is one of the May Fair colors because the Shiapiarelli suite is one of the iconic suites of the hotel. One of the things about the service industry is that it's the little things that make a difference, those special touches and things that make you feel at home and make you want to come back. You can have a stunning hotel, but if the service is nothing, then why come back? The service of The May Fair, and the Radisson Edwardian group as well, is fantastic.

Returning to my discussion with Charles Oak, the GM, he expanded a bit more on his favorite hotel: "We are trying to be London's friendliest five-star hotel. Not best or most professional. Just London's friendliest. Because I firmly believe that if you're friendly from the outset with people, people are going to want to do business with you. Even with a few mistakes, they're still going to want to do business with you because your mindset is part of doing business and wanting to help. We have generally very friendly people. The rest just follows very naturally and very easily. . . . I think the days of the doorman and the bellman and luggage porters and reception staff making judgments on guests based on how they appear are long gone. I remember my own initiation in this regard, as a Savoy trainee. I was there for four years. . . . That was in 1986. I was only nineteen years old. . . . So I was extremely, extremely young. But the formality – you know people, if you'll remember, at The Savoy couldn't check in unless they were wearing a jacket and tie! Now, our core market here is entertainment, media. You can't make a judgment based on how guests look when they *all* look the same, i.e., t-shirts, ripped jeans.

"When I was at The Savoy, you'd be asked to make a reservation, then go to the history file, and they would have to be there. You call them up and say, 'we're full' unless the name was one that you recognized or was in the file. (Which somewhat begs the question – how did you get into the file in the first place? Probably needed to be vouchsafed for by someone who *was* in the file.) Charles lamented that a lot of The Savoy's Art deco furnishings were sold prior to a renovation. "All those seats are gone. All those wonderful stools and chairs that were all made for it. I don't understand why they did it. The *piano* was sold!"

"That Cole Porter supposedly played on," I interjected.

"Cole Porter *played* on it!" he said.

"By the way, thank you very much for my room. It's nice to see Berkeley Square," I said.

"A pleasure!" Charles responded. Our conversation then drifted off to the "Nightingale Ball" held in Berkeley Square. The Ball derives from the Cole Porter song with the lyric, "And a Nightingale Sang in Berkeley Square."

While Oak waxes poetic, I'll slip in here a few last second tips on staying at the May Fair:

◊ Best View: Ask for a room on the back facing Berkeley Square, one of London's most beautiful squares. At night it turns into a mini–fairyland when the old–fashioned street lamps are lit.

◊ Surprising Savings: The periodically offered "Advance Purchase Program" which must be paid for 10 days prior to arrival, includes a 20 percent discount; no cancellations. And, it intermittently has a 2–for–1 lunch or dinner deal at the hotel's delightful Amba Bar & Grill.

◊ Afternoon Tea: served from 3 to 6 in the hotel's Amba restaurant, is $17 for tea and scones and $32 for tea, scones, finger sandwiches and pastries.

" . . . and that's why I love Cole Porter so!" How true, Oak old friend, how true. I often think that the British think of Cole Porter the way we Americans think of Noël Coward. As one of our own. Well, it's time to depart from Berkeley Square, the nightingales and Charles Oak. We're on a very tight schedule. Next up, Grosvenor House.

Chapter 17

Grosvenor House

Like The Savoy on The Embankment, the Grosvenor House was built on land that formerly housed a manor house. Lord Chetwynd lived there first, followed by the Duke of Cumberland, son of King George II. In 1506, Lord Grosvenor moved there, hence the name Grosvenors. But one hundred years later, and especially after World War I, a commercial building boom took London by storm just as it had in New York with its Plaza Hotel rising on the site of an old Plaza in 1907. A. O. Edwards, together with architect L. Rome Guthrie and Sir Edwin Lutyens started work on their grand new hotel in 1927. "An insult to the good taste and aesthetic judgment of the citizens of the metropolis," one reader huffily wrote in to *The Times of London*. But as the Jazz age gasped a last breath of spring, The Grosvenor House opened in May 1929.

Today the "Great Room," one of the largest banquet halls in Europe, still houses the annual Art & Antique Fair which began in 1934. One of the highlights of the 2008 Art & Antique Fair was "The Winter Egg" by Carl Fabergé, given by Tsar Nicholas II to his mother on Easter, 1914. Four inches high, it is carved from rock crystal and white quartz with diamonds, platinum, gold, garnets and moonstone. His mother, Dowager Empress Marie Feodorovna, gave her son gold and diamond Easter egg cufflinks, made in 1907 by Fabergé's chief work master, Henrik Emanuel Wigtram in St. Petersburg. Less costly was an original Marc Chagall lithograph signed in pencil and inscribed by the artist.

Fabergé aside, The Grosvenor House never claimed to be London's fanciest hotel. Nonetheless, because of its sheer size, Park Lane location, and strong affiliation with Buckingham Palace, it has become over the years a magnet for foreign dignitaries as well as for inventiveness. One evening at The Grosvenor House there was a large cocktail reception given by the Russian Ambassador. At the appropriate time the Ambassador thanked the guests for attending, saying with a smile, "As you say here, 'up with your bottoms.'" His bottoms might have been out of line, but his heart was in the right place.

For four years Grosvenor House was a beehive of interior decorators, painters, and plasterers blending rich colors of new furnishings with cream walls. Call them "classic contemporary," with Art-Deco influences from the hotel's origins in many of its bathrooms. One London hotel that I didn't spend the night in, I can't personally attest for the comfort of the extensively researched "Marriott bed," nor had the pleasure of luxuriating in the 300-thread count cotton sheets. But this luxury flagship hotel of the J.W. Marriott brand reminds me of the grand and alas long-vanished hotels of America's Atlantic City such as Haddam Hall where I stayed as a boy. (Haddon Hall formed the nucleus of Resorts International Hotel Casino.) The most prized thing is the hotel's annual Art & Antique Fair. However, just try and take more than memories home!

The Fair is held each year at Grosvenor House Hotel. Here are some tasty samplings from the lineup in 2008, which I believe will give you, far better than I can, a sense of just how serious these folks are about culture and fine things in general:

"A commitment to excellence has been at the heart of The Grosvenor House Art & Antiques Fair for more than seven decades. The quality of exhibitors and the works of art they display are central to the Fair's enduring success. . . . new dealers will join such established Grosvenor House favourites as Colnaghi-Bernheimer, who last year had a very successful Fair selling amongst other things a fine portrait by Nicholas de Largillière; Johnny Van Haeften, one of the world's leading specialists in Dutch and Flemish Old Master paintings; and Moretti Fine Art with their wonderful stock of Italian Old Master paintings. In counterbalance, the Modern British movement is much in evidence at the Fair . . . Modern furniture and contemporary classics will be shown by Linley and Peter Petrou as well as by Lefevre Fine Art who will be exhibiting contemporary furniture by Philippe Anthonioz while examples of art that was created at the dawn of civilisation will be exhibited by Rupert Wace Ancient Art and Basel-based expert Jean-David Cahn.

"The design of the Fair is inspired each year by a different historic building, providing an English theatrical backdrop to the works of art on display. This year Woburn Abbey has been selected for the theme. Set in a beautiful 3,000-acre deer park, Woburn Abbey has been the home of the Dukes of Bedford for nearly 400 years.

"The Charity Gala Evening is on Thursday, 12 June, which is the Fair's first public open evening, and consists of a Private View of the Fair from 7-9 pm, followed by dinner and entertainment in the Ballroom themed La Vie En Rose. The Gala has raised over £2.7 million over the last five years. All proceeds from this evening will go to the benefiting charity, the International Fundraising Committee of the British Red Cross, which this year celebrates the centenary of its Royal Charter."

During World War II the Grosvenor House became the Allied Forces Officers' Club, serving more than five million meals to 300,000 officers. After the War, celebrities flooded it such as Orson Welles, Sammy Davis Jr., Muhammad Ali and Ella Fitzgerald. Marriott International has and continues to return the hotel to its former [rose-fresh] glory.

Grosvenor House is closely linked to Grosvenor Square, one of the largest and most historic squares in London. The American Embassy is on one side, the Millennium Mayfair Hotel on another. The Canadian Embassy faces the American one across the square. It is really only a long block from the front entrance of Grosvenor House.

In his *Letter from Grosvenor Square*, John Gilbert Winant, United States Ambassador to Great Britain during World War II, reveals the beauty and the patriotism that dominated the Square where the Mayfair Millennium now stands and the entrance to Grosvenor House is but a long stone's throw away:

"One evening in the spring of 1941, just after my wife had arrived in London, we went to dinner with the Prime Minister and Mrs. Churchill. They were then living in the "Annex" in Whitehall. Although Number Ten Downing Street had been trussed up to withstand bombing and was used in the daytime, at night the Prime Minister and Mrs. Churchill moved to the Annex which was the nerve center of the war control system. It was the first time I had been there, and after dinner Mr. Churchill took me down into the basement where I saw the communications and map room. The building, which housed these headquarters offices below ground and the Prime Minister and his family on the first floor, was an administration building in Whitehall which had been reinforced with steel and concrete. It was a stronghold which would be held in the event of invasion and from which the direction of the High Command Could be maintained.

"I remember dinner as a pleasant family occasion, although we were all aware that there was a raid on. The Germans came over early that night. When it was time to leave, Mr. Churchill stepped outside with us. There was a complete blackout but for the searchlights sweeping the sky. Bombs were still dropping; we could hear the booming of the anti-aircraft guns and the rattle of shrapnel falling in the streets. Even in the dim light we could see the shimmer of rain on the pavements. Mr. Churchill arranged for our return in two armored cars. We went the rounds, leaving others of the party at their homes and then returned to the Embassy. No damage had been done there."

People sometimes still poke fun at the British for their "stiff upper lip," for being a bit stoical. As the above passage makes clear, they came by that trait the hard way. This calm in the face of disaster is indeed a national trait and certainly pervades the staff's of London's grand hotels. It's not just the guards at Buckingham Palace who are famously imperturbable.

One of my most pleasant memories of the Hotel was having dinner there facing Hyde Park. Howard Hartley, Senior Sales Manager of The Grosvenor House, invited me and a guest to the Park Room for dinner. My guest Arabella Huddart and I feasted on a silver platter of shrimp, crayfish, and oysters before a main course of steak and salmon. Outside the Park Lane traffic whizzed by and birds sang in Hyde Park.

Shane Krige, general manager of The Plaza Hotel in New York, has fond memories of his time working at The Grosvernor House. "I lived in at The Grosvernor House. I lived in the hotel. Here at The Plaza I live out. You know, when you have kids it's a bit easier. It's not a very difficult business; it's dealing with people, it's relating, and it's tying it all together. Because there are so many things that can go right in one day, and there are so many things that can go wrong in one day, but it's how you choose to be engaged and look at the detail." Mr. Krige believes that a hotelier, a general manager, and all an historic hotel's employees must realize that they "are a part of history" and cherish that.

I'm certainly glad Grosvenor House and Grosvenor Square

survived the London Blitz. Of course it's still a pretty exciting place in peacetime, as well. But that's London for you. Every street corner you turn, it often seems, is like stumbling upon another volume of fascinating history in a great library. Unfortunately, we're going to have to put down this particular volume now and move on to the next. Which, by the way, is Mayfair's own The Dorchester.

Chapter 18

The Dorchester

When Marlene Dietrich did her one-woman show at the Café de Paris in London, she stayed at The Dorchester. Her show was a huge hit, and Dietrich's generosity with the staff and fans is noted by Charles Higham, in his book, *Marlene, The Life of Marlene Dietrich*. Higham says the owner of the Café de Paris, Major Donald Neville-Willing, was particularly astonished that one of Marlene's employees herself behaved as if she were royalty.

"Neville-Willing notes, 'A fantastic thing happened. Marlene had a dresser. She was *very* important. When she arrived at the Dorchester she was told there was a room where the ladies' maids ate their meals. She said, 'I'm not goin' to eat in no room where the ladies' maids are at. I'm goin' to eat in the goddam restaurant. And you see to it, Major Baby!'

"She used to sit in the restaurant in her glory, ordering the most expensive dishes on the menu, *pâté de fois gras*, smoked salmon, rich desserts. The handsome waiter who always served her was crazy about her. She was in the *clouds* over him.

"She used to take Marlene's precious dress home every night: Jean Luis did it and it cost *thousands*. One night very late I had a phone call. She was hysterical. She screamed, 'Dunno what I'm gonna do! I went home with that goddamn waiter for the night and I took Mama's dress in a box. Well, I've gone and left the dress at his place, and I can't remember the *ad*–dress! Where does that guy live? It's the only dress we have for the show. She'll kill me!'

"I told her, 'How would I know where my waiters live?' 'It's in a place called Soho!' she said, very distressed. 'Well, I can't ring all the bells in Soho,' I told her. 'You'll have to wait till tomorrow.'

"There are several versions of what happened next. The most colorful has the dresser finally discovering the waiter's address from an employment agency. She rushed to his lodgings, located the box, threw it into a cab and got to the Café de Paris exactly five minutes before Marlene arrived to change for the evening's performance."

Cary Grant, who was born Archibald Leach in Bristol, England in 1898, naturally had a great affection for his native England and London. One time, he went to do the film version of E. Phillips Oppenheim's novel *The Amazing Quest of Ernest Bliss*. It costarred Mary Brian who Grant dated in London. In her book, *Evenings with Cary Grant* Nancy Nelson quotes Brian that, "Naturally, I was bowled over. Not only was Cary good–looking, but he had a great knack for making you feel as if you'd known him forever . . . we danced at the Dorchester and went to private parties. At a very formal party at The Savoy, I told Cary about a crazy game played with tissue paper. You put it against your nostrils and then hold your breath to keep it there. Your partner has to get in a strange position and take it off your nose. Cary thought it was uproarious. He started it at our table, and soon the whole ball-room was doing it!"

The Promenade at the Dorchester is the hotel's answer to long–vanished Peacock Alley at New York's old Waldorf-Astoria Hotel, at 34th Street and Fifth Avenue, where ladies of the day promenaded in all their finery. The 165–foot long Promenade at the Dorchester is only one of the magnificent nooks of the hotel that seems, especially on cloudy days, to float above Hyde Park like a petite *Queen Mary II*. "The Promenade is astonishing: As I entered the elegant balconied hall hung with vast crystal lanterns, and caught sight of the formal marbled, gilded, and pillared vista ahead, I thought its apparent size was achieved by mirrors, but walking down its 165–foot length I found it to be no illusion," says the author of *Historic Hotels of London*. Its Art Deco façade cradles one of the most magnificent penthouses in all the world with its goldfish pool guarded by a graceful statue of Leda and the Swan. Opening as a penthouse in 1930, the Sultan of Brunei has restored it to all of its Thirties panache from the bar with the hand–painted birds in gilded cages to the Terrace Restaurant, which has menus second to none in London hotels.

To get the lowdown on the high life at the Dorchester, I rummaged around in their historical archives. This is what I turned up:

Like many of the great London hotels, the Dorchester has played host frequently over the decades to royalty and political figures, from home and abroad. No less than Princess Elizabeth attended a dinner party at the hotel on the very day before her engagement to Prince Philip of Greece was announced, on the 10th of July 1947. Perhaps more telling, the Dorchester is also where the prince chose to stage his stag party the night before the actual nuptials. He has subsequently been a regular guest of honor at the hotel. Of course, he would in any case, but he does seem to hold a special place in his heart for the Dorchester. It's not all pomp and circumstance with the Prince Consort. The Prince is well known as an expert after–dinner speaker, a skill which he gets frequent opportunity to display at all the events and charity functions filling his schedule. A surprising number of these fes-tivities take place at the Dorchester, and it was a particular ban-ner day on the 26th of October 1990, when the subject of the event at the Dorchester was the Dorchester! The Prince showed up to unveil a plaque commemorating the reopening of the hotel fol-lowing a two–year closing for refurbishment.

London's hotels probably should have been given a special award for the service many of them performed during the Second World War. You know, the entire British "leisure industry" seems to have risen to the occasion during the war. The great cruise ships were transformed into troop ships or hospital ships, and many of London's finest hotels were likewise used for various aspects of the war effort. The Dorchester was right there in the thick of things. In fact several MPs (members of Parliament) as well as some service chiefs (of the armed forces) moved into the hotel on a semi–permanent basis. General Eisenhower, in charge of the entire European theater of war, established his headquar-ters in the Dorchester in 1944, the year of the Normandy invasion.

The Dorchester has also attracted more than its fair share of figures from the literary and artistic worlds. First of all, the hotel established the famous Foyles Literary Luncheons, but then, beginning in the Thirties, the hotel also played host to such world–renowned writers as novelist Somerset Maugham (he of "Rain," and a frequent guest up until his death), the poet Cecil Day Lewis (who not only was poet laureate of Britain but the father of actor Daniel Day-Lewis, to boot), and the painter Sir Alfred Munnings (a superb English equestrian artist). Nor has the hotel's literary leanings slacked off in recent decades, having frequently welcomed both Jack Higgins, the international best–selling author of thrillers such as "The Eagle Has Landed," and Jackie Collins, the international best–selling author of what I can only describe as romantic thrillers, and also the younger sister of actress Joan

Collins, as guests.

Famous actors and actresses who have stayed at the Dorchester makes up an even longer list. One who became a life-long regular was Danny Kaye. The multi-talented actor even once appeared in cabaret at the hotel at fifty pounds a week in the Thirties. Elizabeth Taylor, although not always showing up with the same husband, was another frequent guest. Ms. Taylor also hosted movie premier parties at the hotel, as well as dinners some years ago in the Penthouse Pavilion, which, by the way, is listed by English Heritage and was designed by Oliver Messel. Ralph Richardson, who often was working nearby in the West End or over at the National Theatre, liked to scoot over to the Dorchester on his motorbike for a bite of lunch.

Other prominent guests who caught my eye as I glanced down the long, long list are Nelson Mandela, Woody Allen, Barbra Streisand, Diana Ross, Glenn Close, Karl Lagerfeld, Arnold Schwarzenegger, and Sharon Stone. Now, I don't wish to give the impression that all of these celebrities stayed at the hotel at the same time. That would have been hectic.

Sandro Micheli, the pastry chef at Alaine Ducasse Restaurant at the St. Regis in New York, told me his favorite hotel in London is The Dorchester. "I really like The Dorchester. I do. I think it is one of the top hotels in the world." I always pay attention to pastry chefs.

On a tour of some of the suites, my tour guide said, "This isn't one of the biggest ones but we have some of the deepest baths in London. Which you don't notice until you get in them! But Charlton Heston is on record as saying he loved them because they're one of the few baths in London that he could actually get his knees underneath the water!"

"I didn't get married there – and I didn't even get divorced there! But I made my first London films while staying at The Dorchester overlooking Hyde." So recollects MGM screen legend Arlene Dahl, who graced the films *Women's World* and *Journey to the Center of the Earth*, among many others. "And getting up at 6 a.m. while the Queen's horses were going by. And every once in a while when I had a day off I'd have tea at Claridge's. I have stayed there a couple of times but my favorite hotel is The Dorchester – because of the view. Getting up in the morning so early at least I had something to fill my eyes!"

Society star Pamela Harriman was born in 1920, was married in the fall of 1939 to Randolph Churchill, only son of Winston, had a baby shortly thereafter, and spent much of the war with her in-laws, as well as (it has since been revealed) sleeping with a variety of interesting and powerful men, a career she continued after her divorce from Randolph in 1946. She lived in Paris and enjoyed Aly Khan and Gianni Agnelli as well as others, then married Leland Hayward about 1960. She ended up marrying Averell Harriman, one of her wartime lovers, in 1971. He died in 1986. Bill Clinton appointed her ambassador to France in 1993. She died at The Ritz pool in February 1997 after her daily swim. Rumor has it she was having a thing with a pool attendant, which I don't mention to be indiscreet but simply out of sheer awe at the woman's lifelong vitality.

In *Life of the Party. The Biography of Pamela Digby Churchill Hayward Harriman* by Christopher Ogden, Ogden writes about Pamela's war-time stay at The Dorchester:

"She (Pamela) moved as quickly as she could to the city, where she took a top-floor room at the Dorchester Hotel on Park Lane for six pounds a week.

"Everyone who could get into the Dorchester wanted to stay there. The only hotel built with steel-reinforced concrete, the Dorchester was thought capable of withstanding all but a direct hit by German bombs. The hotel was jammed except for the vulnerable top floor. Up there with Pam was Clarissa Churchill [niece of Winston], her former Downham classmate, who was now a relative by marriage.

"During bomb raids, guests pulled their mattresses into the corridors. Pamela and Clarissa ran downstairs and slept in the inner foyer in the first-floor suite of Australian prime minister Robert Menzies. The charismatic Menzies was in London attempting to negotiate with Churchill a means of conducting the war without destroying the Empire, a negotiation that so deeply divided the two that Menzies made a futile attempt to oust Churchill from office. . . .

"Her six pound weekly bill at the Dorchester included breakfast, but the rest of the time, Pamela was on her own. . . . Wednesdays were the one night she did not have to worry. . . . Every Wednesday, Emerald, Lady Cunard, hosted a dinner in the Dorchester for friends. [Emerald was not a real aristocrat, nor was Emerald even her real name. She'd changed it from Maud; she was married to Sir Bache Cunard, grandson of the shipping line founder, but her great love was Sir Thomas Beecham.]

"An urban Lady Baillie who specialized in café society, Emerald staged enchanting meals at her London home at a circular table of lapis lazuli which reflected the candlelight and the gilt epergne of the naked nymphs and naiads centerpiece. Her guests were an eclectic mixture of handsome men, social wits, clever women, writers, musicians, diplomats and politicians. . . .

"With the onset of the Blitz, she shut up her house and table, but the gatherings continued when she moved into the Dorchester. Her hotel salon was packed with so much valuable French furniture – a welter of velvet and gild, busts by Houdon and Mestrovic – that it looked as though Sotheby's were using Emerald's quarters as a storeroom.

"Pamela, young, pretty and well connected, was always welcome. She had learned a great deal from observing Emerald entertain ... In March, 1941, within days of her twenty-first birthday, she was in high spirits walking down the Dorchester corridor to Lady Cunard's suite ... Emerald hugged her and introduced her to two Americans who had just arrived in London: John Gilbert Winant, the incoming U.S. Ambassador . . . and Averell Harriman, Franklin Roosevelt's Lend-Lease expediter. Harriman smiled at the young beauty. She stared back. He was the most beautiful man she had ever seen.

"On this night's attack, the bombers seemed to come straight up Park Lane over the roof of the Dorchester. Detonations could be heard close by in Mayfair. There was no way Pamela could return to her sixth-floor apartment. But there was no need to huddle in Prime Minister Menzies' foyer. Averell had a safe ground-floor suite and asked her to stay with him."

This is the very thing which makes the great London hotels so special. Any place in the world can throw up a huge magnificent edifice and hire five-star staff and fly in lobster and whatever else it takes to score high in those hotshot tourist guides. But it's very difficult to reproduce great history. A place like the Dorchester has its marvelous ghosts, all of whom are still staying here, if you listen closely enough.

Which isn't to say the hotel doesn't have its more recent admirers. Jano Herbosch, President of Broadway's Drama League, a non profit group supporting and promoting the Broadway theater, calls The Dorchester "a great place to stay!"

Time to rouse myself once again. We're off to the Hilton Park

Lane. Don't worry. It's not far. I'm sure we'll make it there in time for afternoon tea.

Chapter 19

Hilton Park Lane

"We have a wonderful array of people from all sorts of different areas ... also celebrities. Even your wonderful Paris Hilton comes through and stays here. She always gets a lot of attention. This location, with the wonderful suites we have on the 26th and 27th floors and the Park Lane suites overlooking Hyde Park – many of the personalities ... just love it. It is the best view in London and they know it is a hotel that has a great support and services and we have a whole host of people," said Michael Shepard, the General Manager of the Hilton Park Lane, looking every bit like a London matinee idol himself, over breakfast.

"For me, in this business of hospitality, reputation is everything. So every day we go out and our reputation is as good as our last contact and our last meal. Reputation is fundamental," he added. You come away from an interview with Shepard feeling that not just all is right with The Hilton Park Lane but all is right with the world. He's got a twinkle in his eye that says "this day – sure it will have its problems but it will be fun in the end!"

Certainly Mayfair's only "skyscraper" hotel, The London Hilton on Park Lane may be a classic but it has no pretension of being old world. Fred Astaire and Ginger Rogers would have been right at home at the Dorchester or the Mandarin Oriental Hyde Park, formerly the Hyde Park. Yet in one of its sumptuous, artfully appointed suites on 26th and 27th floors your mind may go whirling. One has a steam room, another a Jacuzzi. But unrivaled views of Mayfair, Belgravia and Buckingham Palace together with its location and service challenge even The Savoy's preeminence. Mr. Shepard had been General Manager of The Savoy for several years, and his experience and polished approach have helped the London Hilton Park Lane scale new heights. *Traveler Magazine* named the Hilton "Best Business Hotel in the U.K. 2007," and it was named "England's Leading Business Hotel 2007" by World Travel Awards.

"The London Hilton is one of the world's finest hotels and in winning these awards we're proud to bear the standard for our industry in this country," Mr. Shepard told me. "We consistently strive to provide an exemplary service and an unforgettable experience." And after a drink one winter evening at the Sloane Club in Kensington, I dined at Galvin at Windows soaring twenty-eight floors above Park Lane. No night view of London could be complete seeing it from this pinnacle of Mayfair. Here you can look down your nose – not haughtily of course – at the garden, lawns and lake (a small one) within the high walls of the Buckingham Palace gardens, serene, evergreen sprinkled with flowers like heavenly throw rugs. Galvin's fare is just as delicious. And the lights of London spread out like super-sized quilts below. Queen Elizabeth opens up Buckingham Palace for her famous teas, personally greeting some of the many who attend civic or private charity work, the ticket of admission.

"You have to be of the moment, interest the fashionistas, the entertainment sector," Mr. Shepard continued. "Our nightclub, Whiskey Mist is so successful now that it has been purchased by Blackstone. Their strategy is very much on global expansion of their brands . . . with different vision in different parts of the world. What makes a company is legendary properties. Last night, we did Sienna Miller's party."

To see just why the London Hilton on Park Lane is considered quintessential luxury, step into one of its fifty-six suites. They have all been individually designed to rank among the most luxurious and elegant hotel living spaces in the world, and after my stay there, I heartily agree with that ranking although I did not have a suite *per se*. First off, consider the views. Ah, the views! And in the lounge, breakfast, high tea and evening drinks are set out with the hotel's compliments.

Mr. Shepard sincerely likes people and he started humbly enough in the hospitality industry, as he explained to me, "in this property as a receptionist. And within two years I was actually on a fast track. And then became front office manager and later was transferred, in 1979, to open a new hotel as executive assistant manager and then spent the next fifteen years abroad, in the Middle East and had a number of management positions in hotels like in Istanbul and manager of hotels in cities such as Athens, Corfu, and Cairo and then back to London when I became opening general manager of the Langham Hilton in Portland Place. I stayed there six years with Hilton. I was appropriated to be the

Managing Director of The Savoy for six years during the time that Blackstone, the private equity company, bought them out . . . and then in 2003, the Chief Executive of Hilton called me and asked if I had any reason why I couldn't come back."

Mr. Shepard explained that the significance of the hotel "was more than the fact it was just a tall tower – it was the first international company to penetrate what was traditionally a very conservative industry. After the austerity of the war years [World War II], until the 1950's, hotels were demure places. They were owned by a few families; it was very much an aristocratic business to be in. Many were landowners, and the owners who operated their own hotels were people of moneyed background, generally speaking. Then you had the expansion of the 1960's, and in 1963 this was the first international hotel to open. It was razzmatazz, Zsa Zsa Gabor, Liza Minnelli. Elizabeth Taylor came with Barron Hilton. It was just amazing. And there was almost shock in the traditional British hotel scene. Of course, it was a very different building. It wasn't a building out of the Victorian era – Claridge's, The Savoy, and so on. And there were those in society who didn't like it and they would come to enjoy entertainment. The story is the Queen objected and certainly it took a long time before the Duke of Edinburgh put a foot in the place. But I have met him here. I have met Prince Charles here a number of times, and all of the other children including Princess Anne who comes here regularly to support different charity functions. I've hosted dinner with Prince Andrew, Prince Edward. Certainly we're making good headway with the younger generation (of royals)."

"Is it true it had to get a special dispensation from the Queen?" I asked.

"Well, there are all of these stories," the debonair Mr. Shepard continued. And then abruptly stopped. The British aren't much for telling tales out of school about the Queen. It's not that they fear repercussions. Not at all. It's just that she's so nice, no one wants to offend her.

He added his aim is to give everyone at the hotel a great experience – including the employees. "Well, I coach and mentor a number of young people, and what I say to them is, you know, you're interested in coming to hospitality. Remember there are two types of people: those that like to be with people, deal with people, and service people, and there are those that feel very awkward and uncomfortable about it. And there's nothing wrong if you fall into the second category. You just shouldn't work in this business. If you work for me, what I expect is that you wake up, whether you are doing a morning, afternoon, or a night shift – whenever you wake up to come to work, you jump out of bed, you put a big smile on your face and you say, 'I'm going to please some people today.' And when you jump into work, you've got to please people. If you don't feel like that, do me a favor, go home, go to bed. Don't come to work because if you come on work on your shift with an attitude, the guests will feel it straight away and so will your work colleagues, and it's not fair."

Ah, if only one could get this courtesy in every profession! Maybe we really would have world peace, at long last. With high tea to boot.

With respect to the Whiskey Mist Bar, Mr. Shepard commented, "Well, people say the drinks are expensive. Of course they are in any night venue. But what we do is we say you can buy a bottle, whatever it may be, say a bottle of vodka or a bottle of scotch whiskey, and we put their name on it so that is their bottle behind the bar, and they know that they can come back in, they've bought the bottle, and they can come back in and have a couple of shots. It does engender loyalty and belonging. So it's a smart little gimmick."

Later, from my room high above Hyde Park, I can see the Duke of Wellington's home, its beautiful garden, closed gate, Hyde Park in the distance, Buckingham Palace's gardens in the late afternoon's golden sun . . .

It was then fitting that I had dinner at Trader Vic's Restaurant at the London Hilton Mayfair where the late Victor Jules Bergeron brought contentment to millions of people over the years. I had had dinner with "The Trader" several times at his restaurant in The Plaza Hotel. As you might imagine, he was quite the character. He had lost a leg to tuberculosis, but the great promoter that he was, he felt that was far too prosaic an explanation – so he started telling a story of how he lost the leg to a shark. The odd thing is that, as brilliant as he was in public relations, he never wanted to publicize all the great charity work he did. What a guy. I stopped downstairs to the Plaza Vic's as much out of fond memories of him as a yen for fried shrimp the way only Trader Vic's can prepare them: plump, jumbo shrimp, lightly fried, crispy outside and succulent within.

Having opened in 1963 (within the first Hilton hotel built

outside of the U.S.A.), the French Polynesian themed restaurant is one of twenty-five Trader Vic's around the world, renowned not only for their exotic island atmosphere and blend of French, Oriental and American cuisine but for its celebrity clientele. "Trader Vic's has offered people an island escape in the heart of Mayfair for almost half a century and has been popular with many celebrities during that time, from Jimi Hendrix to Jenson Button," boasts General Manager Dusan Sofranac. "Our laid back atmosphere goes back to the restaurant's Californian roots and when mixed with the potent cocktails, mouthwatering food and great music it makes for a special experience." Trader Vic's began in California in 1932 when the late Victor Jules Bergeron built little more than a cozy luncheonette across the street from his father's store and called it Hinky Dink's.

I had previously gone to the Trader Vic's in The Savoy Plaza with my father. My stepmother, Rebecca Morehouse, warned me to not let him have more than one powerful Mai Tai, a traditional hallmark of the restaurant. Several years later, in my rebellious late teens, I took a date to Trader Vic's, ordered lavishly and "signed" one of my father's business cards as payment. Two days later, I heard about it from my mother – my father had registered his horror at the incident.

At Trader Vic's the guests have included Charles Bronson, Winston Churchill, Sidney Poitier, Ernest Borgnine, Ursula Andress, Sean Connery, Roy Orbison, Martin Luther King, Warren Beatty, Lesley Caron, Ella Fitzgerald, Peter Finch, Julie Andrews . . . Now that is a truly varied clientele. One wonders if Charley Bronson and Winston Churchill showed at the same time, maybe even shared a Mai Tai. Why not? They're both tough guys. Stirling Moss has been a regular since 1964. Paris Hilton is a "newcomer," which is a bit odd since as an actual Hilton heir she practically owns the joint, and, probably, although he didn't mention him, Anthony Quinn. It seemed Anthony Quinn – and New York Post's Cindy Adams – practically lived at Trader Vic's in New York when it was in the basement of the Plaza and undoubtedly everywhere else they went where there was one.

"I just had a guest yesterday, or the day before, he was here on the opening day in 1963, and he was amazed at how little has changed and, even looking at the menu, he said he can't remember," the London Trader Vic's restaurant manager told me. "So I said okay and I went and I got a menu from 1963 and I said, 'there you go. 1963. 2009! There's quite a few dishes that are the same. The presentation changes slightly to appeal to modern customers but that's about that. . . . It's not cuisine at the highest level but it is simple food cooked well." To show the appeal of its signature drink, the Mai Tai, he told me this strange woman came in and "she took one, you know, she stuck some peach juice in and just made a mess. The second time she came to see me she said 'put some water in it.' Again, it wasn't good. The third time she came, she doesn't change anything. That is the end of the Mai Tai story. Now, she comes in, Mai Tai straight away. Another victim!"

In 1932, Hinky Dink's mix of potent tropical cocktails and Americanized Polynesian food quickly made what became known as Trader Vic's popular places in Northern California, New York and around the globe. "Since we opened in 1963, the Trader Vic's here in London has been in the same location, the lower ground floor of the London Hilton on Park Lane. In fact, the 453–bed-room hotel has the only Trader Vic's in the U.K."

"The menu combines an array of cooking styles including steaming, grilling, wok stirring or slow roasting in the signature Chinese wood fired ovens," a promotion piece states. "Dishes include steamed sea bass Cantonese style and Indonesian rack of lamb."

My impressions of London hotel managers, who in their own way were top directors and producers of great shows in every sense, were molded by knowing some of the best in New York. And I think this as good a place as any to tell you about a few.

Webster's defines *hotelier* as an owner or manager of a hotel. But a good manager does more than administer, just as a good artist does more than paint. "A good manager of a good hotel has a love affair with that hotel," the late Alphonse Salamone, region-al vice–president of the Hilton Corporation and long–time man-ager of The Plaza, once told me. "And I don't think you can be a really great hotel manager unless you have that love affair. If you've been at The Waldorf or The Plaza, it's always there tugging at you a little bit. Wherever you go, wherever you are, you're a part of it, and it's part of you." Former New York Hilton Hotel manager, Jorgen Hansen, didn't flag the feeling in such flowery terms but told me, "There are times when all of us are a little bit of a romantic. We like to see that brought back a little bit. I think that on certain occasions you can bring it back. And, certainly, despite its comparative youth, the London Hilton Park Lane brings it back. But where you can't bring it back is to a modern aristocratic hotel; you can bring it back in the Jade or the Astor Gallery or the Basildon Room at The Waldorf–Astoria very easily. You also have personnel there who have been married to The Waldorf–Astoria for thirty or forty years, and those people take pride in bringing an era like that back occasionally." Hansen is a former manager of The Waldorf.

Some hoteliers inevitably come to revere the crystal, carpets, clocks and even the elevators and boiler rooms as one would a good friend or book; others seem to have within themselves all the qualities that make a hotel a home away from home: order, joy, tranquility, and its outward expression, harmony. And people are indeed entering their home, their heart, for a night, a week, a year. The finest managers are really theatrical producers in one sense, presenting both the magnificence of their buildings as well as their hotel's service daily, hourly. It really is a lot like staging a grand drama every day on the fly. Without a net.

Hilton, of course, is probably the best known name the world over when it comes to hotels. The London palace is just one of the Hilton corporation's international crown jewels. The story of how they got to be that big and that famous is a long and complex one. But there was one very important turning point, and it took place in my home town, New York.

When Conrad Hilton became "The Man Who Bought The Waldorf," it was a perfect match between man and building. He probably knew more than any person alive about being an owner; and The Waldorf was brought into existence by the best owner before him. Conrad owned two hotels in California, another in Mexico, one in New Mexico and a string in Texas. Horace Sutton says in his *Confessions of a Grand Hotel* that it wasn't until December, 1942, when Hilton finally made up his mind to buy the towering beauty on Park Avenue, although he had carried its picture around in his wallet for years. "I came east and I was standing across from The Waldorf on Park Avenue, and I looked over at it and the thought came to me, 'Why not?'" he told Sutton. "The more I thought about it, the more I was determined to do something about it."

Hilton could no more be dissuaded from buying The Waldorf than the sun from rising. As early as 1942, Hilton defied the advice of his financial advisers and started to buy Waldorf bonds at a phenomenal four-and-a-half cents on the dollar, or bonds worth $500,000 for $22,500. But his dream would have to wait seven years more, during which time he added a few more New York trinkets to his collection: The Plaza Hotel and the Roosevelt Hotel.

The Waldorf, it is true, hadn't started to be a money-maker until 1942 and though it was doing much better in the last years of the decade, buying it was still a risk. But Hilton reasoned that the publicity value alone was priceless.

But when negotiations took a serious turn and really big money was at stake, Hilton couldn't persuade the board of directors of the Hilton Hotels Corporation to go along. So he did what he did thirty years earlier – used his own money as the nucleus of a buying group. Final say about any takeover had to come from The Waldorf-Astoria Corporation, which financed the hotel's construction, and the New York State Realty and Terminal Company, which had put up $10 million of the original cost and had power of veto on the board. He won both.

Then "nothing stood between me and The Waldorf," he wrote in *Be My Guest*, "except about $3 million."

But there was something, or rather, somebody, else. Her name: Alice Statler, widow of Ellsworth Statler, who coined the phrase about the three best things a hotel can have going for it, "location, location, location."

Hilton was bidding against the Statler chain and although his price was right, and although his chances were good, they were threatened by the fact that the late Mr. Statler didn't particularly like him. She herself occupied a suite in The Waldorf Towers. Elsworth's one-time secretary, she had become a close friend of Frank Ready, Jr's mother, who had also been a secretary. Knowing about the friendship, "Hilton called my father and said, 'I know you're close to Alice Statler. See if you can mend the way,'" says Frank Ready, Jr. "When Conrad Hilton took over The Waldorf, my mother thought, 'Here's the end of this regime.' But Conrad Hilton set my father up so well that she got very soft for Conrad Hilton. So when my father told her the story about Alice Statler, she went up to see Alice Statler and said, 'You'd be doing us a great favor. I was worried about what he would do to Frank, and he's such a great guy.' And when they went down to the meeting, Alice said, 'O.K.'" One by one, the monetary puzzle was pieced together, $250,000 here, $500,000 there, and on October 12,

1949, Conrad Hilton became "The Man Who Bought The Waldorf."

The Waldorf, like most grand hotels worthy of the name, was and is a mixture of antiquity and modern convenience. By all means put in the computerized telephones, and the lightning check-in and check-out, no matter. But remove the wooden-paneled operator-driven elevators in the Towers, the bronze clock in the main lobby, or other old-world ornamentation, and many patrons won't return.

"The Waldorf always has one foot in the past, and it has to remain that way," said Salamone. "You cannot make The Waldorf a modern kind like the Hyatt Atrium or the New York Hilton. "I'll never forget, I had a serious argument with some of the Hilton Corporation of America people, where they wanted name tags on employees' lapels. A person in The Waldorf doesn't give a damn whether the waiter's name is Jerry or Joe. He doesn't come here to address him as Jerry or Joe. He comes here to escape the A&P and the real world. And in that context I used the expression 'a fairyland.' The day it veers from that is the day it's in trouble. Because you might as well go to something else. But I had non-believers above me and below me. But that's why the owners of The Waldorfs and The Plazas have to be very, very careful, number one, in who they make manager, because you can get a 'square peg in a round hole' type of manager who will hurt a Waldorf or hurt a Plaza. These hotels must maintain that delicate position, in fairyland, because they do not have the modern equipment of the new modern high-rises. That's something that the staff often does not appreciate, and even owners sometimes do not. Hilton did. When Mr. Hilton took over The Plaza, there was a lot of ridicule, about this big hand coming in to take over The Plaza. I would venture to say that if Mr. Hilton had not taken over The Plaza, it may have been torn down."

Before I tiptoe away, one more instance of sizzling New York-London synergy. Sienna Miller was being fete-ed at the London Hilton Park Lane while I was there. She's an example of an American performer making it big in London. She was born in New York City and her mother, Jo Miller, ran Lee Strasberg's acting studio in London.

Sienna was thrown a party in the London Hilton Park Lane's Whiskey Mist Bar during Fashion Week (in February 2009). Not long after the actress would strike gold on Broadway in the title role of the Roundabout Theatre Company's American premier production of *After Miss Julie*, in October 2009. Playwright Patrick Marber transposed August Strindberg's 1888 play *Miss Julie* to an English country house during World War II. Incidentally, Ms. Miller's erstwhile boyfriend, film star Jude Law, who appeared with her in the film *Layer Cake* was starring in the title role of *Hamlet* just around the corner from the American Airlines Theatre where *After Miss Julie* was playing. Small world, the worlds of entertainment – and love!

Well, this Hilton Park Lane is one big building, but these whisper quiet elevators will jet us out of here in no time, which is lucky, since we're already due at our next destination, the Berkeley – transplanted in spirit if not bricks and mortar from Berkeley Square, where it reigned for many decades.

Chapter 20

The Berkeley

Although I stayed at The Berkeley only once, it remains in my memory as one of London's premiere hotels. I always think of Boston's Ritz Carlton, now the Taj Boston Hotel, when I think of the Berkeley. It has the refined air of a fine country club dance ballroom. In another sense it's what I call a "cotton candy hotel": light, airy, plush, almost ethereal.

Located in Wilton Place, just around the corner from Hyde Park Corner and "Number One London," where the Dukes of Wellington lived, the understated Berkeley fairly shrieks class from its magnificent penthouse pool – which can be opened to the sunshine when the weather permits – to its elegant main restaurant and more casual "Buttery."

This is not your grandmother's Berkeley, which was on Piccadilly Street, as the entire hotel has moved since the last time granny stayed there. Some of the antique clocks, wood paneling and an entire room designed by Sir Edwin Lutyens, however, made the move and now grace the new Berkeley hotel. Sir Edwin Lutyens patterned some of the carpets after a 13th century design he discovered in a French cathedral. Michael Inchhold and other top designers styled some of the 130 guest rooms and 25 suites.

But the coupe de la resistance is the Berkeley's rooftop swimming pool, the roof of which opens to sunlight and, like the roof of the Starlight Roof of The Waldorf–Astoria in New York used to be, is used to the max in good weather.

To hear more about the Berkeley I talked to Paula Fitzherbert, who is herself a public relations legend. She's the personification of the hotels she represents – exacting, gracious, warm, and someone who relishes pomp and history. Here's what she has to say about the history of the Berkeley and the hotel's famous Blue Bar:

"When it was decided to rebuild The Berkeley from its old location in Berkeley Street it took some time to find a suitable site elsewhere. The present site was acquired with the co–operation of the Grosvenor Estate. The land on which the hotel was built has close connections with the Army. The hotel is situated on what was once the parade ground of the barracks of the First Regiment of Foot Guards, later renamed The Grenadier Guards (hence the name of the nearest pub – The Grenadier).

"The decision not to use the whole of the area was based on the fact that the hotel clientele favored the 'old' Berkeley because it was primarily a small deluxe hotel. To build a totally different Berkeley would have alienated all the hotel's faithful guests from all over the world. It was therefore decided to limit the accommodation to less than three hundred beds and to design the hotel so that its main ground floor and interior layout gave the impression of a private house.

"The distinguished English architect, Brian O'Rourke, who took the greatest care to ensure that it blended in with its surroundings, designed the hotel. The Berkeley opened on this site in February 1972.

"To ensure the hotel has the appearance of a private house, there is no standardization within the accommodation. The shape, design, decoration and furnishings of each of the rooms and suites are different.

"The Blue Bar opened in November 2000 at The Berkeley, the five star hotel in Knightsbridge. David Collins has created this fifty-seater bar in his own inimitable style. He has also incorporated the style of top British Architect Sir Edwin Lutyens, who originally designed the wood carvings in the room, which survived from the old Berkeley when it was based in Piccadilly.

"The bar is located off the lobby of the hotel, and the most outstanding feature is the striking color of the room, which Collins has termed 'Lutyens Blue'. Other features include a white onyx bar, chairs covered in pale lilac crosshatch leather, cream faux ostrich leather stools, and a black crocodile print leather floor inspired by Lutyens' use of black in his designs. The blue cracked gesso wall covering, with red iridescent powder brushed into the cracks gives a warmth and texture to the room. Fashion designer Amanda Wakeley likes Stolichnaya on the rocks when she visits the Berkeley's Blue Bar, her favorite in London.

"Collins' reputation for dramatic lighting is evident in The Blue Bar. The central light fitting is an authentic Lutyens design known as 'The Cardinals Hat,' which he created for Campion Hall near Pembroke, with broad flat glass rims to diffuse the light, and elegant suspended tassels."

"The bar is not a period recreation of Lutyens because time moves on, and the hotel moves on. My brief was to establish a design concept that was in keeping with The Berkeley but with some contemporary vibe!" explained David Collins himself of his latest venture. The bar offers over fifty different whiskeys, a wide range of champagnes, and some classic cocktails including the specialties, Ginger Cosmopolitan, Orange and Lime Caipiroska and The Lutyens Gimlet.

"There is also," Ms. Fitzherbert continues, "a selected range of wine by the glass, and a specially created 'Grape and Smoke' menu designed to pair cigars with carefully chosen wines to enhance the connoisseur's enjoyment of his chosen cigar. Suggested pairings include Organic Bonterra Viognier 1998 which has great richness and a long fruit finish matched with a 'Punch Punch,' a balanced spicy choice. Alternatively choose Shafer Merlot 1997, Napa Valley, full but soft on the palate, with a long aromatic finish making it perfect with a 'Hoyo De Monterrey, Epicure No. 2.'"

The Berkeley has the distinction of having not one but two celebrity chef restaurants. Celebrity chef Marcus Wareing's Berkeley Hotel restaurant Petrus derives its name from the famous chateau by the name in the Bordeaux wine region of France, renowned for some of the world's finest wines. The other is Gordon Ramsay's Boxwood Cafe with favorite "starters," including fried oysters with fennel and lemon and chilled melon soup. Even tea at The Berkeley has its celebrity accents. How about "Ralph Lauren nautical striped raspberry short glass," "Valentino zesty lemon floral crunch," "Balenciaga monochrome striped chocolate éclair" or "Elizabeth Hurley Beach fuchsia vanilla bikini biscuit!"

The Berkeley's crown jewel, even by neighborhood hotel standards, is that rooftop swimming pool, the roof of slides like the starlight roof of The Waldorf-Astoria in New York. Its only real watery rival is the magnificent Olympic-sized pool at the Four Seasons Canary Wharf.

I am presenting my interview about The Berkeley with Paula Fitzherbert in almost its entirety. Simply because there is no better, more eloquent source of information about the fabulous hotel, and because she's so much fun to talk to! She speaks of The Berkeley as she does Claridge's, as if it were her own house.

Indeed, as an historic landmark, it really belongs to us all.

"Claridge's is more of a place to be seen," I noted to my charming interlocutress.

"Yes, it's a much more theatrical experience, really, which is how we position it here," Paula told me.

The whole encounter at that moment struck me as a scene right out of a great West End play. Exposition, to be sure. I'm a playwright myself, you know. This was a light comedy, perhaps, with two debonair characters, she elegantly attired and coiffed, me rather raffishly suited in blue blazer and open-throated chalk-striped shirt. While the rendezvous was decidedly businesslike, there nonetheless was a certain crackle in the air, with two professionals good at their jobs doing what they do best. The two characters, as the curtain goes up, are discovered seated on a sun-splashed catty-cornered couch of the world renowned hotel's lobby . . .

> PF: (*casually*)   The Berkeley is actually the baby of the family, 'cause it's actually only thirty-five years old. And of course Claridge's and the Connaught are over a hundred years old. So again, it has that sort of heavy handed history that they have on them, but the Berkeley doesn't have so we get away with some sort of lighter touches, sometimes, as well. An informality, because that's the way that the world is these days, as well. I think people really want some informality but still done with style and polish. . . .
>
> WM: (*intrigued*)   You know, that's right. The world is going that way, and I'm not under dressed, but there is the – there are other people that wear this for work, these days.
>
> PF: But at The Ritz Hotel, you still have to wear a jacket and tie to be anywhere, and we very much as a company took the decision *not* to do that. I think we actually had Bill Gates staying in one of the properties, and of course, he came down in his Ralph Lauren polo shirt. (*sips her cognac*) I've worked for the company for ten years. And during that time we really did insist on that dress code. But in ten years, the whole world has changed now, you know, and you also have to be very careful not to judge people by what they look like or

what they're dressed – some of the coolest and richest people are the ones in the jeans and the t–shirt . . .

WM: (*slightly confused*)   Now this was when Bill Gates came to Claridge's?

PF: (*devil-may-care*)   I think it must be Claridge's 'cause Claridge's in those days did have a very strict dress code . . . maybe it was Gordon Ramsay's restaurant – I think you need a jacket; I don't think you need a tie. I think The Ritz in London is still the only place where you need to wear a jacket and a tie. . . . Yes, in their formal dining room. And I think in the tearoom as well. Which is love-ly if you're visiting and you're on special occasion, but I think if you're a guest staying there it's a bit exhausting. . . . Now The Connaught is really, of all the hotels, the most traditional and it is almost in a way the one that people personify as coming to England, and being in the heart of England. (*gestures with her hands*) Wood paneling, the old oak staircase . . .

WM: And some people say it's the best hotel in London.

PF: And a *lot* of people think it's the best hotel in London. It's not cutting edge. There's nothing new and funky there or anything like that and that's what people go there and stay for. The good thing is there's some-thing for everybody.

WM: (*glances around*) Yes, I love the cutting edge nature of the decorations here at The Berkeley though, in the rooms.

PF: You're in an eighth floor room, I think?

WM: Yes, yes.

PF: They're small but they're nicely – the attention to detail is very nice in those rooms.

WM: Yes. Beautiful. And beautifully – it's decorated but it's not overly decorated in a sense. You get the sense it's very tasteful. You know you can be in a room which is overly decorated and this has – I like it very much and I can see where it would attract the younger clientele.

PF: (*suddenly excited*)   Yes, yes. Definitely. We pick up the youngest age of the people staying in the properties. . . . It was an interesting thing; most people don't even know there *was* an old Berkeley. Although the Blue Bar,

I don't know if you managed to get in there, which is sort of one of London's top bars. But all the paneling in there actually came from the old Berkeley but then it was given a treatment by David Collins. He painted it that electric blue which is what made it so cool and popular really.

WM: (*deep in reflection*)   I've been to The Claridge's bar, and that's a happening place.

PF: (*encouraging*)   Yeah, it is. And it's quite interesting how London, I mean again, in the last few years nobody really ever used to come drink here in hotels and then I think it was really David Collins and what he did at Claridge's bar and then he subsequently did here, and I think will eventually do at the Connaught, is develop bars, and now it's almost a bit like the Hong Kong society. People actually do come to hotels to hang out and drink.

WM: That's good. I mean that's good for clientele.

PF: Which is good. Even as a tourist, you don't always want to be somewhere where it's full of tourists. (*laughs charmingly*) You want to feel like you're going somewhere the London crowd are hanging out, and you're part of the scene that would be happening anyway.

(WM *nods, lightly whirls his martini*)

PF: (*studying him*)   So when were you last in London?

WM: (*thinking*)   It was in December.

PF: Oh, okay. So you're quite a regular visitor over here.

WM: I'm actually going to stay at The Savoy after staying at The Connaught, and I know you know the folks over there, including Susan. There's a bit of concern that they're going to close The Savoy . . .

PF: (*searching her memory*)   Oh, you mean Susan from the archives?

WM: Yes, yes.

PF: Yes, well I used to work for The Savoy as well. Before – of course The Savoy was all part of our family. We were The Savoy Group before we broke away when The Savoy was sold last year. It's Pam Carter, who has been the PR director over there – a very good friend of mine. And Susan. who heads up the archives. I think –

there is talk – I think they will close The Savoy for a certain length of time. I'm not quite sure how long it's going to be, but I think only to improve it and, you know, put it back to its glory days, really. Because it is, in a way, the most legendary hotel in London, The Savoy. But over the last couple years, all the others had so much money spent on them that unfortunately it seems somehow to have slipped by the wayside a little bit.

(*Both are lost in their thoughts for a moment.*)

PF: There's Boxwood Café which is a slightly more informal restaurant on the other side. . . . . I'm sure you remember the days when there was the old hotel dining room – they're rather grand – and they'd usually be sitting there empty except for some grannies in the corner! And in fact the Berkeley was one of the first hotels . . . that actually had a free-standing restaurant by a big name chef. And since that, that's become quite a big trend here in the U.K., you know, Nobu at the Metropolitan and now we have Gordon Ramsay at Claridge's. . . . And it works very well. It really works very well. It does bring people that are coming in and using the hotel as a restaurant, really, yeah.

WM: (*warmly*)   We went to see "Mary Poppins" last night.

PF: (*surprised*)   Oh, did you? And what did you think?

WM: I was disappointed.

PF: I was very disappointed. I know people who rave about it and loved everything. But I found it – nothing will ever be the film, you see, for me, and I just, you know . . .

WM: That's part of it, but I think part of it was just a mish-mosh. They haven't been able to decide what it is. They need someone to write it more clearly – the book.

PF: I think a lot of it is based on the book, but it's quite lax on a bit, isn't it?

WM: It needs a rewrite. That's one of the rumors in New York that one of the reasons it didn't come over, aside from maybe not having a theater, is the American version needs more work in it or something like that.

PF: Because it *will* come to New York?

WM: Yes, it's scheduled to come in October. Now the

second act is much better, and I think that it just could be cut with a blue pencil – go through it, and the story . . .

PF: (*frowning*)   Yeah, it wasn't magical for me.

WM: (*suddenly remembering*)   Would it be possible to get a checkout at around three or four o'clock?

PF: I'm not actually sure. I would say 'yes' but we're a hundred percent full tonight so let me double-check on that. Maybe if you can have checked out, we can send your bags over to the Connaught for you or something like that, if that would help.

WM: That would be fine. When's the normal check-out? Like one o'clock?

PF: Twelve o'clock. One o'clock. Yes, yes. Of course, if you want one o'clock. (*crisis over, both relax*) . . . I took my son to New York about two months ago for the first time. Oh, he just loved it. New York's so exciting a place to go to when you're ten. His favorite thing – I've never done, because I usually go on business so I usually am at bars or restaurants or whatever – but we went on the Staten Island ferry for the first time which was fantastic.

WM: Where did you stay?

PF: We stayed at a place called SoHo House which is down in the meat–packing district opposite the Gansevoort, so we had that kind of – it's run by a guy that has SoHo House here in London. It's a private members club with swimming pool on the roof, but it's very cool and lovely. But it was hilarious because we woke up at about two in the morning and looked out the window thinking, 'what is' – and it was just like in the middle of daytime. The traffic. It was hilarious! Wall to wall stretch limos and everything. I've been there a few times and it really was – I mean, the first time when I stayed there, I came out and they were hosing down the blood off the streets. It really is still the meat market area as well.

WM: (*helpful*)   But it's a big club area.

PF: Oh, big club area. My god. Tell me about it. They had to put extra strong, sort of double glazing in and things like that because it really is so noisy. It's extraordinary.

WM: (*matter-of-fact*)   Is there someone at the Berkeley I could talk to who remembers the old days?

PF: (*crestfallen*)   No. We have nothing. We have a few old photographs but we really do not have – we're not like The Savoy where there's Susan whose an archivist, or anybody here who has any historical knowledge of the old Berkeley. . . . The Connaught is different; the Connaught actually has a Connaught history book which I can make sure gets in your room. There is a book there, and the general manager, Anthony Lee, who I think is not there this week, has worked there for over twenty years, so he is – he certainly – if you want to speak to somebody at a later time he would actually be the man to speak to. But the Connaught is much more historically – I'll make sure the copy of the book goes into your room so you've got that, so it's all done for you, there.

WM: What about any other long–term employees there?

PF: At the Connaught? Yes, there's a lot of employees at the Connaught that have worked there for a long time.

WM (*suddenly hopeful*)   Yes. Maybe if there's one I can talk to . . .

PF: Well, okay, all right. I'll make sure . . .

WM: And you can tell them I'll be very discreet. (*grins*)

PF: Oh, no. When you go into the Connaught, you'll find there's pictures there of Cary Grant, Rock Hudson and Lauren Bacall and all those faves, Princess Grace of Monaco, everything. They all used to stay there and they're quite happy to talk about things of those days. Jack Nicholson always stays there, and, no, it's – Ralph Lauren, I think, stays there. No, it's very popular but very discreet hotel.

WM: My dad used to stay at The Savoy starting in 1928 or something, and he was a drama critic in New York and I have a story that his widow wrote that I'm going to include in my book. He gave a party in one of those suites at The Savoy and Humphrey Bogart and Lauren Bacall came, you know, they were on their way to *The African Queen* and that kind of thing. He was the same kind of Humphrey Bogart he was in the movies.

(*She scowls at a nearby bouquet in a vase.*)

PF: (*explaining*)   I'm on the warpath today because the flowers are supposed to be changed today – some of them look a bit dead already – so I get very uptight about that. The flowers are my area here so, as I say, I've been on the warpath. They should be changed today. We use a very special florist actually that does it – in fact, they're so special that every year they're flown over to the, they do the *Vanity Fair* party at the Oscars. They literally – Graydon Carter just loves them so much, he flies them and their flowers over to do the party which is quite extraordinary.

WM: (*mildly incredulous*)   To Hollywood?

PF: Yeah. In L.A.

WM: Wow, that's amazing. That's beautiful.

PF: Yeah, it is. It is.

WM: (*checking his notes*)   How long have you been at the Berkeley now?

PF: I've been here, oh, about eight years. Far too long, really.

WM: You have your office here?

PF: I'm based here but I look after the Connaught as well.

WM: I know Andrew Anspach who managed the Algonquin for many years. He swore by the Connaught, you know.

PF: (*privately delighted*)   Oh, really. It does have this slightly legendary status even though it hasn't had any whizzy, new things, but you know, sometimes it's just not about doing whizzy, new things. Sometimes it's about just standing still, and it has a sort of timeless elegance about it and an attitude of spirit that some of the other hotels could learn from, certainly.

WM: (*reconsulting notes*)   Now, the original Berkeley wasn't in Berkeley Square?

PF: No, it was in Piccadilly actually. I know, it's funny isn't it?

WM: (*unsure*)   Right in Piccadilly Circus?

PF: No, no. Further along. Opposite – by the Ritz, down that Piccadilly. On the corner of Berkeley Street, actually. That was why it was named ... (*grins*) Berkeley Street on one side and Piccadilly on the other.

(He suddenly realizes he's been monopolizing her
precious time, jumps to his feet.)

PF: Oh, well lovely to meet you!

WM: *(extends hand)*   Great to meet you.

PF: Thank you for my book on The Waldorf–Astoria, as well.

WM: Oh, you're welcome.

PF: Well, it's a great privilege to write a book like that, isn't it?

WM: Yes. I must say the Towers is a special place; it's probably one of the nicer hotels in New York

PF: I've seen some of our people stay there . . .

And then, suddenly, she's gone, almost like an apparition. Was she real, he wonders? Yes, fortunately, quite real. Even if the rest of The Berkeley, and especially its service, seems a little too good to be true.

It was time for me to be off too, to my next multi-star destination. I thought a little salt air in my lungs might be nice, so I took myself to the Four Season's at Canary Wharf.

Chapter 21

Four Seasons Canary Wharf

This is not your mother's Four Seasons. Four Seasons Hotel London opened in 1970 and was called The Inn on the Park with oversized, sleekly designed rooms and steps from both Green Park and Hyde Park (which it overlooked). The Inn on the Park, festooned with genuine antiques and its own garden, became Chairman Isadore Sharp's blueprint for his hotel empire in thirty countries.

Closed for a major renovation when I was in London, I was offered a visit of a one-bedroom suite with breathtaking views of the Thames. It made me think I was back on the island in the St. Lawrence River that my family was given by New York stage star Irene Purcell. In fact, it's hard to separate the Thames from the 142 rooms and suites at the Four Seasons Canary Wharf. Like a view of the Mediterranean from a hotel in the south of France, the water and the room seem to blend into one. Picture sitting on a blue couch, champagne in hand, toasting a companion and the River Thames. Downstairs on the lobby level the Quadrato Restaurant entices with its Thames River vista and immaculate, how–do–they–do–it–in–diners–full–view? kitchens. The blond paneling in the restaurant is reminiscent of that in the suites above Quadrato.

The Four Seasons Canary Wharf is built on the site of the old West India Quay where ships docked three abreast unloading precious spices, silks and tea from the Canary Islands and other alien ports of call. Redevelopment of the "docklands," as the area was called, started in the 1980's, and guests find themselves not only next to London's newest business district but within ten minutes of the Tower of London, with its Crown Jewels, and the Tower Bridge, and Royal Observatory in historic Greenwich.

At Quadrato, I sat next to the owner of Dress Circle, one of London's – and the world's – best musical theater CD and drama books stores. Starting with a first course of roasted scallops with Parma ham and parmesan crust, fig reduction, moving on to a pasta course of homemade spinach tagliatelle with porcini mush-rooms and thyme; these were followed by a main course of seared wild sea bass with trompette mushrooms, celeriac, carrots and tamarind reduction.

After dinner I swam in the twenty-meter (65-foot) infinity pool after a few minutes in a hot tub the size of other hotels' pools!

"Famous for Business; Fabulous for Fashion."   So goes the hotel's brochure on Canary Wharf shopping which reads like a Fifth or Madison Avenue inventory: Hugo Boss, Gant, Church's English Shoes, the Body Shop, Reebok Sports Shop for a few. The services rival them: Citibank, Barclays Bank, the Gentry Hair & Spa and the Little Unicorn Day Nursery. But as I walked around, fanned by fresh breezes from the Thames, I saw a different scene. The various sized sailing merchant ships huddled at attention in slips as numerous as horses' stalls in Saratoga, once America's horse racing capital. It all had me conjuring up in my mind that glorious empirical past that Charles Dickens awakened me to as a boy. Hooray for the Four Seasons Canary Wharf!

At one point, I sat down with the Marketing Director of the Four Seasons Canary Wharf. Here are some notes from our meet-ing: *she worked at Four Seasons for ten years . . . hotel ten years old in December . . . Canary Wharf area being developed for 2012 Olympics . . . deals tend to be on the weekends as with the rest of London hotels; otherwise try to maintain rates . . . water taxi takes you to Tower of London, Greenwich, Royal Embankment . . . she's from Tipperary, Ireland . . . Isadore Sharp, head of Four Seasons, based in Toronto and visits in the summer . . . celebs can drive incog-nito into garage and get to their floor from there; this isn't necessarily a place for celebs who want to be "seen" . . .*

My own first taste of the hospitality and ambiance that have become hallmarks of Four Seasons was staying at the former Inn on The Park on Park Lane, which became London's and the world's first Four Seasons Hotel. Modern, but with a luxurious, warm flare; a different world – and, yet, a completely comfortable one! Isadore "Issy" Sharp, the well-respected founder, Chairman and CEO of the privately owned Four Seasons, notes, "The reason for our success is no secret. It comes down to one single principle that transcends time and geography, religion and culture. It's the Golden Rule – the simple idea that if you treat people well, the way you would like to be treated, they will do the same."

He continues, "There was no vision, there was no grand

dream, but there has always been a consistent thread and it propels us forward today, as we continue to grow globally, and that's service. . . . One way to characterize Four Seasons service would be to call it an exchange of mutual respect performed with an attitude of kindness. . . . I sat down with our communications experts and wrote down the fundamentals of our culture, which is based on the Golden Rule – to treat others as you wish to be treated. A lot of companies talk about having a culture, but we knew we had to walk the talk if we expected it to thrive in our hotels."

Mr. Sharp, who once worked in the construction business with his father, graduated in architecture from Ryerson Institute of Technology in Toronto. He opened the first Four Seasons, a modest motor hotel, in Toronto in 1961. Among his long list of accomplishments, Mr. Sharp has received Lifetime Achievement Awards from the International Hotel Investment Fund, the American Lodging Investment Summit and the Ernst & Young Entrepreneur of the Year Program. He recently penned a book on the history and philosophy of his company called "Four Seasons: The Story of a Business Philosophy."

"When you return time and again to a much-loved hotel, it is easy to be blinded by sentiment; to see the patina of one's own nostalgia rather than the pockmarks of reality," one travel journalist wrote on visiting Four Seasons Park Lane. "For this reason, I find myself holding my breath when I return here, hoping they have innovated a little; done something that will serve to surprise.

"A few days prior to our most recent visit, a reader had written, bemoaning the dated state of most TVs and sound equipment in deluxe hotels, saying that he expected at least the same quality as at home, but preferably something better. Oh dear, I thought, remembering the dated TVs at Four Seasons London. Imagine, therefore, my delight to see that plasma screens were gradually being installed throughout the hotel; that the wondrously comfortable Sealy beds were now uniformly topped with crisp white Frette, bordered by ginger thread; and the flowery bed covers were gone.

"The changes were subtle, but reflected what is going on in our own homes. The look remains traditionally English, accessorized by an ever increasing display of locally sourced antique furniture, but now there is a lightness of touch, an absence of frilly swags; a cooler style of artworks festooning the walls; a lick of color on the white architraves.

"At lunch in Lanes Restaurant, I was, once again, surprised by the excellent cold buffet. Service, throughout, represented the benchmark for London, and at breakfast, there were families, couples and noticeably contented celebrity guests who were all so at ease that it really did feel like home.

"The newly renovated Four Seasons Executive Suites, with Park view balconies, such as number 901, really impressed me, as they are perfect for couples. We stayed next door in our usual two–bathroom Park Suite, numbers 902/904, which was looking the best I have ever seen it. You can connect thee large suites with an Executive to form a superb family suite. The very quiet Apsley Suites, such as number 330, which have two bathrooms, are also completely redone. The specialty suites, which all have terraces, such as Vanity Fair, offer huge amounts of space for entertaining and are also redesigned; but even if you opt for a standard Superior room, such as number 703, you will find a very fresh, appealing look.

"Unlike some, this hotel refrains from showcasing its numerous famous guests, but offers instead a homely, comfortable retreat, with consistently excellent service. It may not be the trendiest of choices, but in terms of hotel–keeping, it defines quality."

Very nice account, although for a while there I thought I was playing bingo with all those numbers. The great thing about the Four Seasons is that it gives you, really, a rather different experience than the usual superb in–town London hotel. You may not get that feeling of walking through great history here, but you will get the "new" London, the high–tech, gleaming glass and steel London best represented by the Millennium Eye Ferris wheel on the Thames. London really is simultaneously an ancient and an ultra–modern city. It is only up to you to choose which.

We, however, have to get a move on if we're to make our check–in time at our next hotel, which, I believe is, The Milestone. Yes, indeed it is. Come along. Don't dawdle. There's still too much to see and do, and eat! More wild sea bass, anyone?

Chapter 22

The Milestone

As has been said of The Connaught, "if there wasn't a Connaught, it would have to be invented," I say so, too, about The Milestone . . . and The Goring . . . and The Haymarket. At least those were my musings late at night, after I had settled into the Milestone's Mistinguett suite for which I vainly hoped Mistinguett or her modern day equivalent would appear; earlier I had dined downstairs in the vaulted wood–paneled dining room. Ordering steak, I was content. Annell Kendall, the incredibly gracious public relations person for Red Carnation Hotels (and of which the Milestone seems to rival only the Chesterfield for the unofficial flagship title). Against the fire, three figures were silhouetted: Annabelle, I knew. And I would meet Varun Charmay, perhaps the world's greatest trumpeter of the luxury travel business with his luxurytravel.com website and videos reaching dozens of countries. And there was the porcelain–featured Julia Record whose chiseled face and impeachable graciousness disguised a workaholic public relations executive who had herded up the literary lions of travel and other magazines in their dens as head of PR for The Savoy Group. Julia would accompany me to a dinner Chairman Kwek hosted in his Millennium Mayfair hotel where she held court – and more than held her own amongst London's hot restaurants.

Here I was, like Thomas Wolfe decades before, walking, to use Wolfe's own words, on "the queer, blind, narrow, incredible, crooked streets," at The Milestone, from the Kensington Garden suite where you are served breakfast overlooking Kensington Gardens. The split–level Club Suite lounge has a court area upstairs and bedroom/lounge below decorated with red wallpaper, red–motif paintings and prints. The lounge, with a plush white sofa and animal print pillows, features a billiards table. The hotel's Princess Suite has a canopy bed right out of "Aladdin," yellow–gold walls and plush, gold carpet. But my heart belongs to where I stayed – the Mistinguett Suite, named after the famed

Folies Bergère star, Mistinguett, with glorious posters of her in full costume or, more accurately, not so full costume.

Mistinguett starred in a silent film in 1908, a year after her first engagement at the Moulin Rouge. The name of the film was "L'Empreinte." She went on to costar with Maurice Chevalier at the Folies Bergère in 1917. She had, or at least so the legend has it, a torrid love affair with the much-younger Chevalier, and it's said she was the great love of his great love life. Mistinguett died in 1956 with a funeral in Paris that rivaled the one for Rudolph Valentino. Her career had spanned half a century.

Looking at my travel notes, I see I've jotted down "I have arrived." Actually, I got there the day before, deposited my growing belongings – growing with press kits and hotel brochures – and went off to another hotel, this one courtesy of British Airlines. The Hotel Mela, the most high-tech of all the places I stayed this trip, brought me momentarily back down to middle earth (though still better than I'm normally accustomed to) before I stayed in the Mistinguett Suite of The Milestone. Where it was back up into the stratosphere.

I also loved the hotel's blue-tiled "resistance pools" – and it like all the suites is complete with flowers and plants. Yet the most distinguished feature of The Milestone, with 45 rooms and 12 suites, is its sense. "No request is too large, no detail too small," is Red Carnation's and the Milestone's motto.

"Our valued guest is second to none and that having once experienced the Milestone, our guests will not want to stay anywhere else," promotion material for the Milestone proudly proclaims.

A member of the Red Carnation Hotels Group, and overlooking Kensington Palace and Garden, the Milestone has two staff members to every guest and a whole host of services including canapés, ice and lemon provided each evening for guests staying in suites.

The Milestone took a top honor, akin to Lindbergh's solo flight across the Atlantic for hoteliers, when *Travel & Leisure* in the June 2008 issue said this: "London's Milestone Hotel, is the No. 1 hotel for service in the world."

"Excellent service isn't easy to define or measure – it's the sort of thing that falls in the category of 'you know it when you see it.'" Maria Shollenbarger continued in *Travel & Leisure*.

"Any number of luxury hotels provide the requisite high-thread-count sheets, acres of Italian marble, and teams of butlers, but great service is something else. It should be more or less invisible – except when you want it. And then, of course, it should be at your fingertips instantly. A bit of prescience is required – so as to know what guests want before they ask for it – and resourcefulness is also key. At London's Milestone Hotel, the top hotel overall, when a guest expressed an interest in rare antique toy soldiers and tanks, the concierge located a dealer the next day."

Aside from the Mistinguett Suite, my other favorite room in the hotel is the Oratory, where I breakfasted one morning. Originally the chapel of the private mansion, the Oratory is a "grade 2"-listed period Victorian room, next to the hotel's Cheneston's Restaurant. Its arched, stained-glass windows and nearly eleven-foot ceilings add to its rich Victorian luster.

I was part of a "non-incident" in the Oratory. I was meeting with a tremendously attractive young woman, Zelmira Koch, who I have worked with in New York. She had a new job, based much of the time in London, and was excited about getting married to her boyfriend. She got to the hotel first, thinking our meeting was 8 a.m. It was in fact at 9:00 a.m. When she arrived I was discreetly asked if I wanted to dine in the "chapel" part of the dining room – for maximum privacy. I told the restaurant manager it "wasn't that kind of meeting." We had a wonderful breakfast, and "Zel," as everyone calls her, told me what hotels she likes best.

The buck at The Milestone stops with Andrew Pike, the establishment's debonair and extremely friendly general manager. Pike, who joined The Milestone in October 2005, leads a team of ninety employees. He strongly believes, and ultra-satisfied guests attest to it, that "having once experienced The Milestone, our guests will not want to stay anywhere else."

Directly across from the Royal Family's Kensington Palace, with views of Kensington Gardens, The Milestone is located in a Victorian mansion built in the 1880's. Actually comprised of two grand houses, No. 1 Kensington Court was constructed from 1883 to 1884. First Baron Redesdale (1837-1916) occupied the house and was the grandfather of the famous Mitford sisters.

The six Mitford sisters (and sole brother) undoubtedly spent time at their grandfather's mansion during sojourns to London from the country where they were schooled by governesses. (Their father feared, in part, that they might develop thick calves as a result of playing field hockey at school!) The stylish, beautiful, elegant – but outlandishly behaved – sisters were known as much for their social romps as they were for their controversial political views, and they were constant fodder for the tabloids of the day.

Nancy, the eldest was a moderate socialist and penned numerous books from "Love in a Cold Climate" to biographies including "The Sun King" about Louis XIV. Pamela married millionaire physicist Derek Ainslie Jackson only to live out her days on a farm as a "poultry expert," with her companion, Giuditta Tommasi, an Italian horsewoman. Diana married an heir to the Guinness Brewery fortune, then left him to live with, and eventually marry, Sir Oswald Mosley, head of the British Union of Fascists; the pair spent some three years in prison for their political views. Unity, the fascist, was friendly with Hitler and so distraught at the conflict between her beloved England and Germany that she shot herself in the head, becoming a semi-invalid for the rest of her short life. Jessica, the communist, saved money up as a child in her "running away account" and threatened to "escape" on numerous occasions. The youngest sister, Deborah married Andrew Cavendish, the Duke of Devonshire, and the pair turned his family estate, Chatsworth, into one of the best preserved estates in the country. Hmm, she seems to be the black sheep of the family.

In 1933, The Milestone was used for guests who had been invited to the marriage, in Brompton Oratory, of Margaret Whigham to U.S. businessman Charles Sweeny. Mrs. Sweeny later became the Duchess of Argyll and was immortalized by Cole Porter in his song, "You're the Top":

> You're the nimble tread of the feet of Fred Astaire
> You're Mussolini,
> You're Mrs. Sweeny,
> You're Camembert.

Here are some of the things that make the Milestone different, according to Mr. Pike and his colleagues. However, I shall be the ultimate judge (at least here) of that:

Perfectly located within the Royal Borough of Kensington and Chelsea, overlooking Kensington Palace and Gardens and Hyde Park beyond. (Granted.)

Just minutes from The Royal Albert Hall and excellent shopping in Kensington High Street, Notting Hill Gate and Knightsbridge. (Undeniable, if at times a tad unaffordable.)

Stunning Grade Two-listed architecture, a country mansion set in the heart of London. (Self-evident, regardless of what that "grade-two" business means.)

Individually designed and decorated bedrooms with custom made fabrics and original artwork.   Many of the rooms have views directly over the park. (I didn't visit every room, but I'm willing to take their word on this.)

Six beautifully furnished two-bedroom apartments attached to the hotel with full hotel signing privileges, perfect for extra space and longer stays. (Again, though I wasn't invited, I won't hold it against them.)

Cozy lounge with fireplace and library in which to relax whilst enjoying views of Kensington Palace and Gardens. (Ahhhh, yes.)

Choice of traditional Stables Bar and contemporary Conservatory Bar in which to enjoy cocktails and excellent range of fine wines by the glass. (In – hic! – dubitably!)

Full on site leisure facilities including heated resistance pool, fully equipped gym, sauna and treatment room with resident beauty therapist on call. (I'm afraid the beauty therapist threw up her hands in my own case, but the facilities are state-of-the-art.)

Bentley limousine car service with Hotel Chauffeurs providing transfers and tours. (Once around the park, James!)

Bose I-Pods and docking stations in each room. Free unlimited wired Internet in every bedroom and free wireless Internet throughout the hotel. (Absolutely true, but please don't use the laptop in the pool, thank you.)

24-hour butler service and two members of staff to every guest. (I didn't count, but it certainly seemed that way.)

Child friendly hotel with full range of children's menus, bathrobes and slippers, personalized welcome gifts and child minding service. (Don't mind children myself, but the tiny tot services are stellar.)

Bespoke meetings, weddings and events arranged by a dedicated team. (You provide your own bride or groom, of course, but otherwise they're likely to do everything else for you.)

Green Tea or glass of Champagne served on arrival. (Delish.)

Choice of 30 soaps offered to guests staying in suites. (Showering with 30 soaps can be a challenge, but the aroma is fantastic!)

Different old-fashioned sweets provided each night at turn-down. (Yum.)

Bedtime book and reading light provided on first stay at turn-down. (What? No butler to read a beddy-bye story to me?)

Canapés, ice and lemon provided each evening for guests staying in suites. (Starting to get a little full, actually, but maybe just this one more . . .)

Pet friendly hotel with pet preference forms, pet menus, pet bedding, pet minding and dog walking amongst services available. (Didn't bring my pet python, but it doesn't get out much anyway.)

Choice of pillow types including anti-allergy and orthopedic. (The more pillows, the better, is my motto.)

Extensive range of menus with emphasis on British seasonal cuisine. All dietary requirements catered for and zero use of convenience foods. (How convenient!)

Andrew Pike, General Manager of the Milestone, took me on a personal tour of some of the suites in the hotel and as he did, talked a bit about the different features. "We've got fifty-seven rooms here so it's quite small by London standards," he said. "It's been a hotel since the 1920's. Originally, it was two private townhouses with two different architects. It's Grade 2 listed so we're not allowed to change the outside."

Aha! So that's what "Grade 2" means. But I'm interrupting.

"Our company, Red Carnation, took it over in 1999. It's had continuous investment put into it. Every one of our rooms and suites is totally different. I'm going to pick a couple to show you."

Short walk down the hall. Master key out, presto.

"A lovely little balcony; sleigh bed. We have a lot of antique furniture. We bring in beautiful antiques and pieces from all over the world. Because every room is different people have particular ones that they love to use. This one is particularly nice because of the balcony. They're very English in style."

My note: Some rooms/suites have private terraces. This is a very private hotel – very British. It's the kind of hotel people will come to who want lots of luxury and personal service – but they don't necessarily want to be recognized. Yes, I know what a bother that can be.

"Fifty–seven rooms with over a hundred staff here . . . so that means that every one of our guests get shown around the hotel, shown around their room or suite, normally a complimentary glass of champagne upon their arrival or green tea. If you stay in one of the suites, there's a knock on the door and we come up with a beautiful basket of soaps and they can select whatever soaps they want for their stay. Wi–Fi is complimentary throughout the hotel.

" . . . We think if people are paying 300–400 pounds a night for a room, we do not charge for the newspaper or the Wi–Fi . . . " Indeed. Why Fi, otherwise?

"You're not nickel–and–diming people," I say, trailing along.

The master key is whisked out again.

"This is one of our split–level master suites . . . I take it it's okay to say it's particularly liked by gentlemen because you've got the wonderful table here – you can dine on it, have a meeting. And you've got a pool table here. Some of the wallpaper is hand-painted to look like shelves of books so you've got a library feeling here. You're facing Kensington Palace – just through the trees there. And the beautiful gardens of Hyde Park, so it's a great, great location.

"We had some guests once who were staying with us, and they wanted to have tea at The Ritz and they asked me, 'How do we get to The Ritz from here?' 'It's ten minutes in a cab.' I told them. 'No, we want to walk it,' they said.

"So we mapped a little route for them, and they would do the route from here to The Ritz in the Park. In fact the only time they had to cross the road was at Hyde Park Corner and St. James' Park. When they got back, we asked them how long did it take and they said forty–five minutes. You can actually explore London quite a bit just walking.

"If you're staying in some of our rooms, you have the choice of not one but two kinds of bathrobes. We've got a thick toweling robe and what we call a 'waffle weave' which is much lighter. And it's all about little extra comforts. We're big on fresh flowers. They're everywhere. Quite a lot of white orchids. They're across the hotel.

"We have nine junior suites, and we've also got two two-bedroom apartments for longer stays . . . with a fully fitted kitchen. Our standard rooms, however, start at around 300 pounds."

At the outset of this book I told you I'd be keeping my eye open for savings and specials at these otherwise expensive hostelries. The Milestone, believe it or not, does have a couple of good smart "buys." For one, a complimentary glass of champagne (or green tea) is yours upon arrival. You can sip either while you listen to the Bose MP3 players and docking stations in every room and suite. Furthermore, guests in suites receive canapés every evening. But here's the real savings – periodically, the Milestone runs a special that for every two nights you stay in a suite, the third night is free. Also, its "Showtime Package," which includes a full English breakfast, dinner and two tickets to a theater of your choice starts at $680/dbl.

Last but not least, afternoon tea is served from 3 to 6 in the Park Lounge and the Conservatory. It costs a quite reasonable $20 for tea and scones and $40 for tea, scones, finger sandwiches and pastries.

A milestone is a marker by the side of the road which tells you how far you've come, or have to go. However, when you reach this Milestone, you'll know you've arrived.

Chapter 23

"41"

My next stop was a sister Como hotel to The Goring, "41." "41," you say? Well, if you're in London and ask a taxi driver where "41" is – you will most likely have finally stumped a London cabby. It's a bit of a secret in London.

"41" has to be the most unusual hotel I've ever stayed in. First of all, it seems much larger than it is. It's only one floor. But you'll be floored by this floor. Its twenty-one deluxe guest rooms and four split-level suites are all on one level at 41 Buckingham Palace Road. Really, though, it's the top floor of the Reubens Hotel, including what used to be that hotel's ballroom.

But "41" is different in other ways as well. Its "executive lounge" is like the living room of a great manor house. (In fact, this is something true of all the hotels in this book – you're staying in a great manor house with many floors – with the exception of 41, of course). Across from the Royal Mews, where the Queen leaves and enters Buckingham Palace, the first thing you notice when you enter "41" is the black-and-white checked marble floor cradled by a mahogany corridor. As I mentioned, the double-height Executive Lounge is like a salon in a manor house. But what I have not yet mentioned is that the master bath in the second-floor bedroom of the duplex has a "secret " door – it actually isn't so secretive and could well be a storage closet in any other bathroom – but it leads to the mezzanine of the Executive Lounge. Several times, I'd surprise guests as they used the two "complimentary" computers here and I walked past them to a traditional afternoon tea of complimentary cheese and crackers of every sort.

The New York Times raved there's "no better cocoon in England's capital" than "41." "41" came in sixth in Europe in service behind The Milestone, first in Europe, Hotel du Cap-Eden-Roc in Cap d'Antibes, France, and the Mandarin Oriental in Munich, which won second place.

"41's" courtesy and attention to detail extends to early check-ins and late check-outs. It's all in black and white, without hard and fast rules about late checkouts, merely the fact you may, *may* be "subject to a supplementary charge." No threat. No warning. Just a polite notation. And cancellations can be done only the day prior to arrival – *not* the week prior or some such. The Executive Lounge's "pantry" with its assortment of cheeses and cakes is for guests on a complimentary basis. This note: "Our bright and airy Executive Lounge provides round–the–clock dining, including from 8:30 p.m. the opportunity to "plunder the pantry." Resident manager Andrew Gortchacow writes to guests. To a cheese–and–cracker pantry raider from way back like me this may well be the epitome of Temptation!

"We trust you will agree '41' offers the very highest standards of comfort and luxury," Malcolm Hendry, general manager of "41," writes to each guest.

"It would be a pleasure to meet you in our stunning Executive Lounge, which is open from early morning when we serve a delicious Continental and English breakfast, through until late when we can tempt you with after dinner drinks. As General Manager, I would be happy to answer any queries you may have. I would also welcome any ideas or comments on any improvements we can make and invite you to contact the Resident Manager for a complete tour of the facilities."

The closest New York hotel to the spirit and comfort of The Milestone or "41" is The Lowell. "The reputation we enjoy as your 'Home away from Home' is never taken for granted and we strive consistently to exceed your expectations," says Ashish Verma, General Manager. "Each and every member of The Lowell Family of employees is dedicated to ensure a most pleasant experience for you and for all your future visits as our honored guest."

The Lowell's website also says, "One might think that this 1927 landmark building, situated on a peaceful tree–lined street is in the heart of Paris. The Lowell Hotel, however, is centrally located on Manhattan's Upper East Side, between Madison and Park Avenues, steps away from Manhattan's famous museums and New York City's world–renowned Madison and Fifth Avenue boutiques and shops. From the architecture to the service, this hotel reflects discreet aristocratic and understated European elegance.

"A liveried doorman ushers the guest to an Empire Style reception desk with no registration lines. The "hotel intime" atmosphere is complete with lobby designed by Dalmar Tift III which combines Art Deco touches, French Empire Style furniture with lustrous golden scalamandres, chiaroscuro walls and a rare desk console signed by Edgar Brandt. The lobby is contiguous to the famous Post House Restaurant, the entrance of which is separated by an original 1920's door.

"The management, who is highly respectful of their elite customers' privacy, run this New York-European haven like a 'pied-a-terre,' a home away from home. The Lowell offers forty-seven suites and twenty-five deluxe rooms, all of which are uniquely decorated with exquisite antique furniture and upholstered in fine fabrics. 18th and 19th Century prints, Chinese porcelains, wood burning fireplaces, libraries, full service kitchens and marble baths with brass fixtures complete the elegance offered in these comfortable suites. The Lowell provides Bulgari bathroom amenities, VCR's, DVD and CD players, all wireless high speed Internet access, and points for PCs and fax machines in all accommodations. Eleven suites also have private terraces. A writer for *The New York Times* recently encapsulated the mission and atmosphere of the hotel by stating: The Lowell would scream class, if class did that sort of thing!"

One might even say of the Lowell is that it is a London hotel in the heart of Manhattan.

Chapter 24

The Chesterfield

The portrait of Winston Churchill gazed down at me, slightly to the left of the large, round table where I was writing parts of this book. But the diminutive awning of the Chesterfield Hotel, jet black with a red carnation stamped above the word "Chesterfield," told little of the glories of the hotel itself, hidden away in the middle of Mayfair like a lost treasure. Let the grand hotels such as The Grosvenor House pridefully belly up to Hyde Park. The Chesterfield, like the protagonist in "The Little Engine That Could," may not have emerged from the back tunnels of Mayfair, but in service, style and ambiance, it can compete with the big boys.

Thomas Wolfe, perhaps the greatest epic American writer since Herman Melville, settled in a Mayfair "service flat," from where he wrote a friend, John Terry, that he had "a valet like Ruggles of Red Gap." This anecdote courtesy of Andrew Turnbull's marvelous biography of Thomas Wolfe.

I'm in one of the Chesterfield's luxurious suites, which with its 107 rooms and suites, reflect the mood, formality and informality of an English cottage populated by none other than those great international stars of stage and screen Vivien Leigh and Laurence Olivier. Their country house was a small converted abbey but the Chesterfield is like the vibrancy of their personalities – at once indulgent and yet, like Cleopatra's asp, skilled in leaving its mark, albeit a beneficent one. (Cleo being a role Ms. Leigh played with kittenish expertise in the film of Shaw's *Caesar and Cleopatra*.) Sit in the cozy bar, with green leather covered stools and iced champagne right before you, and you are Mr., Mrs., Ms., or Miss Chesterfield!

Rising from a seat at my round table I'd go around a plush gold-colored couch to a cavernous bedroom several steps below the bedroom entryway, overlooking a charming terrace.

The Chesterfield's sweet but with a bite, like a cappuccino purchased on Mayfair's Half Moon Street nearby. Around the corner, literally, is Shepherd's Market, as quaint a gathering of mews, renovated horse stables and pubs as you'll find in all of London. Shepherd's Market takes its name from Edward Shepherd who was granted a license to hold a cattle market several days a week. The area, in the very heart of Mayfair off posh Half Moon Street, is a Greenwich Village–type enclave in the midst of rows of mansions and multi–million–pound townhouses. You expect to see Charles Dickens' Oliver Twist amble down one of its narrow lanes although it's literally miles from London's East End where some of the book of *Oliver Twist* was set.

"I tell my managers, don't employ people with experience; employ them with the right attitude," Oliver Raggett, the General Manager of the Chesterfield, told me as we sat in the hotel's clubby bar. (Despite the name, he's no relation to Mr. Dickens' famous urchin.)

The Chesterfield opened in the Thirties as an independently owned and operated hotel of another name. It became part of the Red Carnation Hotels in 1982 when it was renamed "The Chesterfield." "At the heart of Red Carnation is Mrs. Tollman, our Founder and President" Mr. Raggett explained. "I've worked for many different companies which have been by shareholders and dividends. Of course, you want to make some money! But at the end of the day, Mrs Tollman wants us to run hotels that everyone is proud to work for."

"The Tollman family see the staff as the heartbeat of all of their hotels and even in the worst of times there have been very few, if any, redundancies. I'm really, really fortunate. Because we have this hotel listed as a four–star property, but provide service that is at five–star level. I've got a staff of 140."

"Why only four stars?" I asked.

"We don't have facilities like a health club, and some of our bedrooms are smaller than you would find in a five star."

"The staff are passionate about their jobs. And it's not done by chance. They love their jobs. In the last three or four years, it has been very tough to find staff because there were lots of opportunities. And, in England, working in hotels has never been seen as a profession. So I've said to my managers: Don't necessary employ people with experience, employ them because they have the right attitude . . . so we've been quite successful getting people in here who want to work." Of course, when Mr. Raggett says "attitude" he doesn't mean it as we would in the States, he means a *good* attitude.

"I've got many, many guests who have over a hundred 'stays' at the hotel, that's not nights but coming back to the hotel more than one hundred times. Our most regular guest has 390 stays! That's not nights. He's come back 390 times! Many are corporate people who live outside of London and use The Chesterfield as their base. We also have many people from America who are over ten or fifteen times a year.

"It adds up. Because we treat our staff a little better, we get the right people. Guests come back and see the same faces, staff who may not be valued in so many of the brand hotels because of the transient nature of the job. I've been here two and a half years and am one of the shortest serving members of the team.

"Andrew, the General Manager at the Milestone has been there for more than five years and so on. Guests like the stability; it really does mean something to them."

Here's an example of how great staff can make a difference, as Mr. R recounts: " . . . the Saudi Embassy (a block away) accidentally cut through a cable outside. We lost all our power, no lifts, no water. So for five hours we had no electricity and we didn't have one complaint. We didn't hide away in our offices, we were out front tackling the problem head on, welcoming guests, explaining the problem and keeping them informed. Everyone went away happy. Of course, it's not a nice thing to happen but . . . . Another thing. We don't try and nickel–and–dime our guests. About a year and a half ago, we installed Wi-Fi and internet and provide this at no charge. It was a great move, we could have made a substantial additional income by charging but we've made so many friends and generated a lot of goodwill by providing it free of charge"

Thanks you very much Mr. R for a very pleasant, if brief, stay, and for all the genial conversation. Well, once again I must rouse myself from an extremely comfortable couch and "lift" myself upstairs, pack and move on to the next item on the agenda. Ah, well.

Chapter 25

The Metropolitan Hotel

The Metropolitan is a member of the COMO Hotels and Resorts, our old friends, which indeed are defined by a special Asian spirit: a commitment to servicing guests to ensure total relaxation and rest. "We nurture each and every one of you, bring families together, and for business travelers, pre-empt the smallest need to ease your day-to-day cares," a website promotion promises. "This detail, passion and integrity makes each stay unique. It defines not just our service standards but the soul of each property. This is because we want you to feel the essence of the destination – in food, architecture, and the way we help you navigate a place, to experience its many layers. So whether it's a private island in the Indian Ocean or a city hotel at the heart of Bangkok, COMO Hotels and Resorts – an award-winning, privately owned company – knows how to make memories last."

Wow. I've had best friends who've never treated me that well. COMO Hotels is not unlike that other new major force in the world of high-end hospitality, The Millennium & Copthorne Hotels, Plc, the globe-spanning domain of Chairman Kwek. These are companies who specialize in hotels but have a sophisticated international understanding. In the new global economy, it strikes me that this is an indispensable quality. When you run a major luxury hotel in a major city these days, your clientele will be truly international. The more you can genuinely relate to a wide range of customers who themselves have a wide range of customs, the more likely, it stands to reason, you are to be successful. Or, at least, to please your guests.

Which isn't to say that a hotel like the Metropolitan isn't at the same time delightfully English. With a scrumptious afternoon tea all their own. Here again I must refer to my audio notes:

De'Light tea – olive oil muffins, scones made with 50 percent light flour and 50 percent potato flour so not "stodgy" – more crumbly; low-fat crème fraîiche rather than clotted cream; organic desserts; cupcakes use lowfatlow fat cream cheese, less sugar (and more natural like fruit purees); no-bread sandwiches are little pots filled with, say, smoked salmon with cucumber and dill sandwiches, roast beef with horseradish – all quite different to other teas

"Instead of having – you'll have your pot of tea but then you can have the ultimate iced tea which can be served either alcoholic or non-alcoholic," Jo James, marketing and public relations manager for the hotel, said. And then we have these really delicious Eco-Tinis – everything sourced from the M25 so it's London gin, the honey is from Soho, all the fruits have come from nearby organic farms ... these rhubarb, raspberries, the pears, everything we use for those have all come from the manager's brother's farm lot. In case you hadn't heard, local naturally grown produce is all the rage in haute cuisine, and even not so haute cuisine, nowadays. No less a figure in England than the Prince of Wales is an expert, and gentleman farmer practitioner himself, on the subject. In fact, it seems the Prince himself has dabbled a bit in the hotel supply biz. Here's a blurb from the Prince of Wales official website on the subject:

"Organic mutton from Home Farm (the Prince's Duchy Home farm) is sent to Calcot Manor Hotel near Tetbury and the Ritz in London. The Prince is enthusiastic about restoring mutton (meat from a two-year-old sheep), to the dinner tables of the nation after speaking to struggling sheep farmers who found they could no longer get a decent price for older ewes. To this end, The Prince launched the Mutton Renaissance campaign."

Not quite sure they have mutton at Nobu, the Michelin-starred restaurant at the Metropolitan. They seem to go in more for Eastern accented cuisine. But one service at the hotel does intrigue me: Something they call the "COMO Shambhala Urban Escape" which offers "a full range of specifically created COMO Shambhala therapies and spa products." And if that's not healthful enough for you, there is also "a well-equipped gym (with personal trainers and yoga practitioners available on request), steam room and power showers" on site. Which is, as they used to say in Swinging Sixties London, outtasight.

It feels like we've barely checked in to the Metropolitan and now we have to be moving along again, to The Halkin. Now that you've been fully revived by those Shambhala therapies, you should have no problem shaking a leg.

Chapter 26

The Halkin

At The Lanesborough and Connaught there is original art. At the Halkin, I was intrigued, yeah enchanted, with the watercolors of musical notes. Were they temples, pyramids or merely the heights of the imagination of a musical mind?

But I soon came to see that the best art at the Halkin was the rooms themselves. I had the most beautiful flower arrangement. Two large pink roses in a glass bowl. I wanted to pack them in my suitcase and keep them forever. My room at the Halkin – from its teak-walled hallway to large, what must have been triple glazed windows – not a sound came in – to the brass drawer fittings on the wooden desk – was a modern museum piece!

In a Como Hotels and Resort brochure in my room I ran across a photo of the Como Hotel on Cocoa Island in the Maldives. It was a scene which was tranquility itself. "Solitude is happiness for one who is content," a caption read. And that's the Halkin. Contentment. Now, if The Goring is looking back at a sort of family palace – the Halkin reminded me of my grandmother's home in Ithaca, New York, with the dark wood paneling, the over-stuffed chairs, but with a kind of buzz her house never, ever had – the Halkin somehow manages to be "now" but without being in-your-face contemporary. It's comfort, peace, success arrived.

Actually, it is the fanciest parking garage in the world! Conceived, created and owned by Christina Ong, the Halkin's weathered Georgian façade bricks, Portland stone and arching windows, surrounded by a luxurious green grass ribbon on one side, Belgravia embassies, mansions, and sprinkled with converted horse-carriage houses rival the nearby Lanesborough directly on Hyde Park Corner. And to say the Halkin is "green" is an understatement. Even its carpets were chosen for their basic earth and sky tones. Lucid pale blue on the fifth floor, sand and russet red on others.

Australian chef David Thompson brings Royal Thai traditions to Nahm, the Halkin's Michelin-starred restaurant that opened in 2001 and where I had lunch with the hotel's attractive, articulate director of public relations, Jo James. Light poured through the arched windows of the restaurant, rippling on the pale gold walls. This airiness is reflected throughout the hotel with the heart of the hotel's design concept being "expansion of space." Valentino Vago painted the mural entitled "skyscape" on the ceiling of the atrium lobby to enhance this seamless space theme.

The Halkin is about sunlight and mews and grass and most of all, serenity. It is a rose of Belgravia. Even Nahm is a teak, gold and russet refuge reflecting some of the discreet chic of the hotel's forty-one bedrooms. Australian chef David Thompson spices the freshest possible vegetables, fish and meat subtly, artfully in Royal Thai tradition. While I was in residence, I was fortunate enough to have lunch with Jo James, whose leading lady good looks and effervescent personality reminded me, albeit in quite a feminine way, of Al Pacino, an idol of hers. In fact, along with the press kit she left me a card depicting Pacino and bearing this Pacino quote: "Vanity is my favorite sin."

I had both "breadless tea" (at the Metropolitan) and lunch with Jo James of the Halkin. Jo filled me in on many things Halkin.

"Originally, the hotel's building was a car park, which was turned into the Halkin," Jo told me. "So that was the first COMO hotel and the reason it's called COMO is because its Christina Ong and Melissa Ong, the owner and her daughter, respectively. (And whose combined initials, of course, spell COMO. The hotel has no connection to either the Italian lake or the American singer.). The vision for the Halkin was to create the first boutique hotel, so very pared-down luxury, very understated style, 41 guest rooms, very personal and individual style of service."

As for the Metropolitan, Jo explained it was:

"A rather dowdy, four-star hotel, which came up for sale. What the new owners wanted was a hotel with a destination restaurant and a destination bar, hence Nobu and the MetBar. Prior to MetBar you didn't go to a hotel for a night out. The Metropolitan introduced a policy of membership chosen by 'movers and shakers' in the media and celebrity news world. Kate Moss and other models hung out here. MetBar opened eleven years ago and the market is now saturated. You don't pay to become a member; you are invited to become a member. Many guests are music oriented and Oasis, Kings of Leon, Duran Duran are happy to guest D.J. for free! The Johnny Orson show launches in March – like an old David Letterman–style T.V. set and when members come to the bar, they're watching an exclusive T.V. show just for them – very spontaneous, no rehearsal.

"Halkin, on the other hand, is much more discreet than cutting edge, on–the–forefront. Other Metropolitan guests include Kings of Leon, Fu Fighters, New Kids on the Block, Pussy Cat Dolls. The Brit Awards crème–de–la–crème staying here next week."

Jo turned out to be a regular font of info. Here are some other "Jo notes" as I call them, a short–hand version of our interview:

"Celebrities include Bruce Willis, Cameron Diaz, Denzel Washington, Giorgio Armani . . . very happening, fun hotel . . . a main hotel for London Fashion Week; third floor rented out by designers as show rooms . . . Madonna has stayed here in the past . . . Boris Becker was a MetBar habitué . . . Mayfair pays a fee to be Fashion Week official hotel but Metropolitan has a natural relationship.

"The Metropolitan guests tend to be younger than those at The Halkin. I also talked to its manager. Halkin clients' average age spans 40–60 and the Metropolitan range generally is 28–50, on a very generalized level – having 'made it big' versus 'trying to make it'! . . . London's Nobu has been a success since its beginning and is 'the restaurant,' . . . no paintings on the rooms' walls – the room is the painting; design doesn't include clutter – wide open spaces – cleaning is actually more of a challenge . . . It has always attracted and looked after people from the music industry.

"We have such a cross–section of people that stay here; we do have the people who work for the corporate operation – we have from one end those who might be senior VP, VP level of a multinational company down to an 18–year–old from, I don't know, Tennessee or Pennsylvania, wherever you want, just starting off a band in America and trying to make it big in the U.K. And you know, you can spot one of them standing here and drinking beer out of a bottle while another over here is drinking Cristal champagne out of the finest crystal glass. So that cross–section is certainly something that is very exciting to work with because of the challenges and the requirements that the different type of people have, and the fact that they can live together in this type of environment is as welcoming to one set as it is to the other. And that's nice – it gives the hotel a buzz."

It was while talking to Jo that it dawned on me for the first time that the London grand hotel experience is now quite varied. I think you could have said not that long ago, a few decades, that there really was only one overall type of style, that exemplified usually by The Savoy or the Ritz or even the smaller "classic" British hostelries. But nowadays, with London the international financial center that it is, as well as a cultural mecca, there are all sorts of hotel "styles" to be found, especially in the top tiers. As Jo herself told me, "The kids stay at the Metropolitan and the parents or grandparents stay at the Four Seasons." I didn't have to reflect long which category I myself now fit into. One hotel manager asked me if I wished to accompany him on his daily jog, around Hyde Park, which is a good five miles per circuit. Thanks, but no thanks. Now if it were only twenty years ago . . .

Jo James obligingly expanded a bit on this "age-gap" phenomenon: "At the Metropolitan you have the Met Bar and Nobu; we can get away with something a bit more racy at the Metropolitan whereas the Halkin is slightly more laid back, discreet." Specials at the Halkin have included one called "all about me and you get free access to all the movies, a box of chocolates in your room on arrival, a gift for you to take home, and some really nice toiletry amenities. So they relax and indulge themselves. There's a fabulous family package at the Halkin called 'Family Affairs in Belgravia.' And the kids get milkshakes and cookies and the parents get champagne in two interconnecting rooms for Easter (a deal for £500 for two rooms)."

Rates, in general, charge according to "availability." But unlike many hotels, you will see a parity of rates across "all demand channels," Jo explained, on the hotels' own websites and travel vendors, "with all of our hotels, our eight properties, we have a rate parity program."

The Nahm offers master cooking classes eight times a year. "It's a huge sellout with both our U.K.-based customers but also our international," she says. "Real food enthusiasts get up early on Saturday morning. They learn how to make a complete meal, and everyone sits down together for lunch with food that they've prepared. The first three dates this year have already sold out within a few days of the dates being published." Both the Halkin and the Metropolitan are members of Como, which is now Christina Ong's global brand. In "Home from Home," Como's newsletter, you'll not only find some news of Mount Street, a ten-minute walk from the Metropolitan and twenty from the Halkin. The newsletter, in fact, provides a pretty good snapshot of the attractions of this area of town, even if some of the names have changed since publication. In other words, it gives a sense of what it's like to stroll around the neighborhood:

"It began with Marc Jacobs. In February 2007 the designer chose this pretty Mayfair street, with its red-brick buildings and bijou charm, to site his flagship store. It's easy to see the attraction.

"Others have followed. The neighborhood, quietly sandwiched between Berkeley Square and Park Lane, is suddenly the new hot spot, alive with London's fashion crowd and a roll call of retailers rumored to be eyeing up real estate. The biggest new openings have included the intergalactic Balenciaga flagship. From creative director Nicolas Ghesquière and artist Dominique Gonzalez-Foerster, the space features a multi-leveled ceiling in orange Perspex and white lacquered metal racks reaching out with clothes from a spacecraft structure.

"French shoe designer Christian Louboutin, famous for his red-soled shoes and dagger plinths, is another to grace the wide pavements with the opening of his European flagship. And Aesop, the cult beauty brand from Sydney, Australia – featuring all natural skin, body and haircare products – has also chosen Mount Street for its first UK standalone store.

"At the far eastern end of the street quintessential English outfitters Alfred Dunhill has found its spiritual home in grade two-listed Bourdon House, once the Duke of Westminster's Mayfair residence. The Georgian building now provides three floors of retail space including an impressive Dunhill emporium and the Discovery Room housing custom menswear and leather. Alfred's, Dunhill's inaugural private members club, can also be found here. There's a restaurant nurtured by Executive Chef Mark Hix, a private dining room, a 'dishonesty' bar and four bedrooms, one a replica of the Dukes own sleeping quarters. It is by invitation only. However non-members can still visit the spa, private cinema, humidor and cigar keeps.

"By night the neighborhood is reeling in some well-heeled punters. Another private members' club, widely acknowledged for its bona fide exclusivity, is George, created by Mark Birley (also behind Annabel's and Mark's Club). You'll find it at numbers 87–88.

"Scotts fish restaurant has recently reopened after a £3 million refurbishment. When Kate Moss celebrated her birthday here last year she joined a celebrity clientele that includes Jemima Khan and Harold Pinter. Leather banquettes and twinkling mirrors ooze glamour while occasional splashes of modernity include some spectacular art and a gleaming crustacean bar piled high with shellfish.

"Just around the corner at Farm Street veteran club owner Piers Adam has teamed up with film director Guy Ritchie to revamp an 18th-century watering hole, the Punch Bowl. The pair has given it a thoroughly British makeover with flower baskets hanging outside and candles wedged in Champagne bottles.

"And finally, if you're in the area, don't miss a quick peak at Timothy Taylor's new gallery. His second in London, this exciting venue gives more space to Taylor's favorites such as Bridget Riley, Sean Scully and Fiona Rae. Designer/architect Ron Arad will be showing at Carlos Place from March."

You see? Just as I've been trying to tell you all along. London of late offers the best of both worlds, the classic and the ultramodern, sometimes cheek-by-jowl on the same street.

Even the hotel brochures can be startlingly modern. "Palette of aubergine, cream and white created by Keith Hobbs of United Designers." So says the extravagant mauve cloth-covered Como Hotel and Resort brochure, which further explains that the Met Bar downstairs is "a cult classic among the music, media and fashion crowd."

"It's hard to comprehend just how much of a history hotels have," Jo, who does PR for both the Halkin and the Metropolitan Hotels, in case you hadn't noticed, stated. "When you work in the hotel industry, it kind of reminds you why you got into the hotel industry in the first place. The fact that the hotels are glamorous and you know they've got so much energy and kind of lots of secrets and you're kind of part of that world – I'm really enjoying it."

Having lunch at Nahm, I could certainly see how she came to that conclusion. I felt like I was dining in a sea. A South Sea, most likely.

"Yes, beautiful, yes. So you've got – one of the things with the restaurant and the hotel, it's very understated, so even though you've kind of got use of gold, kind of texturing, it's still very tastefully done as opposed to being very shiny surfaces and things like that. But everything's been handpicked."

When he got to London the Nahm chef wanted, according to Jo, "to do something super, super authentic. So he had a collection of memorial books that date back hundreds of years. Apparently there's a tradition in Thailand that when a female member of the family passes over, they actually have a memorial book for her, including her superstitions, recipes, all these kind of things. And so he had a collection of over a hundred of these. So all of the recipes that are on the menu actually date back – and then he's added obviously a slightly modern twist on that, more modern ingredients. One of the nice things about Nahm is that it hasn't been kind of pared down to suit a Westernized palate – there's a lot of authentic flavors. . . . All of the fresh fruits, vegetables, the spices and everything all come over every week from Thailand, so everything's super authentic. All of the proteins come from the U.K., from various farms.

London Fashion Weekly had one of its kick-off parties at the Met – throughout the first floor, including the Met Bar and in suites above. I had invited Julia Record, a prominent and exceptionally nice London hotel public relations executive, to join me and we poked our heads into some of the suites in which (possibly) tomorrow's name designers had set up shop temporarily.

I think the last time London buzzed with this much modernity and style was the fabled Swinging Sixties, when the Beatles and Stones and Carnaby Street seemed to have taken over the entire city and suddenly extremely distinguished gents in bowlers were letting their hair grow long and their trousers flair. From what I hear, it was a pretty wild time. Wish I'd been there. But I'm getting a strong flavor of it now here at the Halkin and the Metropolitan. "Oh, yeah, baby!" as that infamous Sixties swinger Austin Powers would say.

This time I didn't even have time to unpack. And here we are off again to the next luxurious lair. Which is, namely, The Lanesborough.

Chapter 27

The Lanesborough

The Royal Arts Commission, the Georgian Society, English Heritage and the Victorian Society played a hand together in transforming what had been St. George's Hospital, built in the mid-1800's and designed by William Wilkins, architect of London's National Gallery, into The Lanesborough. In 1719, Viscount Lanesborough had erected his country estate on the site.

Hyde Park Corner is really the center of London. You can think of it like the hub of a wheel, where you have Victoria, Knightsbridge, Park Lane, etc., acting as the spokes of that wheel, the main arteries of London. Truth be told, over the years, many a big wheel has stayed at The Lanesborough.

"This is the essence of London," writes world-renowned interior designer Trisha Wilson in her book, *Spectacular Hotels: The Most Remarkable Places on Earth.* "Butler service. Tea offered upon arrival. A change of clothing pressed immediately."

Mere steps from Buckingham Palace at Hyde Park Corner opposite Hyde Park and Constitution Arch (or, originally, Wellington Arch). My son, William, and I pulled up to the hotel – which marks the spot upon which Viscount Lanesborough built his country home in 1719 – in a tri-wheeled foot-taxi. "Welcome home!" the doorman exclaimed as Will and I climbed out of the vehicle which had come to a stop right next to a Rolls-Royce and a Bentley and a Jaguar. After all, it wouldn't be London's most luxurious and well-run hotel if the staff looked down their nose at any way guests got there.

As for its architecture, Wilson, who knows hotels better than just about anyone on earth, goes on to describe the Great Hall as "an impeccable, ordered space offering the grandest sense of having arrived. . . . The inlaid wood floors are incredible, especially those in guest rooms. Grand arches, moldings and details stand out with elaborately draped bedsteads, window treatments and period furniture defining interior residential style."

At the same time, Wilson waxes ecstatic about The

Lanesborough which, she exclaims, "bowls me over." And where she likes to summon a butler "around the clock or reserve the Royal Suite, which includes a butler and a chauffeur–driven Bentley at your service." And, in fact, every room, every suite, has butler service. Ask for a car to take you to the West End or airport and, while it may be a BMW instead of a Bentley, it's at your beck and call.

As you've seen, this is not really a book entirely about London's magnificently designed and built hotels. It is also about the people who made and love those hotels, love staying in them, and you can no more really separate them than Peter Pan from his shadow. Well, actually, you can separate Peter Pan from his shadow, but – you know what I mean.

Take Geoffrey Gelardi for example. He is the personification of The Lanesborough Hotel. Gentile, soft–spoken, impeccably groomed and dressed and yet with a sense of humor that made him never seem stuffy. He blends into the refinement and beauty of the miniature city that is The Lanesborough and is one with it. Then there is Andrew Pike, general manager of the Milestone Hotel London. "My role at the Milestone is to lead our team of over ninety employees to ensure that the service and product we provide is second to none."

Trying to make all guests feel like kings and queens is the main goal of Geoffrey Gelardi, Managing Director of The Lanesborough Hotel who has been with it since day one in 1991. A fourth generation hotelier, Gelardi spent some of his early years learning the business "washing dishes, waiting on tables and bartending." That is, he learned the hotel business from the bottom up. "I worked my way up through the ranks in a fairly concise manner, starting off at trainer level," he says in an interview with the *Independent Newspaper UK Limited*. Gelardi comments, "I don't have any degrees and in this industry I think your qualifications are really what's on your resume. My father, who was president of Trust House Forte in North America, said to me: 'You can go and spend three years at school or you can work as a staff member for three to four years.'"

Mr. Gelardi's late father worked at The Waldorf–Astoria and Trust House Forte to name a few. His grandfather simultaneously was manager of The Savoy in London and The Waldorf Towers. He himself is managing director of The Lanesborough and vice-president of operations for Rosewood Hotels & Resorts, overseeing Rosewood Group hotels in Europe, the Middle East and Asia.

Mr. Gelardi is a hotel rarity: a third generation hotelier beginning with his grandfather who, as Mr. G recollects, "was first manager of The Savoy up until, I think, 1928, and then in 1928 he was at Claridge's," and then The Waldorf-Astoria opened in New York in 1932, and he became, jointly, manager of The Savoy and The Waldorf Towers." And "Father did command a presence; written on his gravestone is 'a true gentleman.'" Mr. Gelardi himself worked at The Waldorf from about 1974 until 1976 as a graduate trainee and assistant food and beverage manager. He talked further of his illustrious grandfather:

"Well, he did originally work in the lower echelons of hotels but he did most of that in Italy and then when things became tough in Italy, he was actually on his way to North America when he stopped off in London because he ran out of money. He was actually a lawyer by trade, and for whatever was going on, the First World War and all that kind of stuff, he was also, by the way, I'm not sure it's a good thing or not, but he was also, when he lived in Italy, he was the catering director for Mussolini. Whenever there was a big function, they would call my grandfather in to help coordinate it and all that stuff. Anyway, he decided to go to North America and he got to England and needed some more money so he went to work in the hotel."

"Catering director for Mussolini – must have been in the Twenties?" I asked.

"Long before World War II. Eventually, I'm not sure exactly – when he got to London he wasn't the general manager. He got promoted to general manager at The Savoy, and then when he left The Savoy and got to Claridge's in 1928, and then in 1931 he was asked or requested to help open The Waldorf-Astoria, in 1931. He was actually given the post of general manager of The Waldorf Towers. So he was, I believe, the very first international general manager in the world, who was actually running two hotels simultaneously, although he wasn't running the whole Waldorf. I think Lucius Boomer was the original general manager. . . . I have a picture behind my desk of my grandfather standing up giving a speech to the whole of the original executive committee for The Waldorf-Astoria. It has the housekeeper there, with all their signatures. So he used to take the Queen Mary back and forth, and take my father with him actually sometimes. And then my father also worked at The Waldorf-Astoria as a receptionist in the

Towers. And when I went there in '74, I was working in all the departments, and I went to the Towers for a little while with Rene [Sautier] at the time, and this fellow came up to me and, he was an old chap, and he said, 'I understand your name's Gelardi?' And I said, 'yes, it's Geoffrey Gelardi.' He worked there; he was the head bellman. And he said, 'well, my name's Gelardi, too. Hi, I'm Ed Gelardi.' And I said, 'Well, that's amazing!' He said, 'well, what's amazing? Your granddaddy gave me the job here.' He was a second cousin and he'd been working there I don't know how many years – something like forty or fifty years and was still there. So that was sort of interesting. But, yeah, my grandfather. I have his memoirs. He was a prolific writer and very, very eloquent. I mean, far more eloquent than I ever – or even my father was – and he writes beautifully. I'm hoping to write my own book, actually, in the not too distant future. Three generations of hoteliers, along with the stories that go along with it. . . . It's amazing to see how he focused on exactly what we focus on today."

Mr. Gelardi said so much that I had to scribble down some of it; herewith my further notes of our discussions: *London led the way in going to formality without stuffiness . . . The Bellaire and The Lanesborough are his two 'children' along with his three literal children . . . tries hard to create a very friendly atmosphere . . . all of the doormen are fourteen-year veterans (from when the hotel opened); same with all but one of the concierges (one's been there a mere ten years) – they have Big John, Little John, and Old John . . . story of the £3,000/night guest with the list of five-to six complaints (i.e., wilted flowers) who gave his list to his hotel driver who told the concierge who told Geoffrey who wrote an apology letter the next day . . . hotel owns their own cars, including a Rolls-Royce Phantom. Even their cars have a proud history!*

Comparing The Lanesborough to Claridge's and The Connaught, Mr. Gelardi pointed out, "The Lanesborough is a very modern building, I mean, the guts are modern. Technologically, we're one of the most advanced hotels in the world. Certainly when we opened, we were the first one that had private line faxes, private phones in every room, and so on and so forth. Today, we still have leading edge technology: we have Wi–Fi, we have high–speed Internet, we have movies. . . .

Notes, part II: *Flat-screen TV's go up and down into cabinets . . . only hotel with triple-glazed windows . . . "we have the highest ratio of staff to rooms of any hotel in Europe and probably North America. I have over 270 staff full-time plus additional staff that we bring in."* . . . *butlers not part of housekeeping or room service like other hotels — complete area of their own with mandate to look after guests' every need* . . .

He went on. "We have a little computer on each floor that tells them when the guest is in and when the guest is out. So when you leave your room, they're supposed to go into your room – I often know when my butlers are doing a good job because I'll get a phone calls from the guests saying, 'somebody stole my shoes!' Because the butler's been in there, he's taken the shoes out to clean them, and he just hasn't gotten them back quick enough."

Yet more notes from Mr. Gelardi: *Even dry cleaning and pressing is done in-house . . . as managing director, needs to supply three elements: enough staff, enough equipment and enough training. "Then I can be demanding because they have their crutches." . . . run the highest rate and often the highest occupancy making this statistically the most successful hotel in London . . . thinks the St. Regis is the best hotel in NYC . . . Caroline Hunt likes the little rooms on the fourth floor because they're cozy, even though she can afford anything . . . Bill Gates has been a guest . . .*

And here are my random notes on The Lanesborough in general: *Can do civil service weddings . . . beautiful glass atrium in Westminster Room on Lower Ground Floor (building on a slope so can be accessed from different levels) . . . little garden . . . Wedgwood blue Wellington Room . . . Royal Suite is partly free for a tour later . . . building was hospital then vacant . . . fireplaces purely decoration today . . . great shower water pressure . . . double room with gorgeous high ceilings . . . wood paneling in many rooms . . . triple and double glazed windows . . . double suite like a library . . . pop-up television with large screen . . . Full Royal Suite stretches length of corridor but can be divided up . . . gorgeous with what appear to be antiques; free standing tub . . . French princess was proposed to in a £30,000-a-night suite with 1,000 roses, etc. – she declined but married the man within two years; either The Lanesborough or the roses did the trick.*

Michael, Front Office Manager of The Lanesborough, looks and sounds like he walked out of Noël Coward's "Tonight at 8:30" play. Debonair, with almost Cary Grant good looks and Michael Redgrave voice to match, Michael would have been very much at home on the stage. In fact, however, he's on stage every day and night at The Lanesborough. "We had a few odd concepts when we opened the hotel which didn't work. One was not to have menus in the restaurant. People couldn't get their head around that at all. For the soft opening we did try it for a couple of days

. . . and it just didn't work.

"They'd say, 'What would you like for breakfast, Mr. Morehouse?'

"You'd say, 'What have you got?'

"And they'd say, 'No, no. What would you *like?'*

"People just needed something in front of them. We used to say if you wanted to eat Lobster Thermidor standing on your head in the lobby, you're more than welcome. Imagine that! Never say 'no.' And I don't think the Japanese have got a word for 'no' which is quite interesting. Instead of saying, 'no,' you say 'wouldn't you rather,' and steer them somewhere else."

"'No problem' – it triggers something. Because if you say don't think of a blue tree, what do you think of? 'A blue tree.' Anyway, instead I got him to say, 'It's a pleasure . . . ' Anything apart from a double negative – and the word 'problem.'

Novelist Thomas Wolfe, through his alter ego George Webber, spends time in London and reflects about his own, not butler, but woman servant who looked after him in his novel *You Can't Go Home Again.* "No problem," was not part of her lexicon. "In truth . . . Mrs. Purvis, the servant had a divided loyalty, and yet, in a curious way, she also managed to convey to each of her employers a sense that her whole-souled obligation belongs to him, and him alone." Ditto for the butler at The Lanesborough and other hotels.

If a very great part of a great hotel is "location, location, location," as the old saying goes, The Lanesborough can be thought to have the best location in London. "We've got the Palace on one side and the Duke of Wellington on this side."

At the same time the hotel counts service as equally important. "Architecture and furnishings may create an unparalleled package, but The Lanesborough's service bowls one over," says Trisha Wilson in her book on great hotels of the world. "This life recalls that of a very fine London townhome, quite unequaled, and perhaps the closest thing I'll ever come to being treated like royalty." This, coming from Wilson, is no ordinary endorsement as Tricia has been around the world more times than an astronaut and stayed at more of the best places than even some kings and queens.

I was told upon arrival at The Lanesborough by my butler it would be more economical for me to have a suit, rather than a shirt, pressed. All the butlers here are under the watchful eye of head butler Sean Davorn, who was a butler in a magnificent private abode earlier in his career (and who has since, I hear, moved over to The Savoy).

Service *par excellence* is not easy to come by these days. "It's getting more and more difficult to get people with that compunction to serve," Michael continued. "People no longer, or very few people at least, feel that they want to be subservient . . . I think the word servant conjures up some negative connotations that in order to serve well, . . . while there are still people who want to serve well and do their job properly and understand the concept of being a servant, but basic philosophy is a difficult one to get across these days. But when you have someone like Sean who really understands it and is able to deliver it, it's a rare case these days. But certainly he does try and instill this into his butlers. And does a great job at that.

"The type of butlers we want these days are much more interactive. Because people don't have butlers these days as they used to . . . and if you have a stoic butler, it scares the heck out of everybody. Even the butler's waiting too long . . . for a tip, before they go out the door, I think that's terrible. . . . Nobody merits serving but no one likes having the guests' feet wiped on them so to speak. A lot more was tolerated in the past.

"Let's face it – no hotels are cheap in London at the moment. And people don't mind paying a lot; I think they are getting value for their money. That's the key to feeling you've got the attention and you've got what you paid for, and that makes such a big difference compared to our competitors. . . . we are the forerunners for having this type of service but none of the others have matched it yet."

Did I tell you about the champagne upon arrival? That was a good start!

"Also complimentary tea to wake up in the morning," Michael reminded me. Who could forget that? "It's a great start in the morning, your butler bringing that and then your choice of paper. . . . For myself, personally – and I've worked in Claridge's and other top hotels so I am quite familiar with these properties – but this is *unique*, this property. It's like a private house. As the head butler I like to consider it as a private house. And," he said with a twinkle in his eye, "I'm looking after the private house, so to speak! And that's what I think we do. We try and create an atmosphere which is homey compared to Claridge's.

"I think this is far more of an 'English feel' and this is a very typical English house. When you walk in it isn't a 'hotel-ey feel.' Everything wasn't in your face. Things were hidden away quite nicely. . . . and the counter bars in each room are quite unique. It doesn't matter if you're paying seven or eight thousand pounds a night or 400 pounds a night. They are in every room. There's no difference in the service you get. All you ever get in the hotel is more space.

"When you add up all these things, it is value for money that you get.

"Although the initial room rate is expensive, I think you get value for money and I think that makes such a difference to people. We have laundry returned within four hours without an extra charge. Most hotels charge an 'expense' fee. I think this is a little oasis in Hyde Park that someone can chill out at."

How nice. You and the champagne can chill at the same time. Ah, luxury.

"We do it while you're out . . . also making sure no one goes into your room without going through the butler. . . . I hope that with the corridors, we don't have people with trolleys which spoils a hotel. As I say, it is a very English hotel – in England. If I go to New York, I want to stay in a very New York hotel.

All right, so long as we're being so frank. What about Claridge's?

"Claridge's to me is a hotel, and yes, Claridge's had its glory days. But I don't think they have the service detail we have here. . . . It was a very elegant hotel. They're known for that. It's a fabulous staircase and the whole hall oozes elegance. There's no question of that.

"You can have a beautiful building but if you don't have a food staff and the right attitude and the right ambiance, it won't happen," head butler Sean explained. "For example, when a butler comes to me it takes three months before he is actually let near a guest. Qualified – it doesn't matter. He has to understand what *our* standards are and what *our* guests expect.

"Someone once asked me for wild goat's milk. And I had to send to Wales for it. I had to send the chauffeur the whole way down there. It cost fifty pounds for the chauffeur.

Actually, though Sean may have been too polite to bring the matter up, the goat's milk was a walk in the park compared to the zebra's milk. According to Britain's *The Sun* newspaper, in a 2006 story, then husband of Liza Minnelli, David Gest, asked his butler at the Lanesborough to get him a pint of zebra's milk. Frankly, the hotel thought Mr. Gest might simply been having some fun at their expense. (Or, at ten thousand pounds a night, perhaps at Mr. Gest's expense.) Nevertheless, Sean Davorn eventually found a shop which had frozen zebra milk. "Luckily, I remembered a fellow who'd helped me before. Sure enough there was a shop at the top of Regents Park where you could buy the stuff. It was £15 a pint and the guest had a pint every day."

Of course, various milks from around the world are not all that the hotel provides its guests (or its Gests) As the head butler continues, "Say you want your bath run at 6:30 and a gin and tonic and I'll have it ready for you."

"Any kind of toiletries?" I inquired.

"If the guests wanted it, then we got it. It didn't matter, as long as they get what they want," Sean said.

Hyde Park Corner may just be the best address in the World. Sure The Plaza in New York isn't bad. So, too, is 1040 Fifth Avenue where Jackie Kennedy Onassis lived. But the Dukes of Wellington lived at Apsley House, also known as "Number One London," between Mayfair and Hyde Park between The Lanesborough, the Dorchester, Four Seasons and Buckingham Palace. Were the original Duke of Wellington alive today, and he had a choice in the matter, he may have chosen The Lanesborough instead of "Number One London" across the intersection as his number one abode.

Sometime later I had the great good fortune to get to talk to Paul Gayler, celebrated chef of the Lanesborough.

"As you know yourself, every day's different in the hotel business," he told me. "There's one challenge today. There will be another one tomorrow. It's not a job you actually ever get bored in . . .

"I'm a great believer that every cuisine has its master . . . but I've got quite a good knowledge of cuisines across the board because I've got an interest in it."

He's also authored many books. "I've just finished my eighteenth book now."

Paul also has a prominent place in a book called *The Cook's Book*, written in collaboration with fifteen chefs from around the world.

"Years ago, when I started out, the hotel's occupancy was

the main thing," Paul continued. "If a restaurant succeeded or didn't wasn't important. But everything now – if you have a bar, it must make money. If you have a restaurant, it must stand alone as a viable business. It never used to be the case. They made their money on room occupancy . . . It's all changed and I think for the better."

Well, as they say, the proof is in the pudding or eating and my meal, arrested by glasses of non-vintage Taittinger Brut Réserve and 2005 Tignanello, Antinoi (80 percent Sangiovese and 20 percent Cabernet Sauvignon from the Chianti Region in Tuscany) was fit for a Wellington, let alone a lowly Morehouse.

But traveler take heart! Believe it or not, the Lanesborough also tries to give its clientele great value for the dollar or pound.

"When one travels a lot, it's very annoying when every time you want to go on your computer, you have to fill in your name and your room number and 'I agree to this' and 'I agree to that.' And then they charge you anything from 10 pounds, 20 pounds, 30 pounds! And you pick up the phone and is it an arm or is it a leg?!" Michael explained to me. "So our whole philosophy is based not on nickel-and-diming people – and giving great value. And we know we're not the most inexpensive hotel in the world. But we have done surveys that show the amount you can save if you check into some of our competitive hotels, we picked four hotels – I don't want to say which ones – but we use scenarios that you would make two three-minute phone calls to the United States, which is not that many, that you'd have two bottles of water, that you'd have a small bowl of fruit, that you would use the internet obviously, that you would watch a movie and have one outfit pressed. And the least expensive hotel charged 78 pounds (for these items) and the most expensive hotel was over 170 pounds, just in little extras that probably everyone will use at some stage."

Does the business traveler save with avoiding phone charges?

"Absolutely. We used to have people where their phone bill was greater than their room bill . . . the leisure traveler doesn't use the phone, for example, as much but certainly value for more is always good."

International singing star Michael Feinstein, whose career really took off after appearing at The Algonquin in New York, told me one of his fondest London memories was singing for a private party at The Lanesborough Hotel. But Michael Brooks, an executive with Sony Music, who loves going to Feinstein's at The Regency, the posh nightclub at New York's Regency Hotel named after Michael Feinstein, says some of the top London hotels regrettably have turned down overtures to have cabaret because they like things just the way they are, thank you.

Speaking of New Yorkers, Broadway theater producer Stewart F. Lane has produced a number of shows in London including "Ragtime," which was revived on Broadway in 2009. Lane had loved staying at The Lanesborough – no relation! He did a book signing in the lobby of Broadway's Palace Theatre, which he co-owns with the Nederlander Organization as well as operates. As he talked about Broadway in the Seventies I thought back to London and how much each city had changed since then. "The Seventies were a terrible time for the Broadway theater," Lane said "Theaters were white elephants." Crime, drug, prostitution had turned the once venerable Times Square into one of the world's most garish red-light districts. Soho in London also had the distinction in those days of having more sex and more shops per block than any district in London. Now London's Soho is a film and media center and the Soho Hotel caters to many in those industries.

We're getting horribly spoiled now. We'll never be able to return to New York and live in peace without butler service. But, in the name of journalism, we must push on, enduring all. Luckily, there will be a smooth transition, at least, at our next scheduled destination, which happens to be the hospitable realm of Tim and Kit Kemp.

Chapter 28

The Soho Hotel

Americans in London do manage to get together! "After we did a reading of the musical *Ghost*, Alexandra Silber (a costar of a London production of *Carousel*) came by and hung out with us for a little while."

So said TV, film and theater producer David Garfinkle who is co-producing the blockbuster musical, *Spiderman, Turn Off the Dark* on Broadway, and *Ghosts* in London, and who swears by The Soho Hotel.

"I ended up eating there a lot, I was just working so hard. We stayed at The Soho Hotel on and off for a little over a week. We were doing a reading of *Ghost* so we stayed at The Soho Hotel which was just down the block from where we were rehearsing. Actually, we were divided up into a couple of hotels, but that was one of the ones . . . a lot of film and theater people stay there and the Covent Garden. Garfinkle and his fiancé, Merle Grant, a fabulous singer and dancer in her own right, are not alone in their praise of The Soho.

. . . Liv Tyler stayed in Duplex at one of the Firmdale hotels . . . Scarlet Johansson stayed a long time at Covent Garden Hotel while doing Woody Allen's Match Point *which also featured the hotel . . .*

I had breakfast with the incredibly beautiful Angela Mannerson at The Soho. She filled me in on the eye-catching and unique murals adorning The Soho's restaurant Refuel, and at Oscar, the restaurant of another Firmdale London hotel, Charlotte Street. "Both murals were painted by Alexander Hollweg. Refuel's features some cars, which hints at the site's previous life as a car park. Whilst Oscar's features murals painted in the style of 1916 frescoes entitled 'Scenes of Contemporary London Life' by Roger Fry and his Omega Workshop. Kit adopted this idea and commissioned Alexander Hollweg with the scenes of 21st century London as inspiration." We both cast an appreciative eye over the Refuel's mural. "It's very colorful and adds a lot of activity to the room, doesn't it?" opined Ms. Mannerson.

"On Sunday afternoons, we host the Weekend Film Club where you have a champagne afternoon tea or a three-course lunch/dinner, and then watch the movie of the week in the hotel's private screening room," she continued. "It is only £35 and such a wonderful experience because you get to obviously dine in a nice restaurant and then go and relax in a very, very comfortable screening room. The experience is very different to viewing a movie in a massive cinema, and it is also very good value for the money. Many business travelers arrive on a Sunday and they want to do something but nothing too tiring, so enjoying good food followed by a film is quite a relaxing thing to do, but constructive at the same time. It's been very popular. Films shown are ones that are at the cinema but not yet out on DVD, and it could be something like *Australia* and they've got *Slum Dog Millionaire* lined up in a couple weeks; upcoming ones would be like *The Reader.*"

Each hotel has a large DVD collection at the concierge and popcorn cartons . . . Soho has more of a "pop" style or edge to it and strong media presence (being near film and media cos.); Haymarket is a John Nash building (listed) with softer interior, surrounded by theaters, hedge fund companies. etc.; Knightsbridge Hotel has old-world charm, townhouses, modern English (not "chintz"!) smaller scale but still fresh; "this hotel" contemporary London; . . . Tim and Kit like to "layer" old historic, say, fireplace, next to contemporary abstract art . . . museums using café space with better food to draw diners who then see a bit of art in the process — different kind of lure . . . licensing doesn't allow general public into Haymarket swimming pool anymore . . . Soho has a bit of the feel like old Vermont farmhouse with wooden tables.

In some cases I have to defer to Frommer's description of London hotels: they just can't be beat. Take its descriptions of The Soho Hotel, for example: "A former parking garage in the heart of bustling Soho just became one of our favorite nests in London . . . hoteliers Kit and Tim Kemp have come up with a stunner here, a cocoon-like luxury lair in a cul-de-sac off Dean Street . . . all the famous Kemp touches can be found, from boldly striped furnishings to deep bathtubs for a late-night soak . . . the theaters of Shaftesbury and the Ivy Restaurant are only a block or two away."

Eleven hotels are featured in "Location," a booklet which describes itself as the Design Hotels Portfolio. I stayed in three of these in London including The Soho Hotel, the Metropolitan and the Haymarket Hotels. The Haymarket is located in a landmark John Nash building, next to the Haymarket Theatre. Nash helped develop a lot of Regency London. I've toured and dined in some of the other hotels including the Charlotte Street Hotel where paintings by the 20th century Bloomsbury group are juxtaposed with some fireplaces and plush chairs.

Like me and like a lot of people in the hospitality industry, "Location" is a big fan of Tim and Kit Kemp of Firmdale hotels. We've already made their acquaintance, of course, but they do seem to be all over town these days. Perhaps the secret to their success is that they own and design their every property. Their great local touch might explain why they have as yet not expanded elsewhere in the European Union, or even farther afield. On the other hand, why tamper with success? As of last check, every one of their London "boutique" hotels was booked solid.

Wait! Hold the presses! I've just got word that Tim and Kit and Firmdale are at long last dipping their toe in the Atlantic – their first hotel outside of England is scheduled (as of this writing) to open in New York City, a gorgeous little getaway of a place called the Crosby Street Hotel. Finally, I'll have access to my London luxe life in my own backyard.

I couldn't resist contacting old acquaintance Paul Underhill, former asset manager of New York's Plaza Hotel and former President of Millennium Hotels, USA (and former London waiter!), about this potentially momentous move on the Kemps' part.

Paul said, "Probably one of the few things that becomes a challenge in New York is that in New York people expect snappier service. Lunches in England can go on! If I want to talk to you for an hour that's fine but I really want to make my order and my food to come and then I can make the decision. I think that's one challenge they (Firmdale) may have. But on the whole, good service, and friendly service, translates wherever you are in the world. The feel that you, the guest, is important. You can see that the people in the hotel, no matter how busy they are in trying to set up for the opening, are smiling at you. It doesn't matter who it is! You never know who you are talking to in a hotel. And if you get in that habit, you don't think about it, you do it automatically."

When Paul went to London to observe the quality of service at the Haymarket, The Soho and other Firmdale hotels, he came away with this: "No, I wasn't amazed. I was impressed because it is not in your face. It's not like you drive up and are greeted by five butlers! . . . Their service is rather like the decor – you grow into it. You realize that you ask someone a question and they answer it! They follow up and they get back to you!"

Of course I promptly inspected the Crosby as soon as I got back stateside. I immediately felt I was back in London. Even the cobbled street in the heart of New York's Soho art and residential neighborhood whispered London town. Each of the individually designed bedrooms and suites on eleven floors of new construction have full-length, warehouse-style windows and abundant natural light.

Of course, I put more weight on Paul's impressions than my own. Of his own visitation to the new establishment, he stressed that while the "hardware" and amenities of the hotel were of the very highest quality imaginable, the Kemps' overall emphasis is on making sure guests are comfortable. "That starts with the type of doorknobs you have," Paul explained. "The shower, all of those things – if they don't work – if an engineer knows every time he goes up to a room the door is going to fall off, he loses confidence in his product and he can't correct it. . . . But Tim (Kemp) has brought his own man over from London to paint the door numbers. The first thing that arrived in the architect's office was a door and he said, 'This is how we want the door.' There was no if, ands or buts about it. And that's the kind of detail they've done with the purveyors of the drapes. All their hotels are really 'home decorated.'"

On service, Paul said, "As simple as it sounds, it isn't. It is not easy to anticipate what the client wants. That's really what it boils down to. Why is this guest standing in the lobby? Why is he worried? How can I approach that person? And it becomes an acquired sense, if you are interested in people, who come to understand . . . You can have situations where guests don't want you to go over to them!

"The thing I always say is when you're working in a hotel you're on the stage. And when you go to a restaurant you can expect people to look after you. But it's not servile to look after someone. To make someone comfortable and happy. And if you get that through members of the staff then they start to enjoy looking after people! Rather than say to themselves, 'how many more people are going to come in before I can go home!' State of mind."

Thanks, Paul. Now, back to Britannia.

The Soho is not the newest but it is the largest of these properties, and of the Firmdale empire. The others include: Charlotte

Street, Covent Garden, and the Knightsbridge. (Firmdale is expanding in leaps and bounds and it's sometimes hard to keep count of their hotels; they also have the Haymarket and Number Sixteen in London.) Soho, it might be argued, is less of a boutique and more of an old-line grande dame hotel. Every room and suite in it has been decorated differently, but all reflecting some charming aspect of London life.

One might even label The Soho's rooms "large." But The Soho was built from the ground up, not converted from an earlier building. Normally, you would be hard-pressed to find property vast enough and available enough to build on in this otherwise historically dense city. Not only that, but it does seem that every other building in London has been "listed," or protected from the wrecking ball. Well, you may have wondered in the Sixties and Seventies how God could ever have allowed large municipalities the world over to build all those horrendously ugly, enormous parking garages. It's so that entrepreneurs like the Kemps would have something that everyone would be happy to seen torn down so that a beautiful, trendy new hotel could go up. The Soho went up between Dean Street and Wardour Street – right in the thick of London's thriving new "medialand." But they didn't just throw up any new hotel. They somehow managed to make it look new and historic at the same time, with its classy red-brick style, and the floor-to-ceiling "warehouse-style" windows. So, happily situated in Richmond Mews, just off Dean Street, as it is, the hotel opened to near universal rave reviews in the fall of 2004. Even the youngish staff was outfitted with style, in their charcoal Mark Powell suits, lilac shirts, Paul Smith ties and John Smedley knits. Moreover, the service too seems to combine the best of the old and the new – attentive but also relaxed. In the kitchens, Robin Read's seasonal cuisine for the gorgeous Refuel restaurant and bar fits in perfectly.

Kit Kemp, as usual, must have had a ball designing the place. The lobby, for instance, sort of wanders around. Nor is anyone likely to overlook the ten-foot black Botero cat sculpture, which also puts in an appearance on the hotel's stylish stationery. But where, you ask, is the signature tailor's dummy? In this hotel is has been sculpted from clear acrylic and lit internally, and found everywhere, from the check-in desk to the guest rooms. The hotel even found inspiration in the site's former occupation, as the Alexander Hollweg mural in the Refuel Bar picks up on the old "parking-lot" theme.

The hotel offers guests two impressive lounges to choose from. The Drawing Room features impressive art amidst wide oak floorboards and French fireplaces, the whole encapsulated in hues of hot pinks and pistachio greens. If that's a little too intense for you, try the somewhat cooler library, which favors more relaxed lighting, including an oddly meditative neon ladder.

Of course, the main course of any hotel is still the rooms themselves, and they do not fail to impress. The Terrace Suite is perhaps the most jaw-dropping in all of London. Not only tastefully furnished, it boasts wraparound terraces from which you can see pretty much everything in town. If your tastes, and budget, are somewhat more modest, do try the Junior suites. And if you're planning an extended stay, look into the Apartments, which can only be described as genuine swinging London pads. Number 2, for instance, has an open-plan kitchen, large living and master bedroom and a bathroom seemingly carved out of granite with a separate step-in shower – it's more grotto than loo. Of course there's a second bedroom suite with its own private bath. The only problem with it is that you may never want to step out the door.

Charlotte Street Hotel

Surprise, surprise, Charlotte Street Hotel is another Firmdale property which has gotten rave reviews. A five-minute walk from Oxford Street in Central London, it has much in common with the Covent Garden Hotel – the modern English look, the innovation and comfort, the emphasis on quality. Guarding the front door are two enormous gas lamps that transport you, even before you step into the hotel, back to a storied London of Dickens and Conan Doyle.

Inside the hotel isn't bad either. The pale wood floors and dados exude a certain relaxed luxury, as do the regal leather armchairs and the attractive, attentive young staff. This special feel is continued in the hotel's large open-plan bar and restaurant, named Oscar. Central London has never had it so good.

Covent Garden Hotel

Covent Garden is another creation of that mad, magical team of Tim and Kit Kemp. The dynamic duo seem to have taken over London, and absolutely no one is complaining.

As the name implies, this hotel has a fantastic location near the theatre and restaurant districts, almost within shouting distance of the Royal Opera House (otherwise generally known as Covent Garden). It's also fairly near St Paul's of Covent Garden, sometimes called "the actor's church." Its Tuscan portico entrance is seen in some sets of *Pygmalion* and is where Professor Higgins meets flower girl Eliza Doolittle. Some folks later made a fairly successful stage musical of this Bernard Shaw play called *My Fair Lady*. Awwww, g'wan! No, really. It's reported that the Earl of Bedford, who was in somewhat of a financial maelstrom at the time, asked Inigo Jones, second only to Christopher Wren when it comes to London architects, to build this gem of a church – but "no better than a barn." "You shall have the best barn in London!" Jones replied.

The hotel itself couldn't be more discreet, tucked away behind its brasserie-style awnings. Inside, it gets only better, with rich wood floors and eye-catching Persian rugs. Speaking of brasseries, Brasserie Max is just off to the right as you come in, or keep going and talk to the wonderful folks at the reception desk.

The suite that I got the grand tour of was the surprisingly largish Loft Suite number 303, with lavatories up and down – the up one just off the galleried bedroom and the down one branching off from the massive entertainment room. In a hotel like this, every room is an entertainment room, really. Like everything the Kemps do, the redesigning and tinkering never end, so one can never be entirely sure what the place will look like if you stay away for any length of time. There are department store windows which change less frequently than a Kemp hotel.

If a room is more to your taste, try number 3. It's really a high-ceilinged Junior Suite with views opening onto Shaftesbury Avenue. Here, the styling is refreshing pinks and whites, pretty much everywhere. Or, try the Junior Suite number 417. It has those exposed beams which just make you feel like you're really in London, maybe downing a pint with Long John Silver. Number 417 can be quite romantic, too. It's up to you, whatever your fantasy is. Also, keep in mind the Doubles, such as number 412, which boasts a rather unusual cross-beamed ceiling. Really, nothing makes me beam like a good beam, crossed or otherwise. There's just something so storybook about them. Maybe because in the States we hardly ever see them. Mostly it's just plaster and track lighting.

The Kemp stamp has definitely been put on the bathrooms at Covent Garden, very similar to the style at the Charlotte Street Hotel, in fact. The food is auspiciously Asian but not too out-there. The Covent Garden also offers an intimate brasserie setting in its eatery. Or try the wood-paneled, impressively draped Drawing Room with its "honour" bar. Later, work it all off in the gym or the single treatment room. Or simply continue lazing around in the screening room. The hotel sponsors a weekend film club Saturday evenings that includes an attractively priced dinner-movie package.

Like all the Kemp offerings, Covent Garden Hotel is remarkable as well as comfortable. You'll generally find the clientele a tad more mature than at Charlotte Street, and its restaurant is more refined. The Firmdale hotels just seem to keep getting better and better. Who would have thought after all these decades of luxury accommodation that there would still be so much room for innovation?

Knightsbridge Hotel

One thing you have to grant London hotels – they've got the names locked up. What could be more evocative, I ask you, than Knightsbridge Hotel? The very name conjures up so many fabulous images and sensations. King Arthur seems to standing before you. Not that there's much else terribly medieval about this hotel, mind. Knightsbridge, by the way, did derive its name from the bridge that knights of the realm of yore rode over on the way in town from Windsor Castle and other remote regions.

The neighborhood of Beaufort Gardens is a generally genteel residential one. The Knightsbridge is a welcome addition to it, I think. First of all, the area needed it. Secondly, the hotel and the environs go hand-in-gauntlet. The hotel has been designed in the modern style with taste (not always the case); and the setting couldn't be more peaceful and restorative. The hotel offers most of the services a modern traveler or businessman requires these days, except for a fitness room. The rooms have been individually decorated and there are four Junior Suites, which are somewhat juxtaposed in style; the one is earth tones and textures, the other is startling fuchsias and slickness.

The impressive lobby houses Carol Sinclair's remarkable organic sculpture (there's that word again, "organic"), which does go peculiarly well with Peter Clark's rather fanciful collages of classic Knightsbridge dogs – mostly small breeds like Scotties and Dachshunds. After all, how relaxing would it be to lounge under a picture of Great Dane or Irish Wolfhound?

The lobby sort of flows into the Drawing Room, which switches tones on you with its African prints. Keep going and the style switches again to a softer feel in the Library, especially Dominic Berning's clever book lights and that ladder with its rungs lit up. Of course there's an old hearth, on top of which is a John Illsley abstract. Again, the old and the new, mixed like a classic cocktail. Speaking of which, there is another "honour" bar to meet your libation requirements. The staff is another set of genuinely charming, attractive youngsters. Where do they find them? Or is it the result of some sort of crash–course, boot camp–like training school? Eton, perhaps? Rugby? No matter. The results speak for themselves, with those charming accents. The service and the housekeeping are top–notch, too.

As for specific accommodations here, I dipped my toe into number 101, which, they tell me is the largest and best on hand. It certainly looked it. All the rooms, however, are "junior–style" with separate sitting areas. Their Deluxe Doubles are also impressive, I hear. I ducked into number 201 long enough to see that it looks out onto Beaufort Gardens and is furnished in a harmonious way that you couldn't have believed before you saw it with your own eyes. I also got a look at number 302, where the offering is bespoke fabric and tree–top vistas.

The suite I actually stayed in had an extensive balcony and floor–to–ceiling windows that made me happy to gaze out of and thankful I didn't have to wash them. You see, that's one of the great things about hotels. You really can enjoy your luxurious surroundings. If they were in your home, you'd be the one responsible for keeping it all so spic-and-span. It takes a hotel staff to keep house like this nowadays. The seating in my suite consisted of varnished oak and leather clad objects. And on the rare occasions when I grew tired of gazing out those Monticello-sized windows, there was satellite TV in both the sitting and bed-room areas. Further merciful amenities included excellent air-conditioning, a personal safe (into which I placed my few meager valuables if only for the sensation), a DVD player, all the outlets any nerd could want and even a cell phone provided for my use.

Snooping further about the property I could see that the bathrooms generally were of the shiny granite and oak variety, usually with twin wash basins and rather invitingly deep cast-iron tubs. I was notified that not all the baths have separate step-in showers; so you've been warned.

No doubt, unlike me, you'll be gadding all about town at night, but I was thankful for the 24-hour room service, supplying everything a midnight-fridge raider could dream of, from the homemade pizzas and hamburgers to the grilled rib-eye steaks and the Banofee Pie and Carrot Cake.

Knightsbridge Hotel has somewhat the feel of an extremely upscale B&B, but I still have very fond memories from my youth-ful Britrail Pass days of many a British B&B all over this lovely country at which I also felt right at home.

Chapter 29

The Haymarket Hotel

Staying at the Haymarket Hotel was idyllic several ways. First, for me, the hotel staff reminded me of "The Lambs Club" where I lived as a teenager and very young man until I got a job on the *Christian Science Monitor* as a reporter. I had had a reporter's "try-out" on the *New York Post*, something that the Newspaper Guild benevolently set up for up-and-coming reporters. Since I had never written a news story in my life, aside from the few to qualify for a try-out, it was a grueling two months. I'd painstakingly labor on my *Post* stories as if I had been Truman Capote reworking and reworking a novella. The veteran reporters could sit down and whip something off – a half hour. I sat there in the city room for hours, finding the right word for something I had never done before.

Anyway, back to the Haymarket, which may or may not have been a gentleman's club in an earlier incarnation. Before Firmdale turned it into a landmark hotel, it did serve as the headquarters for American Express. And right next to it sits a landmark theater, the Haymarket. It was here I saw a stellar *On the Waterfront* directed and starring Steven Berkoff, and it made me rejoice over what true drama could be. Starring Simon Merrells, who captured the spirit of a young Marlon Brando, who starred in the 1954 movie, I got an orchestra (or stall) seat for the incredible sum of ten pounds by getting to the box office just before curtain time. The Haymarket Theatre had opened in 1824, on July 4th of that year to be exact, with a production of Sheridan's *The Rivals*. In 1994 it had a £1.3 million refurbishment when air conditioning was also installed. The otherwise war-torn year of 1914 saw the premier performance of Ibsen's *Ghosts*. Ralph Richardson played 610 performances of a play called *Yellow Sands* in 1926. But it was in 1925, John Barrymore recalled, remembering all the activities of the first evening he ever spent on the Haymarket's fabled stage:

"I waited until the theatre had become dark and empty.

Then I walked out on stage, stood there, alone, looking toward the black vacuum of pit and stalls, and I knew what the Viscount St. Alban meant when he said that the poets had made Fame a monster . . . I might have quit that same night, had it not been for the sake of Winston Churchill. He was so fond of our family, such a great friend, that I didn't want to let him down."

Offstage in London, Barrymore loved walking through fogs and "felt they were full of romance and adventure." As Barrymore's friend Constance Collier told author Gene Fowler for his biography of the great thespian, "Whenever there was a real fog, Jack was in his element. He became most poetic . . . with his collar turned up and his hat pulled down over his brow as he tramped along in the heavy fog by the railings of Hyde Park."

As I have already touched upon, one of the great traditions of London hotels is for the managers to leave hand-written notes for guests. Here's one from Simon Galic, Deputy General Manager of the Haymarket Hotel: "Dear Mr. Morehouse, A very warm welcome to Haymarket. It's a pleasure having you stay with us. Regards, Simon."

As a result of my play, *Gangplank*, co-written with Mark Druck, Broadway and London producer David Garfinkle told me about staying at the Haymarket. He once patronized the hotel on my recommendation. "I love the swimming pool," David smiled. David was producing a musical version of the cult movie, *Ghost*, with Demi Moore, Patrick Swayze (who as of this writing has tragically just passed away) and Whoopi Goldberg, on London's West End. Another thing he liked about the Haymarket was its location next to the Haymarket Theatre in the epicenter of the thriving West End.

The Haymarket Hotel, along with its five sister hotels, has obviously been a labor of love for owners Tim and Kit Kemp. Kit as design director has poured herself into the decoration of the hotel with its fresh take on English design combined with quirky modern artwork; she defines her style as "English eccentric." Kit in 2008, according to the Firmdale website, "won the prestigious Andrew Martin International Interior Designer of the Year award. Selected from a shortlist of designers by a celebrity panel including Thandie Newton, Twiggy and *GQ* Editor Dylan Jones, Kit Kemp was chosen for her distinctive interpretation of a quintessentially English style. Martin Waller says: 'Kit Kemp has redefined the concept of the city hotel. Her unique perspective brings a flamboyance to interior design without ever sacrificing the essential commandment of comfort!'" Labeled "the Oscars of the interior design world" the awards were set up in 1996 in order to discover and celebrate the talents of the world's best designers.

More about the reclusive Kemps can be gleaned from an article that appeared in *The Boston Post* by Christine Temin.   I learned, in fact, a number of fascinating things about the Haymarket and its renowned designer from this jaunty newspaper item.

It seems that designer Kit Kemp has been quite prolific in her career. She has designed dozens and dozens of hotel bedrooms by now. She also has a charming design signature – the figure of a female mannequin, which stands in the room sharing the same fabric which can be seen nearby, from the curtains to the valence to the cushions.

Of course there was the one time when this rather whimsical touch had an unexpected consequence. It seems one hotel guest, exhausted from her day's itinerary, returned to her room, draped her coat over the obliging female mannequin and promptly dropped off to sleep. Some time later she awoke, spotted the strange figure in her room and nearly lost it.

Kit Thomas got her start in the biz in the mid Eighties. At the time she was working for an architect when she had the great good personal and professional fortune to run into Tim Kemp, who was making his own living by transforming old buildings into youth hostels. The two like-minded youngsters got hitched and soon after opened their first hotel. Other young couples get married (or sometimes not) and like to visit hotels. Not Kit and Tim. They had to start their own. And their initial effort was Dorset Square, which had been a Regency-era townhouse before they got hold of it. The newlyweds turned the property into a splendidly elegant 38-room hotel in English country house style.

That was then. Now the two are a sort of chummy conglomerate, heading a $20 million dollar a year hotel empire with half a dozen small hotels and about as many restaurants scattered about London. Critics now give them credit for being in the vanguard of what's now known as "boutique" hotels, those smaller, fun places to stay. Kit recounts another amusing story about the time she had a devil of a time getting herself and her three casually dressed daughters seated in the restaurant of one of those non-boutique behemoth hotels. It was breakfast and the maitre d' insisted that her girls be "properly attired." Eventually a détente was worked out and they were placed at a table behind a voluminous potted plant. It made Kit realize that there just might be some room in the London hotel market for a place where a mother and her children might be served breakfast while wearing polo shirts.

Hence, you can wear pretty much whatever you want at a Kemp hotel. Even the owners can be spotted in jeans sauntering about their own premises. Which is not to say that their hotels are any less chic than the tony uptown joints. Just less strict. At least that's how many of their regulars seem to feel, including such not un-stylish folk like designer Isaac Mizrahi, actor Albert Finney, model Naomi Campbell, rock star Sting and comic and actor Steve Martin.

Almost from the start, though, both the Covent Garden and its younger sibling the Charlotte Street Hotel have attracted a stellar showbiz crowd. After all, they wear a lot of silk sport coats in Hollywood, but not that many ties. It's often hot there, you know. This affinity for the entertainment industry types shouldn't be a surprise, considering that both hotels offer state-of-the-art screening rooms fitted out with Italian leather recliners.

Charlotte Street even started something they call their "Sunday Night Film Club," which for many guests has provided them with something to do in London on that otherwise low-key night (when many theatres and restaurants are closed). Moreover, this club is open to one and all. For about $40 you're served a three-course meal at the hotel's restaurant, after which you saunter down to the swanky screening room to watch a tastefully selected film. For instance, Kit Kemp has proudly noted, they screened "Chocolat" before its general release. How's that for a nice dessert after dinner?

But these hotels have many swell "touches." Like the "honesty" bar, where you pay for your drinks on the honor (or honour) system. That is, you run a tab and pay the reckoning when you check out. Isn't it flattering to be trusted, for once?

"A hotel should be a haven," Kit Kemp avers. How true. "When guests move the furniture around, we pay attention to what they've done to make the room more comfortable for themselves."

Ms. Kemp also strongly feels that "hotel interiors should be amusing. I do think some of them get so incredibly serious." I'm not so sure about this as a general maxim, but it does work wonderfully as a philosophy at her hotels. In addition to the mannequin motif, Kit Kemp hotel bedrooms have also been known to contain a jockey's weighing station, antique telephones and walls painted to look like wood. Even the artwork hanging on the walls is not your usual hotel landscape and still life. One room features a portrait of a hefty farmer's daughter, who looks about to burp, or given her voluminous dimensions, about to erupt.

The rates at Firmdale hotels can also be less severe, though not exactly inexpensive. For instance, you'd be hard-pressed to find one of their rooms going for less than $200 a night, and the rates can rise to The Savoy – like $600-700 per evening. Though if you go to Knightsbridge, which is their hotel near Harrod's, you can get in the door for under $150. And your room will still have linens by Frette and toiletries by Miller Harris. The Knightsbridge may not have the exhaustive room-service that the big hotels can provide, but as long as you don't require a three-star meal in your room at three in the morning, you should be quite comfortable.

Although I only toured the Covent Garden Hotel, I immediately felt its kinship with the other Firmdale Hotels. The www.firmdale.com website details the new restaurant and bar at the Covent Garden Hotel which, I was informed, had recently undergone a makeover.

The revamped eatery got not only a separate bar area, but a longer pewter bar. Many a British pub offers pewter mugs, but an entire pewter bar? Incredible. The menu also was revamped, with a new emphasis on what they call "British brasserie style cuisine." What this means, among other things, is that there's more fresh, seasonal produce on hand. You have an excellent choice of wines, by the glass, and the restaurant is open all day for the three traditional meals as well as for coffee, cocktails and afternoon tea. Also worth noting are two private event rooms, easily adaptable to serve any function from a chic dining space to a formal corporate boardroom.

According to the website, afternoon tea is "the new power breakfast." Not exactly sure how that works out, unless you're prone to taking very late breakfasts, but I'm sure they know their business. In any event, power hungry or merely peckish for a scone, you can partake at either the "sumptuous drawing room" at the Charlotte Street Hotel, or in the sun-splashed "leafy garden" at Number Sixteen. The Cream Tea will run you nine pounds while the Traditional Afternoon Tea starts at seventeen pounds. Over at the Haymarket Hotel, however, you can dine on the "Cupcake Tea" for a mere five pounds.

Any one of those sounds like it would fit me to a T. But I'm afraid we must be getting along to the next stop on this most luxurious of lines, with a visit to the environs of bustling, good old Piccadilly Circus.

Chapter 30

The Piccadilly, The Gore, and a Little Cabaret

This is not my end chapter so much as it is my odds and ends chapter. I'll leave it up to you whether the ends justify the odds here, but I did want to get The Piccadilly and the Gore in someplace, though they didn't quite merit their own chapter. And while I was at that, I thought I might as well toss a few other fun anecdotes into the salad. This one, for instance:

Like Churchill, Nancy Astor (1879–1964), a member of the House of Commons, who had married the fabulously wealthy Robert Gould Shaw II and Waldorf Astor, was larger than life. A teetotaler who rarely if ever took a drink because of her Christian Science beliefs, she vociferously disapproved of liquor and served none in her St. James Square mansion or country estate.

In the book "The Wicked Wit of Winston Churchill," compiled by Dominique Enright, Enright says "on one occasion WSC had just stood up to address the House (of Commons where she was a member from 1919 to 1945) and was raising a glass of water to his lips when he caught sight of her. 'It must be a great pleasure for the noble lady, the member for the Sutton Division of Plymouth, to see me drink water.'"

Enright also records what may have been, or not, the most famous exchange between the friendly enemies:

NANCY ASTOR: If I were your wife, I would put poison in your coffee.
WINSTON CHURCHILL: If you were my wife, I'd drink it.

Now, back to the hotels. . . .

I wasn't even particularly interested in the Piccadilly Hotel until I learned that Broadway producer Al Woods, who owned the Eltinge Theatre on 42nd Street, liked to stay there.

"The New Piccadilly Hotel has been totally refurbished," quoth the book, "Historic Hotels of London." "Close to Piccadilly Circus, it is within easy walking distance of many West End theaters and cinemas, Burberry's, Laura Ashley's, and Liberty's large stores, and the famous bespoke tailors of Jermyn Street. The interior is palatial. The vast magnificent Oak Room Restaurant has wood-paneled walls decorated with gilded trophies, garlanded leaves and flowers, helmets, swords, and shields in carved relief. Wonderful chandeliers, specially made in Italy, have wide swirling ribbons of glass and delicate crystal flowers glittering among the lights.

"The former chef from Dukes Hotel has been tempted over to run the kitchens, and he presides with sure, delicate touch over the *nouvelle-cuisine*-inspired dishes. His 'Menu Surprise' in the Oak Room Restaurant is at first sight dauntingly long but it consists only of modest-sized dishes. A complimentary mini-kebab of duck was followed by salmon terrine with sauce verte, watercress soup in a tiny cup, and lobster, shrimp, and sole in a piquant sauce. After mango sorbet to clear the palate, there was lamb lightly grilled, a choice of cheeses – all in perfect condition – and a selection of exquisite desserts, finishing with coffee and petit fours. Each of the eight beautifully presented, delicious courses provided most memorable mouthfuls. There is also a comprehensive selection of *á la carte* dishes.

"The modestly sized bedrooms are fairly plainly furnished with reproduction antiques but the marble bathrooms are lavish. Clothes hanging space is surprisingly limited, and has clothes hangers of the irritating sort that are fastened to the rail. Many millions have been spent on 40,000 square feet devoted to recreation and fitness in a vast complex beneath the hotel. This includes a twelve-meter swimming pool surrounded by statuary and lush plants, two solaria, saunas, a Turkish bath, glass-backed squash courts, a nautilus gym, and a billiard room, as well as the Club Brasserie, drawing room, nightclub, and library. All are open to guests and to a limited number of private club members. Some suites overlook the glass-roofed, palm-filled tropical splendors of the Terrace Garden Restaurant. The Bell's Whisky group, which owned both The New Piccadilly and the famous Gleneagles Hotel in Scotland, has recently been bought by the Guinness group. Let us hope the high standards that have been set in the restoration of this stately Edwardian hotel are maintained."

Hear, hear! Likewise, I felt the Gore merited at least a mention:

According to London finance writer, Jasmine Birtles, "A

recent, exciting find of mine in my quest for London hotels that retain character and high quality, is the Gore hotel in Kensington. It's one of those boutique hotels that you would barely know was there unless you were looking for it. Nestled behind the Royal Albert Hall, just by Kensington Gardens, it is a cozy hotel with delightfully baroque stylings. None of those boring, minimalist sofas in twenty shades of brown, this is a hotel that you can luxuriate in. Velvets, golds, intricate carvings and mood lighting make it a relaxing place to escape to. It is unashamedly retro, enjoying its own opulence and comfort. I love it already!"

Before I leave you, I again feel compelled to mention those maestros of the hotel world, the hotel managers. They are like the Broadway impressariosimpresarios of old – colorful, multi-talented, hard-working, and even at times a little eccentric. Many of them are worth the price of admission to their luxurious hotels all by themselves.

And, as I say, many of them might have been great actors too. Certainly I've met a few would be quite at home in "Hay Fever" or another Noël Coward play; they are debonair, immaculately dressed, charming, exceptionally thoughtful. Yet each is a top executive at the top of their profession. They are captains of their superliners with the added responsibility of being chief executives. Their staffs, to a man and woman, reflect their vision and thoughtfulness. The phrase "the customer is always right," sometimes attributed to George Boldt, proprietor of New York's Waldorf-Astoria Hotel, never had a truer ring to it than at London's grandest hotels. Actually, the phrase "the customer is never wrong," was coined by Céesar Ritz in 1908. Marshall Field and Selfridge's used the slightly different "the customer is always right" in later ad campaigns.

In an odd but true way, all great managers, and it must be said that most four- and five-star London hotels have great managers, are like the character Gatsby in F. Scott Fitzgerald's novel, The Great Gatsby, as he relished Daisy looking around the rooms of his huge estate.

"I think he revalued everything in the house according to the measure of response it drew from her well-bred eyes," narrator Nick Carraway says midway into the book. So, too, managers take keen interest in their guests' figurative "ooh's and ah's," it seems to me. Moreover, they are like Nick Carraway, too. Content to stand, for the most part, out of the limelight, simply to be able to take part in the grand drama that they oversee.

Stars in particular have always have loved London hotels. Karen Akers sang with the other American cabaret stars at "Pizza in the Park" in 2009. But, she told me, "I wish he had gotten a hotel, But for the time being, it is what it is."

"She'll [Karen Akers] be thrilled that you're coming," cabaret star and impresario Jeff Horner told me at an after-party for Karen Akers.

"We're spending thousands of dollars in P.R. but not on ads. So we're really trying to micro-market – to find out who the audience is and where they are – and to reeducate them as to what cabaret is because we know that they are there . . . we're nothing very hard (on having one of the hotels pick this up.)"

London has everything in the way of entertainment any tourists or native of Great Britain could possibly crave. The musical *Dirty Dancing*, more a hit in Toronto, started out here as did *Mary Poppins* now at the New Amsterdam on Broadway. But I was rather surprised to get a lesson in American composers from Maude Maggart who was at the Jermyn Street Theatre in February. So was Julie Wilson, whom I just missed and Karen Akers and Jeff Horner who were their great selves on stage. Maude, who New York's *Time Out* called "the New Face of Cabaret," talked for what seemed like many minutes.

"I didn't expect applause after the last number because I know 'Marriage Is for Old Folks' is potentially offensive. It's the song after 'Folks Who Live on the Hill.' I didn't mean it to be offensive. They are two different perspectives. 'The Folks Who Live on the Hill' was written in 1937 and 'Marriage Is for Old Folks' was written in 1965 so you can draw your own conclusion. Why the songwriters felt free or compelled to write about love and marriage and idealism is lack of . . . 'Folks Who Live on the Hill' was of course written by Jerome Kern and Oscar Hammerstein, and 'Marriage Is For Old Folks' was written by Mort Shuman and Leon Carr. And the song that was (sort of) in the middle of those two songs was a Noël Coward song, "This is a Changing World." And I think that Noël Coward . . . may be the best one to bridge the gap between generations and ways of living about the human experience. About love, certainly, about life. I feel that Noël Coward was never dated. If you look at his plays, the lyrics to his wonderful songs, they never seem dated. They only seem – bright! They only seem truly reflective of what the human experience is. I'm a big Noël Coward fan. A proud card–carrying member of the Noël Coward Society. As my esteemed colleague, Jeff Horner, told you tonight, this show is called 'Good Girl, Bad Girl,' and it is about songs that I think apply to either a good girl or a bad girl in the realm of the American Popular Songbook which I think we can agree that the American Popular Songbook, the songs that were written during that era from about the turn of the century, maybe a little bit after that, to about 1955 . . . I know that Irving Berlin stopped writing songs after the Beatles because he didn't know what to do anymore.

"And I realize that the songs I love from the American Popular Songbook category fall into two categories in terms of ones that women sing either good girl or bad girl songs.

"Good girl songs are the ones where the woman or the girl is totally content in her situation. If she has a husband she is very happy to be married to him. If she has a boyfriend, she's very happy to dream about the rest of her life, consisting only of him and their love and their children, and the same old view and holding the same old hand for the rest of her life. And that's wonderful!

"And there is another perspective which is the bad girl perspective, and that is anything other than the good girl perspective . . . the girl who wants a little bit more or is curious about something more.

"And for the rest of the show I am not going to tell you my opinion about what I think is a good girl song or a bad girl song . . . I don't believe that is something such as a good girl or something as a bad girl. Because to be human is to lie somewhere in the middle. The first song you heard tonight was 'How Could Red Riding Hood Have Been So Very Good.' That's a song written in 1926 by A. P. Randolph that was banned on the radio, when radio came around, because it was too suggestive. It didn't out Red Riding Hood into one of the two categories – it suggested that maybe she was bad, probably. I think Red Riding Hood is the perfect poster child on what it is to be good or to be bad . . . she certainly set out on an innocent journey. She was taking food and medicine to her lonely grandmother. . . . She then sang Julie's song from 'Carousel,' which goes in part 'He's your fellow and you love him and there's nothing more to say.'

"What's the use of wondering?"

"What could go wrong within the realm of that melody? Anything could be right. Even myself when I listen to that melody I say to myself, 'Well, maybe that could be okay.'"

Cabaret and Noël Coward are inextricably linked to the great London hotels, The Savoy in particular. Like the hotels, cabaret and Coward are both anxious to please, but also rigorously professional and sophisticated. The great London hotels do have their many differences, but for an American I think this is where they all meet – in providing that wonderful fantasy of high living that Coward and cabaret honed many years ago into an art.

In parting, allow me to squeeze in one London hotel I wished I'd stayed at. That would be the Jumeirah Carlton Tower. I was tipped off to it by a manager (and author, I should add, of a volume on Charlie Chaplin) I interviewed at The Savoy, who used to work there.

Within easy reach of the London's most fashionable shopping areas, Jumeirah Carlton Tower enjoys an enviable location on Cadogan Place and Sloane Street. It overlooks the private garden of Cadogan Place and offers its guests 220 rooms, including 59 suites.

Voted "Best UK Business Hotel" at the Condé Nast Reader's Travel Awards 2008, Jumeirah Carlton Tower is situated in the heart of "fashionable Knightsbridge" and located within walking distance from Harrods and Harvey Nichols department stores, as well as luxury designer boutiques situated on Sloane Street. In addition to its spectacular views over London's skyline, the hotel boasts three restaurants: The Rib Room, Chinoiserie, and Club Room. As if that isn't enough to keep you busy, the hotel also houses one of the most exclusive health clubs in London, the Peak Health Club & Spa. Oh well, not even I can get to everything. But definitely the next time I'm in town . . .

EPILOGUE

From The Savoy, which was considered the greatest hotel in the world for decades and reminds me even today of Noël Coward, Cole Porter, Richard Harris and Bogart and Bacall, to the cozy, almost retiring yet old-world charm and comfort of The Chesterfield, in the very heart of Mayfair – its chic, black awnings remind me of a beautiful woman, reclining in the luxurious Mayfair surroundings, and giving inviting winks to passersby and guests alike – I still can't say I've had my fill of grand London hotel life. If only one could afford to stay forever. At The Connaught, I just felt incredibly right; at The Lanesborough incredibly pampered. Well, as General Doug Macarthur famously said upon being forcibly evicted from the Philippines, "I shall return!"

During nearly four weeks in London in February and March 2009 I stayed in fifteen hotels. Some were ones I had stayed in before such as The Connaught, Milestone and The Lanesborough. Some had amazing celebrity and celebrities; others amazing histories – past and present. All had amazing service and very often, excellent to amazing food.

I'm often asked where I would stay if the hotel tariff was entirely on my nickel. That is an impossible question, for each of the hotels I've described in this book is so individual, so extraordinary, so unique, the question is impossible to answer. Each has a "wow" factor the others lack. In the Chesterfield, for example, I felt extremely at home during my two nights' stay. Secluded away in the middle of Mayfair, it has no grand entrance or park or idyllic park views. I won't say I wasn't awed when I stayed at The Goring that Queen Elizabeth had dined there and paid for her meal.

This quote from F. Scott Fitzgerald's short story "Love in the Night," has long captured some of my love of London's grand hotels, the narrator speaking: "What surprised him most about making love was that it seemed to have no element of wild passion – regret, desire, despair – but a delirious promise of such happiness in the world, in living, as he had ever known." It is that ineluctable element of "delirious promise" that great London hotels dispense with typical British aplomb. It's the kind of feeling that is difficult to put a price on, because it is so rare in the world, and in life.

In the end London hotels are a pilgrimage, an exhibition of London life and history. The mighty Thames, pillar of commerce, Monet inspiration . . . a never-never land of beauty and excitement and expectation. London hotels are all of that and more.

What I've tried to do in this book is to give you an untypical view of London at its best. Sometimes, as great author and illustrator Ludwig Bemelmans wrote in a letter laying out some of his thoughts for his children's book "Madeline in London" (his last book published the year before his death in 1962 when he was living at New York's renowned National Arts Club), illustrations of London look "like Whiskey ads, traveling posters or 'Come Visit England' throw throwaways." But he would, I like to imagine, have nonetheless found a certain freshness in the preceding pages, as I hope have you.

My sojourn through lush London is done, but hotel life goes ever on! I recently (October 2009) had lunch with that hotelier and financier par excellence Chairman Kwek. Long range, he wants to turn his Millennium Mayfair into a six-star property. "I am now trying to find the right interior designer," he told me over a lunch of scallops at New York's prestigious National Arts Club. He seemed to be leaning toward Trisha Wilson of the Dallas-based Wilson & Associates. "She did the St. Regis Singapore," he explained. "It was very well done. I think it is the best hotel in Singapore. She has many world-wide demands on her time. But she personally oversaw some of the work on the St. Regis." Also on the Millennium Mayfair: "One developer a few years ago approached me about buying the hotel. I said it wasn't for sale. He said 'What about joining forces? I promise I will build the best hotel in London, even better than The Lanesborough, Claridge's or The Connaught.'" The Chairman didn't take the developer up on his offer, at least not yet.

"Make sure you let me know when you want to come to Singapore," he mentioned to me as we were getting ready to leave. "I will make sure you stay at the St. Regis there." Hmm. The Far East is exploding of late, the Pacific Rim the global region of the future everybody says, and boasting some of the finest hotels in the world, not a few of which owned by my lunch companion.

Why not spend a month investigating the Far East's best hotels? Hong Kong, Singapore, Tokyo, Shanghai? Twenty-nine hotels in thirty days? Sounds doable. Maybe I will make it all the way around the world like Phileas Fogg after all. Taxi!

Acknowledgments

First, I want to thank my mother, the late Joan Marlowe Rahe, and stepfather, Roderic W. Rahe, for their encouragement of me as a journalist, playwright and author. When my mother died in early 2009 at age 88, we found scrapbooks of clippings of articles I had written. My stepfather, although not in the arts like my mother or father, Ward Morehouse, was always encouraging and provided me with encouragement and some financial support until my writing started to make me a living. My brother, Roderic W. Rahe, Jr. was equally supportive although expressing a healthy skepticism of a writer's financial promise.

Eugene Scanlan, General Manager and Vice President of The Waldorf–Astoria Hotel, taught me not only a love of that grand hotel, but grace and a cool head under pressure. Jean Dalrymple, my father's second wife, and a good friend, expressed a wonderful joy in everyday life as a Huckleberry Finn adventure. "You'll never have it as good as you do now," my stepfather would say to me, seemingly like a broken 33? rpm record. He was right in one sense. In another, his strong work ethic taught me that work and more work would eventually pay off in everything I did.

All mothers encourage their sons. I don't know how but mine did until she died. As I said at my mother's funeral, she was a cheerleader for others' lives and talents. Their success was hers – she rejoiced in their accomplishments, progress, marriages and children. In my case, it was my newspaper career that she always championed. From my early "un" bylined work at *The New York Post*, throughout ten years on *The Christian Science Monitor* to *The New York Post* (plays and books) . . . her greatest gift was "rejoicing in another's good" as it says in the Bible.

I often went to the theater with both my father and mother. With my mother I saw Boris Karloff as Captain Hook in *Peter Pan*, and several years later, Mary Martin as Peter in the musical version. When I was a teenager, my mother, who was co-editor and co-publisher of *The Theater Information Bulletin* and later *Theater Critics Review*, gave me many tickets to Broadway and Off-Broadway shows. My stepfather, as I say, loved going to the shows and encouraged me to go as well.

Like many journalists, my first desire was to be a playwright. I thought, as so many young writers do, that given time I could weave my own version of *The Glass Menagerie* or *Long Day's Journey Into Night* from out of hot, thin air and my own life. I had some early success with a play called *The Actors*, which Frank Rich called "sporadically promising" and "demonstrates a flair for flavorful, well-paced comic dialogue and a keen command of the love and spirit of a vanished Broadway era." It ran as a showcase at The Troupe Theatre on West 39th Street and, on the strength of Rich's review, it managed to move Off-Broadway four years later in 1986.

Like dozens of other playwrights, I'm grateful to those who gave me the chance to put on my plays and write about theater for many newspapers. I list in no particular order the editors, critics, theater managers, directors, press agents and others who have helped me as a reporter for *The Christian Science Monitor* and as a columnist for Reuters, the *New York Post*, *The New York Sun*, *amNewYork*, *The Epoch Times*, and TimesSquare.com.

They include the late Curt Sitomer, the American news editor of *The Christian Science Monitor*, who took great joy in fitting people to a particular "best." In my case it was in New York City. Others who have been helpful and who I've admired along the way include: Richard Watts, long-time critic of the *New York Post*; Chuck Caruso and Lou Calisauno, early colleagues at the *Post*; Clayton Jones, John Hughes, Earl Foell and others from *The Christian Science Monitor*; Matt Diebel and Vincent Musetto of the *Post*; Gary Shapiro, "Knickerbocker" columnist of *The New York Sun* and Seth Lipskey, its editor, as well as Stuart Margues, formerly of the *Post* and the *Sun*; Alex Stonizinski, former editor-in-chief of *amNewYork*, as well as Emily Hulme and Marcus Barum.

To Stewart Lane, my collaborator on *If It Was Easy*, and his actress-producer wife, Bonnie Comley, I owe special thanks for their always exciting Broadway news and friendship. Publicists Gail Parenteau who represents the Ohies, Beck Lee, Tony Origlio and Barbara McGurn. No list of acknowledgments will be complete without mentioning the hotel executives who have encouraged me to write about the history and glamour of their illustrious establishments, including Chairman Kwek Leng Beng, of Singapore and Millennium Hotels; Per Hellman, former general manager of The Waldorf-Astoria; Paul Underhill, former asset manager of The Plaza; Gary Sweikert, former general manager of

The Plaza; Tom Civitano, former vice president of public relations and marketing of The Plaza; and Martin Riskin and George Lang, who epitomize both the excitement and promise of grand hotels and their often equally grand restaurants and banquet facilities.

Special thanks to Craig Rosenthal, Howard [Sandum], Anne Chubbuck, John Grimaldi, John Shapiro, John Nania, Robert Dilenschneider, Greg Collins, Nadia Ghattas, Jared Pearman and others who have encouraged me in writing about the theater and hotels which have made some of our greatest theater – literally, in the case of The Savoy Theatre next to The Savoy Hotel and figuratively in the case of most other hotels.

BIOGRAPHICAL NOTE

Ward Morehouse III is one of the world's most distinguished authors of books on the world of hotels, theaters and travel. A third generation newspaper man, and son of the late, great drama critic and theatrical columnist Ward Morehouse, Ward Morehouse III is also a TV host ("The New Yorkers") and radio co-host, playwright ("The Actors," "Gangplank," and "Beloved Broadway" among others), and Broadway and roving hotel travel columnist. His other books on hotels include one on New York's Plaza Hotel called "Inside the Plaza: an Intimate Portrait of the Ultimate Hotel," and "The Waldorf–Astoria: America's Gilded Dream." He is following up the success of his book on New York hotels, called "Life at the Top: Inside New York's Grand Hotels," with "London's Grand Hotels: Extraordinary People, Extraordinary Service in the World's Cultural Capital," one on Santa Fe hotels (2009) and one on Brussels hotels (2010). At his best Morehouse is a storyteller in the same vein as Fitzgerald or Hemingway but his tales are based almost entirely on real life.

His theater reporting is as colorful as it is dynamic. Of the book, "Broadway After Dark," Bill Hoffman, an editor and writer of The New York Post's Page Six wrote: "'Broadway After Dark' is a beautiful love letter to the Great White Way. Ward Morehouse III and father spin some of the most interesting tales I've ever read about New York's glorious theater district." "No one is more qualified to write the history of Broadway's landmark Hudson Theatre than Ward Morehouse III," writes Frederick M. Winship, United Press International cultural critic-at-large.

INDEX

LaVergne, TN USA
16 February 2011
216800LV00003B/55/P